CLIMATE TRAUMA

CLIMATE TRAUMA

Foreseeing the Future in Dystopian Film and Fiction

E. ANN KAPLAN

RUTGERS UNIVERSITY PRESS
New Brunswick, New Jersey, and London

Library of Congress Cataloging-in-Publication Data

Kaplan, E. Ann.
   Climate trauma : foreseeing the future in dystopian film and fiction /
   E. Ann Kaplan.
     pages   cm
   Includes bibliographical references and index.
   ISBN 978–0–8135–6400–5 (hardcover : alk. paper)—ISBN 978–0–8135–6399–2
   (pbk. : alk. paper)—ISBN 978–0–8135–6401–2 (e-book (web pdf))—
   ISBN 978–0–8135–7356–4 (e-book (epub))
   1. Dystopian films—History and criticism. 2. Climatic changes in motion pictures.
   3. Psychic trauma in motion pictures. 4. Future, The, in motion pictures. I. Title.

   PN1995.9.D97K36 2015
   791.43'615—dc23
   2015004940

A British Cataloging-in-Publication record for this book is available from the British
Library.

Visit our website: http://rutgerspress.rutgers.edu

Manufactured in the United States of America

For Marty forever

CONTENTS

ACKNOWLEDGMENTS

This book goes to press just as public awareness of climate change, long known to be deadly dangerous for humans and the planet, is slowly gaining pace. I am not sure if the book is behind the times, then, or rather, emerging at just the right time for its meanings to take hold. Entertainment media for a variety of reasons have long been producing (and continued post-9/11 increasingly to produce) movies and TV shows about catastrophic collapse of infrastructures. But even links between these dystopian fantasies and climate change per se have been slow to penetrate public consciousness. A *New York Times* article by Alexander Alter on September 6, 2014, however, noted that the post-apocalyptic wave in fiction had evidently not yet peaked, and on December 10, 2014, Jason Mark wrote briefly about "Climate Fiction Fantasy"; he mentioned the 2014 futurist movies *Interstellar* and *Snowpiercer* in his quick historical review of the genre he names "cli-fi." Well, this is pretty much the topic of my book, only I am looking for deeper psychological meanings, for the cultural function of such fantasies, and I show humans as the cause of climate trauma—something media are still reluctant to say. This reluctance may be the reason that, although 70 percent of Americans now believe climate change is real, there is rather little thinking of ways to prevent the dire results predicted by the fictions I study—or rather little looking at what it means to live with uncertain futures.

I have many people to thank for helping me think myself into this difficult terrain. First, let me thank Sally Kitch, director of the Institute for Humanities Research at Arizona State University for awarding me an IHR Fellowship on the topic of "Society, Dystopia and Social Change" for spring 2010. It was there, in discussions with members of that remarkable seminar, that the germ of this project was born. Second, thanks to CHCI colleagues with whom I worked on a Consortium for Humanities Centers and Institutes grant proposal around the same time. I learned much from Sarah Buie, Paul Holm, Ian McCalman, Ann Waltner, along with other international scholars on the executive committee. Third, let me thank Cristina Venegas, then chair of Film and Media Studies at UC Santa Barbara, for inviting me to pursue my climate change research while in residence in the department in early 2012 and 2013. I was delighted to engage in projects related to climate change being undertaken by Janet Walker and colleagues in the Carsey-Wolf Center in those years. I am very glad that collaborative research continues in spring 2015 with new colleagues, like Ken Hiltner. Thinking together with all these colleagues inspired me, and some thoughts no doubt seeped into the pages that follow. However, I am alone responsible for how any ideas turned out.

Inspired by the CHCI work, and as (then) director of the Humanities Institute at Stony Brook University, I was able to initiate Humanities for the Environment Projects with local faculty. With special SBU funding and the support of SBU's new Sustainability Program, we organized a successful lecture series in fall 2013. This included visits by leading scholars in Environmental Studies such as Ramachandra Guha, Elizabeth Kolbert, Sandra Steingraber, Susanne Moser, and Leerom Medavoi. It was a privilege to meet these scholars, and scholar-activists, in person. I learned a great deal from reading their work, hearing their lectures, and participating in seminars with them. More recently, a visit to the HISB by Rob Nixon and Anne McClintock, whose work I already knew, offered more inspiration; they also confirmed the importance of getting our work on human-caused climate change out and available to the general public.

My English Department colleague Michael Rubenstein worked with me on the local grant application to fund the 2013 fall lecture series, and he was a delight to collaborate with then as now. I want to thank him not only for his smarts but his organizational talents—and most of all for his engaging research from which I have learned much. Heidi Hutner, director of sustainability at SBU, has been a strong supporter of my research, and I value her hard work toward establishing Environmental Humanities and Social Change degree programs at SBU. Other colleagues at SBU, including Justin Johnston and Jeffrey Santa Ana, have contributed to my ideas or responded to public lectures or articles in press. I want especially to thank Adrián Pérez Melgosa, whose name appears in several footnotes for offering insights about my research.

I want to thank the students in my course on Environment in Thought and Image, organized to coincide with the environmental humanities fall 2013 lecture series. Discussions with this bright group of graduate students pushed me to think more deeply about climate change. I was challenged to think from different perspectives and was introduced to literature new to me (such as Steam Punk novels, and David Markson's *Wittgenstein's Mistress*). Sophie Lavin was especially helpful over this past year in furthering HISB-related research ideas and practices. She was instrumental in spring 2015 in working with Environmental Humanities faculty at SBU on grant proposals related to climate trauma and resilience. We all owe much to her for her work.

Three students deserve thanks for their work in getting the manuscript ready. Lauren Neefe helped prepare my text for Rutgers Press to send to outside readers. Ashar Foley later continued to work on technical details to shape and format the manuscript. Greg Clinton performed the difficult task of preparing my images for the standard required. I learned a lot from him in the process, and I appreciate his undertaking this time-consuming work. Greg also contributed in a major way toward the design of the book cover, for which I am grateful.

But the person who has really borne the brunt of my increasing obsession about climate change is my husband, Martin Hoffman. Luckily, as a psychologist, Marty only too readily engaged with me about why it is so hard for humans to come together and collaborate on what needs to be done to save the planet (which might well go on without us) but also to save humans as a species. We have had many long discussions about this, emailed relevant articles to each other, and in general tried out many theories. It has been wonderful to engage with Marty in this way over the several years it took to write this book. Our conversations may even entice Marty to write something himself on the issue of how humans got (inadvertently) to be a suicidal species.

My daughter, Brett Ashley Kaplan, has supported me along the journey of getting this book done. As my pressure increased, Brett said to me, "Don't rush it, Mom." I found that wonderful advice. Having just completed her third book, she knows the score.

Let me end with a dedication to my wonderful grandchildren, Anya and Melia. Too young as yet to fully appreciate the climate catastrophe that generations before them have generated, they nevertheless will bear the consequences, along with their children. I can only wish them the courage and the fortitude to bear the effects that continued fossil fuel use will entail. I know they will be at the forefront of efforts to make life bearable for those less fortunate than they as storms increase and resources diminish.

PROLOGUE: CLIMATE TRAUMA AND HURRICANE SANDY

Many of us have our own Hurricane Sandy, and I am no exception. So much depended on exactly where we were when the storm hit. While the Weather Channel on TV, before going dead for us in lower Manhattan, noted the hurricane's trajectory, little attention was given locally to the devastation in Cuba, Haiti, the Caribbean, Puerto Rico, and Canada. This was an international catastrophe, but as experienced by many, it was read as a thoroughly local event.[1]

Some people, like my students who lived in Brooklyn, hardly suffered at all, whereas others living near the New York City, Long Island, or New Jersey coasts had their homes wiped out. My experience was in between these extremes. But let me first caution that, as with all traumatic events, what an individual brings to the situation in terms of psychic strength or vulnerability makes all the difference. Suffering can't be quantified or even compared. There are so many different kinds of pain, so many different calibrations to do with class, race, wealth.

MY EXPERIENCE

Middle-class folks like us, living in apartment buildings without generators in lower Manhattan, got our share of the disaster. During that fateful night, the storm raged outside our fourteenth-floor apartment. The trees on the street below were bending or breaking, the rain very heavy, and the streets empty. But lights were on everywhere, and it didn't seem so bad. The next day I was mainly worrying about a trip to Pittsburgh I was supposed to take and about my work schedule.

But quickly that all changed. There was a sudden power outage. All media were out and with no phone service we had no information to go on. I looked out of the apartment window to see, for the first time ever, the shocking sight of an absolutely dark environment. The Empire State Building, the Con-Ed Building, the Zeckendorff apartment buildings, and other buildings usually lit up, were dark.

My personal vulnerability (a phobic tendency) in a catastrophe like this didn't help. I began to feel trapped in our apartment. We walked downstairs (first of several treks down and up the fourteen long, dark, narrow flights) to talk to the doormen and to get some coffee, food, and water. We finally learned that the outage so far was only below Thirty-Fourth Street and that those who could were moving to hotels or relatives uptown.

I will never forget that first morning, walking around what had been our familiar neighborhood, now utterly foreign with no electricity. I think everyone needs a lesson about our near total reliance on electricity. Seeing at last an open shop, although totally dark inside, we found some cans of Starbucks coffee and handed over our credit card. But it relies on electricity. In this unusual setting, people were freely sharing knowledge about what was open, where to find food, and so on. Someone said there was real coffee over in the West Village.

Going over there, we passed NYU's Bobst Library, and I was surprised to find it lit up. Once inside, I saw an image (one of several) that stayed powerfully with me: Bobst had opened its doors to the general public. The grand wide-open Bobst Library foyer was transformed into a crowded work space with double lines of computer terminals set up along the counters, thanks to NYU's generators.[2] Because of the library access, email and the Internet became our way to reach the world uptown and beyond. Not only was communication opened up, but we could also use the toilets. Later, we realized we could even shower in NYU's gyms. When the library closed, we went back to the apartment, and dragged ourselves up the fourteen flights each carrying as big a bottle of drinking water as we could manage, along with cans of food. We found that if we walked about three flights, then took a rest, walked three more, rested again, and so on, we could manage it. I hated entering the dark apartment. Reading was difficult. So it was pretty much going to bed and trying to sleep.

By now most of the other people had left the building, which made me anxious about strangers getting in. Outside the apartment door, there was just a small glimmer from a single strobe light the doormen had left. Being without electricity made me suddenly aware that hall and stair lights had always been on before, day and night. It was scary to have darkness outside the apartment, and to look out on deserted streets from our windows. No lights, no people. Just dark buildings, like dead people with dead eyes. In the apartment I felt claustrophobic because of the flights of dark stairs that lay between me and the outside world. I hated being in the dark flat but also feared going down the stairs. And feared even more being on the empty streets.

I had a terrible scare on these stairs one day. Coming up on my own, I suddenly realized there was no-one else now going up or down, since most floors had no people on them, and that if something happened on the stairway, no-one would ever find me. I couldn't phone my husband as I would normally do. This brought on a panic attack and I couldn't climb any further. Luckily, as I was trying to calm myself, two women came out of one of the floors. I told them I was having an attack. They went back, got some water, calmed me down, and then walked with me up a flight or two until I felt better. After that, I made sure always to be with my husband on the stairs.

I couldn't sleep at night for fear of what might happen if there was a fire. Since there were so few people around, this was quite illogical. Still, I worried that there wouldn't be firemen to help, water to put out the fire, or doormen to call, given that, without electricity, they were unreachable. I lay in bed, blinds raised, waiting for the dawn to light up the building across the way. The flat was so dark that finally we decided to risk leaving a flashlight on so that, when I got up, there would be light.

Wandering the streets near Bobst on about the fourth day of the outage, we came upon what was to me a shocking sight. Outside the local Gristede's food store, where we normally shop, were mounds of huge plastic bags on the pavement. Management simply threw out the entire stock of what had been perfectly good food. I later found out that, after the frozen food was taken to a dumpster, people managed to open the lock and take home what they could carry.[3]

A big break for us came when some of our friends living on Fifty-Second Street got in touch and invited us up for a shower, dinner, and entertainment. We planned to go uptown every night from then on, eating out and catching a movie. Strangely, we were just on our way to do that, standing outside the apartment waiting for a taxi, when suddenly the lights went on. It was amazing. In a jiffy, our whole situation changed. The electricity was back. But was it really? I was not ready to rely on it and felt afraid to use the elevator until assured by the doormen that indeed the problem with the burnt out hub had been fully resolved.

HURRICANE SANDY AS BORDER EVENT

A bit like 9/11 (if on a different scale), Hurricane Sandy was a border event, a characteristic it shares with Hurricane Katrina. Both disasters had dramatic political, social and psychological impacts and marked a cultural change in the United States, an altered consciousness of Americans as citizens. In the case of Katrina, among other things, there was shame at the racism that emerged from beneath the perpetual cover-up. Governmental inefficiency or worse was also exposed. With Hurricane Sandy, in turn, came a heightened sense of class difference, awareness that the most economically vulnerable people were living in areas most exposed to storm damage. Age differences and mobility, linked to class, featured heavily in people's experiences, as evident in the media reporting. Each catastrophe offered a sense of things being irreversibly altered after the happening, of changed sensibilities, of changed feelings regarding security, safety, stability, and of being unable to rely on the environment.

There is no doubt that the two catastrophes highlighted America's class and race politics, since the people living in the areas most open to drastic flooding and storm damage were significantly minority or lower-class. As with Hurricane Katrina, Sandy provided an example of the environmental injustice analyzed by, for example, Ramachandra Guha and Rob Nixon. In that sense, both hurricanes revealed class disparities that are too often neatly hidden beneath pervasive normative codes (still in play after all this time) of the country as a "melting pot."

In comparison to other people, my husband and I were lucky. We did not lose our house and belongings as did so many, nor were we left abandoned in a flooded house as were others. The elderly were especially vulnerable to being left without recourse, as they were often unable to get up and move away as people were told to do. The scandal of NYU placing its research labs and patients' files on the basement floor of the Langone Medical Center, which was quickly flooded by the storm surge, will go down in history: It was either an incredible error or reflected the sense of climate stability, whereby no-one ever imagined a thirteen-foot storm surge could penetrate that far into lower Manhattan to flood that basement. The medical center's backup generator also failed or was flooded. The image of elderly and sick people being carried down many flights of stairs and transferred by taxi to other hospitals in the area is astounding.[4] But also documented were the unprecedented efforts of doctors, nursing staff, police, and fire personnel in saving all the many patients who had to be moved and transferred.[5]

Sandy was a border event in exposing our complete reliance on electricity. It was a wake-up call in this as in other ways. As Michael Rubenstein remarks, writing about the meaning of electrification in Ireland for Irish literary modernity, "once 'plugged in' to the electrical grid, the citizen is dependent and reconstructs daily life around a technology that exists only as a function of national infrastructure."[6] As he correctly notes, in this reconstruction of everyday life, there "is a nearly instantaneous forgetting that accompanies it. [That is,] The transformation that occurs, while controversial and profoundly lived through at first, leaves everyday consciousness with astonishing rapidity."[7] It was that "forgetting" about electricity in particular (but also plumbing and sanitation) that returned so dramatically, and traumatically, to consciousness when Hurricane Sandy hit. We were reminded brutally of what we had forgotten in that habituation and incorporation of public utilities into modern daily life that Rubenstein discusses. It was a supreme example of what Christopher Bollas (as Rubenstein reminds us) called "the unthought known that asserts its urgency in moments of crisis."[8]

Hurricane Sandy was a border event in a final sense—of the division between scientists who link this extreme climate disaster to planet warming and those who deny such a relationship. Debates in the wake of Sandy revealed, then, a theoretical border. Arguments as to how far the extremity of this weather event was the result of global warming were all over the Internet. Amid the skepticism reported in Wikipedia's Hurricane Sandy site, there was nevertheless agreement that "One factor contributing to the storm's strength was abnormally warm sea surface temperatures offshore the East Coast of the United States—more than 3 °C (5 °F) above normal, to which global warming had contributed 0.6 °C (1 °F). As the temperature of the atmosphere increases, the capacity to hold water increases, leading to stronger storms and higher rainfall amounts." Some scientists saw the abnormally warm surface temperatures as part of some "natural variability," whereas others such as Harvard scientist Daniel Schrag believed Hurricane

Sandy's thirteen-foot storm surge was an example of what will, by mid-century, be the "new norm on the Eastern seaboard."[9]

The noted Stony Brook University oceanographer Malcolm Bowman was quoted widely in the wake of Hurricane Sandy (often in discussions with then New York City mayor Michael Bloomberg). Bowman argued that the city must erect extensive storm-surge barricades around its coast, on the model of those in The Netherlands and London.[10] Others disagreed but had few alternative suggestions. Responses to articles on the web include Jeff Tollefson citing "two studies published in February and March this year [2012] (which) suggest that warming due to increasing ice loss in the Arctic Ocean could be altering regional air circulation, causing a more meandering jet stream."[11] The net effect, researchers say, is an increase in the likelihood of severe winter storms and other extreme weather events across the United States, Europe, and northern China. Although the idea remains controversial, some scientists wonder whether the same phenomenon could lead to an increase in hurricanes such as Sandy and Irene, which last year roared up the coast from North Carolina to New York and came perilously close to flooding the city as Sandy did.[12]

There is general agreement that Hurricane Sandy was a wake-up call not only to the United States but to coastal cities around the world. This is no doubt a global problem, with two powerful industrialized nations—China and the United States—at great risk that rising sea levels will endanger their harbors at the center of global shipping networks. As I go on to argue in this book, global collaboration on dangers facing world economies in the face of climate change is essential before it is too late.[13] If wake-up calls cannot move governmental leaders, humanity's future is bleak. As Martin Hoffman has argued (in personal communication), humans may not be a suicidal species, as some have argued, so much as victims of a strong evolutionary drive to survive. In following our individual drive for securing the material necessities of life—a drive that soon becomes sheer greed—we may end up putting our species at risk.[14]

Indeed, we may have already begun the process by starting to destroy species and the very planet we need to sustain us. In reviewing Elizabeth Kolbert's book *The Sixth Extinction*, Al Gore notes Kolbert's highlighting "the role of man-made climate change in causing . . . the current spasm of plant and animal loss that threatens to eliminate 20 to 50 percent of all living species on earth within this century." He went on to note that many find it "inconceivable that we could possibly be responsible for destroying the integrity of our planet's ecology. There are psychological barriers to even imagining that what we love so much could be lost—could be destroyed *forever*. As a result, many of us refuse to contemplate it."[15]

Such psychological barriers may be a reaction formation to the phenomenon of "Pretraumatic Stress Syndrome" (PreTSS) which I go on to theorize in this book. I situate pretrauma against the more familiar Post-Traumatic Stress Disorder (PTSD), which is a condition triggered in the present by past events. In pretrauma, on the other hand, people unconsciously suffer from an immobilizing anticipatory anxiety about the future. My experiences during Hurricane Sandy reflect the familiar PTSD—that is, I responded to the catastrophe through what it triggered about past traumas. However, having had this experience, I may now suffer from pretrauma—that is, living in fear of a future terrifying event of a similar kind.

Generalizing from my experience, I suggest cultures may now be entering a new era in which pretrauma is pervasive in the public sphere. In this new era, media of all kinds—journalism, the Internet, television, film, and literature—offer catastrophic futurist scenarios. In these scenarios, audiences are invited to identify with future selves in uncertain, dangerous, and ultimately unsustainable worlds. Such identifications result in a pretraumatized population, living with a sense of an uncertain future and an unreliable natural environment. My hope is that, instead of being passively terrified, audiences will begin to understand dystopian scenarios as warning humans of what they must, at all costs, avoid.

CLIMATE TRAUMA

INTRODUCTION: PRETRAUMA IMAGINARIES

Theoretical Frames

"The bravest thing is to take this first step: get real. Facing the truth, and letting it sink in. . . . But coming to grips with the reality we now are in takes time, and it is critical that we give it a quiet space inside ourselves."

—Susanne Moser, "Getting Real about It"

According to the 2014 Intergovernmental Panel on Climate Change, our planet is suffering catastrophic damage from human activities. As Justin Gillis in the *New York Times* noted, "the report was among the most sobering yet issued by the scientific panel." Paul Crutzen years ago coined the term "The Anthropocene" to describe the new era humans have entered in which they represent a dangerous "geologic force." The impact of the realities of global warming on unconscious psychological conditions, cultural discourses, and media representations takes trauma theory in new directions.[1]

Having been preoccupied with trauma in terms of its classic description as related to past events, I realized that *future* catastrophic events could also be traumatic.[2] "Pretraumatic Stress Syndrome" (PreTSS) is a condition that I here situate in relation to the well-known "Post-Traumatic Stress Disorder" (PTSD). The increasing number of futurist dystopian worlds in film and literature in the post-9/11 era evidence severe anxiety about the future in Eurocentric cultures—an anxiety that warrants the term *pretrauma*. Pretraumatic Stress, however, has been little studied. My "discovery" of it came about through looking at futurist dystopian films. Recently some cognitive psychologists have been sufficiently drawn to the concept to undertake an in-depth study that supports what I theorized from the films. In their study, "Pretraumatic Stress Reactions in Soldiers Deployed to Afghanistan," Dorthe Berntsen and David C. Rubin define pretraumatic stress, very much as I have been doing, as designating "disturbing future-oriented cognitions and imaginations as measured in terms of a direct temporal reversal of conceptualizations of past-directed cognitions in the PTSD diagnosis."[3] Their data are drawn from Danish soldiers who were measured before, during, and after their deployment to Afghanistan and complement work on future selves addressed below.

While pretrauma stress in U.S. and other cultures relates to diverse kinds of disaster, in this book I focus specifically on fears about the total collapse of natural and social environments. It seems we are witnessing a cultural shift away from traditional U.S. progressive futurist imaginaries to something dark and ominous. Hoping to find answers as to why such worlds dominate the Western cultural imaginary, and what the impact of a cultural PreTSS might be, I began to study it in the novels and (mainly) commercial films set in catastrophic futures that inspired me in the first place. Although some of the films I discuss are made by Latin American directors and science fiction has been a huge genre in Japanese cinema, it remains to be seen how far the pretrauma film has become a global phenomenon. Some research, like that by Ursula K. Heise, has begun to explore international sci-fi literature so as to bring a global sense of the diverse uses of the genre, but work like this for cinema is not yet complete.[4]

Having conceptualized pretrauma, I was interested to find that Jeff Nichols's film *Take Shelter* (2011) embodied exactly the phenomenon that I was theorizing and that the cognitive psychologists are providing data for. Pretrauma in this film turns into a narrative that demonstrates pretrauma's full force. The protagonist, Curtis LaForche (Michael Shannon), suffers from PreTSS—related to fantasies of violent climate change—instead of suffering from the linked *post*-traumatic disorder.[5] The hero's life is all but destroyed because of his pretrauma symptoms, such as nightmares, flashbacks, hallucinations, depression, and paranoia, all related to his fear that future climate events will destroy the natural world along with his family.

Pretrauma fictions comprise one of two distinct considerations framing this book. First, in studying these fictions, I explore how pretrauma is

FIG. INTRO-1 In a typical shot from his point of view (POV), Curtis LaForche hallucinates a dire weather event to come.

figured in film and what it means for spectators. I analyze the (pretrauma) future selves that viewers are invited to identify with and the potential impact (psychic, political, cultural) of these imagined selves. I also theorize the viewers' attraction to such pretraumatic scenarios in which, through identification, they figure as "virtual future humans." Second, I look at how the circulation of futurist disaster narratives induces a kind of pretraumatic stress, both in the individuals watching the films and in U.S. culture more broadly.

In returning to science fiction and recognizing a new dystopian genre in the disaster films, it is possible to see their proliferation in the wake of 9/11. I have no doubt that 9/11 seriously destabilized an American society that had previously seen itself as secure and invulnerable. If the Japanese invasion of Pearl Harbor was a wake-up call on one level, the triumphal Allied victory over Germany and Japan seemed to settle the question. The destruction of the Twin Towers was a much greater national shock. The attack took place in the heart of a major metropolis, invading the continental United States both internally and dramatically. As scholars have shown, 9/11 continues to haunt U.S. literature as well as its cinema. Elizabeth Kovach, for example, studies the "precarity of personal and national being" in Paul Auster's *Man in the Dark* and Siri Hustvedt's *The Sorrows of an American*, as well as related concerns in other fiction. Kovach shows the explicit situating of these fictions in the wake of 9/11, functioning as what she calls "witnessing hauntologies" in the aftermath of the catastrophe.[6] While the films I discuss in this book are related to science fiction, there are enough differences to suggest a generic subset, which I will call "pretrauma cinema." Within this subset, a further separation can be made between dystopian imaginaries of totalitarian regimes (pretrauma political dystopias) and films preoccupied with the end of the world as inhabitable for humans (pretraumatic disaster films). Along with *Take Shelter*, Alfonso Cuarón's *Children of Men* (2006) is a central text because it uncannily moves in the direction of both political thriller and end-of-the world disaster film.

Conceptualizing the phenomenon of PreTSS offers a new lens for an expanded trauma theory. Future time is a major theme, along with thinking through the meanings and cultural work (including that pertaining to race and gender) that dystopian pretrauma imaginaries perform in our newly terrorized historical era. Such work includes bolstering white male authority via the illusion that government agencies (or their surrogates) ultimately remain in control.[7] Finally, the circularity of representations that both anticipate and respond to historical events is significant. Such representations have a strong affective charge, especially as historical events lead to war or anticipate future ecological devastation. These fantasies function as warnings, a kind of "memory for the future," and I investigate what future there is for memory as these fictional humans come to an end.

Numerous interdisciplinary scholars helped me to frame this project, but select colleagues were especially useful in outlining the two generic subsets it treats. In regard to the futurist political dystopia, Susan Buck-Morss's *Dreamworld and Catastrophe* shows how the collapse of the Soviet Union and the end of the Cold War signaled the termination of an era. As she puts it, "The construction of mass utopia was the dream of the twentieth century. It was the driving ideological force of industrial modernization in both its capitalist and socialist forms . . . this collective dream dares to imagine a social world in alliance with personal happiness."[8] The pretrauma political dystopia emerges from the destruction of this dream, and Buck-Morss's work lays bare the background for the subgenre's cynical, negative politics. Written a decade later and drawing on the experience of a highly evolved global capitalism, Giorgio Agamben's related political analyses add to Buck-Morss's analysis by showing how global capitalism has eaten away at the nation-state in ways that belie the optimism some held for a new world order. Agamben has helped me understand why politics as usual is no longer possible in the current global situation, driven by multinational financial markets.⁹ Governments manipulate politics in order to serve their own economic and political ends, regardless of the negative outcomes for most people.¹⁰

Dipesh Chakrabarty starts from an anti-capitalist, leftist position similar to that of Buck-Morss and Agamben but offers a bridge between their work on political systems and new climate concerns. Chakrabarty shows that, as drastic climate change renders the end of the world a potential reality, we have to revise our leftist thinking. In an era when humans wield a geological force, he notes, "a fundamental assumption of Western (and now universal) political thought has come undone." Important about Chakrabarty's contribution is his questioning as to whether the "geological agency of humans"—an agency that has resulted in what scholars are calling the "Anthropocene era," universalizing Crutzen's concept—is the price we pay for the pursuit of freedom. He suggests that critiques of global capitalism "do not give us an adequate hold on human history once we accept that the crisis of climate change is here with us and may exist as part of this planet for much longer than capitalism or long after capitalism has undergone many more historic mutations." He argues further that "a critique that is only a critique of capital is not sufficient for addressing questions relating to human history once the crisis of climate change has been acknowledged and the Anthropocene has begun to loom on the horizon of our present."¹¹ Leerom Medavoi makes a related—but orthogonal—argument, namely, showing, in his words, "*how much* the environment has mattered to capitalism throughout its history, how central a role it has played, precisely because 'environmentality' is the mechanism through which the milieus of life are assessed and transformed, and rendered more productive [original italics]."¹²

For the second subset, the pretraumatic disaster film, ecocritics and environmentalists are relevant. Ramachandra Guha has long been a powerful scholar in global environmentalism, tracking the history of environmental discourses internationally and stressing contributions by Indian and other rural women often overlooked. Rob Nixon builds on Guha's work in his important research on what he calls "slow violence" and environmental injustice. His work raises crucial questions about race and class in relation to global warming. Meanwhile, Ursula K. Heise's research, largely on science fiction rather than film, offers insights about the interrelationship of theorists of global warming (for example, Bill McKibben) and nonfiction writers (for example, Alan Weisman) with science fiction. Heise also studies the increasing globalization of science fiction and looks at international writing in the genre as well as in ecocriticism. The 2014 research of journalist scholars Naomi Klein and Elizabeth Kolbert (see the afterword) adds incrementally to thinking about human futures, about the relation between climate and capitalism, and about what, if anything, can be done to prevent disaster.

If the scholars noted above eschew psychoanalytic perspectives, in this book I make such perspectives central. Complex questions about human psychology cannot be avoided, and such questions add to the insightful contributions of others. Nor is it sufficient for a critique of capital to omit human psychology. A fourth colleague, Susanne Moser, contributes to my thinking, along with the always reliable Sigmund Freud. Before I met Moser or read her research on the emotions related to climate change, I had used Freud's theories about anxiety and the death drive as a way of understanding why humans seem unable to move forward together to mitigate their drastic negative impact on the planet. From his earliest to his very last work, Freud was preoccupied with trauma and with understanding its mechanisms. In his early 1895 studies of hysteria with Josef Breuer and on through his work to *Moses and Monotheism*, written at the very end of his life, he tried to understand trauma, its symptoms, and its impact in relation both to the individual subject and (as the dystopic *Civilization and Its Discontents* shows) to collectivities, nations, culture. Michael Roth notes how trauma shows us "much about our own preoccupations with catastrophe, memory and the grave difficulties we have in negotiating between the internal and external worlds."[13] This aspect of trauma is demonstrated well by Freud also. In a sense, trauma is for our internal life what catastrophe is externally. Trauma haunts us because of its connection with death, and this link led Freud in 1920 to conceptualize a death drive, related to pretrauma phenomena. The drive shows the subject's future orientation, a looking toward a future death that is partially, if unconsciously, desired.

While Moser prefers existential psychology to psychoanalysis, our ideas are not far apart. We are both concerned about the ways in which extreme anxiety leads to depression and denial. Moser is clearer than even Chakrabarty about the dire situation we are in. The scenario as she outlines it includes our having done much too little, much too late, "resulting in our communities, economies and the ecosystems we depend on being

overwhelmed by the pace and magnitude of climate change, and all atten-
dant losses and disruptions." She continues, noting that "we will experience
a range of essential systems degrading over time, or collapsing outright, but
in either case shifting into completely altered states." Moser believes that we
need a cohort of leaders, "adept in a range of psychological, social and political skills, to navigate the inevitable human crises that will precede, trigger
and follow environmental ones." They will need to guide people, she says, in
"processing enormous losses, human distress, constant crises and the seemingly endless need to remain engaged in the task of maintaining, restoring
and rebuilding . . . a viable planet, and the only place the human species can
call its home."[14]

In regard to psychology research pertinent to my study, I also found
cognitive psychology research by Adam D. Brown and his colleagues to
be useful in shaping my thinking about the impact of viewing future selves
in dystopian films. The concept of pretrauma dovetails in interesting ways
with the team's work on future selves with war veterans. Brown's research
does not dwell on future selves in the context of climate catastrophe and
his temporal focus is different, but the project nevertheless renewed my
thinking about the concept of pretraumatic stress. The idea that imagined
future selves have an impact on one's current view of self is important for
the future selves that viewers encounter in pretraumatic cinema. I ask
what the impact on the viewers watching a pretraumatic futurist scenario
might be in regard to those viewers' sense of their own future self. In what
ways do these identifications also alter the subjects' idea of their future as
human beings facing possible catastrophes? How does the situation of living vicariously in uncertain times in film scenarios change people?

If Nicholas Mirzoeff is right—and I think he is—that issues regarding
the Anthropocene and climate change should now be considered as important as gender, race, and class have hitherto been considered to humanities
research, the question arises as to how we situate the new category in relation to the others.[15] As a feminist, I am most concerned with how gender
needs to be situated vis-à-vis global warming and in how the pretrauma
disaster film unconsciously focuses on *male* as against *female* responses to
worries about a catastrophic future. While the environmental critics and
scholars noted above (especially Guha and Nixon) address issues of environmental injustice head-on, the full force of such injustice appears to be
bypassed in pretraumatic fictions, leaving the serious class and gender

issues to documentaries and academic studies. I return here to Chakrabarty's thought regarding the degree to which conceptualizing humans as a species occludes the poor, women, racialized peoples, and the invisible minorities who are already bearing the brunt of the first waves of environmental catastrophe. If the dilemma is difficult in lived reality, my job is to see what cultural work is performed in fantasies of future climate catastrophe that focus on male rather than female protagonists.

Selected from a very large inventory of futurist disaster films, the films in this project reveal the response of international artists to the dramatic changes described by the scholars mentioned above. Filmmakers and novelists create fictional worlds relating both to the end of "the mass utopian dream of a social world in alliance with personal happiness" and to the destructive geological force that humans now occupy on planet Earth.[16] Utopian discourses have given way to dystopian imaginaries on a scale rarely seen in earlier aesthetic periods. Indeed, the dystopian/utopian oscillation is fundamental to the pretrauma genre addressed here. Films reflect pretrauma operating in culture and discourse along with the twin processes of fear and hope. In trying to understand the complex psychological mechanisms that inhibit humans from coming together to save themselves and the planet, I argue that such processes have first to be grasped and then changed.

But this is a complicated business, with respect to climate-change science and the methods used by humanists to analyze representations of the environment in literature and film. As Kathryn Yusoff observes, scientists have to rely on models that predict future change, and these do not provide absolute certainty. Discussing the 2007 report by the Intergovernmental Panel on Climate Change (IPCC), Yusoff points out that, while "the catastrophe of climate change is excessive and will inscribe all earthly space," we need to pause and ask how we know about the dangers articulated by collaborative climate prediction models (also known as general circulation models, or GCMs). She suggests that we investigate uncertainties, including how much we do not know and how much is difficult to know.[17] Justin Gillis also notes that the potential consequences of planetary warming issued in the latest 2014–2015 report by the IPCC offer possibilities, not certainties. Gillis says the distinction is crucial, but he quotes scientists saying, "You don't need 100 percent certainty for society to act."[18]

Meanwhile, Leerom Medavoi, following Lawrence Buell and Greg Garrard, has critiqued literary ecocriticism for "relying upon the ubiquitous trope of environmental crisis," which, he argues, derives from a Christian religious narrative that "has been secularized and imported into the context of environmental criticism."[19] While I critique the films I study for falling into this trap, I aim at once to historicize (as we must) and keep open the question of "how to live in uncertain times," a phrasing that avoids the apocalypticism prevalent in religious and media discourse and aims to draw attention to a serious reality.[20]

With his 2013 monograph *Hyperobjects*, Timothy Morton, has presented a new theory of the situation humans are in that would seem to upend familiar discourses. It's a terrifying wake-up call, inciting us to notice how far humans are already reeling from the consequences of global warming and how deeply—without our fully knowing it—humans have already been affected. Morton believes the end of the world is already here: humans are living in such a world without consciously knowing it. He believes that "hyperobjects"—of which global warming is the most obvious example—surround us as nonhumans and stick to us, getting inside our bodies as well as our psyches. We only discover such objects once they are here. But it's almost as though Morton has evacuated the cultural, political, and social sphere, lifting the discourse to an entirely different level. At several points in my analysis, I refer to Morton's views, because on one hand they offer a plausible reality, framed as a polemic; on the other hand they leave little room for cultural studies scholarship such as mine, which lies at a level of consciousness before the one that Morton describes. At one point, Morton states that "narratives of doom about 'the end of the world,'" such as those discussed in this book, "are part of the problem, not the solution."[21] He believes such stories inoculate us against the object that is already here. I disagree with him on this point because I see the narratives I work with as alerting us to what might already be here but is certainly in our future. The narratives force us to face horror and fear rather than relax, as he suggests.

Tom Cohen, like Morton, also critiques critical theorists for their apparent neglect of what's happening to the biosphere: "We theorists," he writes, "have deferred addressing biospheric collapse, mass extinction events, or the implications of resource wars and 'population' culling." He chides Foucault and Derrida for not dealing with "ecocatastrophic logics," a confrontation he appreciates in Morton's work. Cohen calls for a practice of "disidentification" and for the "disoccupation [of] the metaphorics of home." Since the publication of his provocative volume, humanities theorists have begun to undertake the work Cohen calls for—if not in as radical a fashion as he proposes.[22]

In this book, as a project in cultural studies, I aim both to document and to critique the proliferation of fantasies of apocalyptic catastrophe in Eurocentric cultures since 9/11. Popular culture seizes on prevailing societal tendencies and in the process, circularly, exaggerates and increases their prominence. Apocalyptic imaginaries about the end of the world continue to emerge and continue to be given space in media reporting. Joon-ho Bong's *Snowpiercer* (2013) and Christopher Nolan's *Interstellar* (2014) are but the latest versions of a world transformed by a climate catastrophe. As Julia Kristeva puts it, "Films remain the supreme art of the apocalypse, no matter what the refinements, because the image has such an ability to 'have us walk into fear,' as Augustine had already seen."[23]

Although fantasies of Armageddon and the apocalypse go far back in biblical history, the form and scale of the concern is new. Chronic anxieties about future catastrophe—trauma as "dystopia of the spirit"—requires renewed attention in a culture such as ours, which may be too preoccupied with trauma, yet in which real catastrophes confront and challenge us.[24] Fear, panic, and anxiety pop up regularly as topics in the media (and indeed the academy), warning people about future disaster and enhancing the sense of pretrauma for those susceptible to such emotions. Widely circulated journals and magazines proclaim disasters of numerous kinds, with cover titles such as "Anxiety" or "How Scared Are You?"[25] Such panic affects circulate in the public sphere and become part of subjective worlds through the media's identificatory and imaginary processes. In circular fashion, the real catastrophes caused by humans generate fantasies that in turn have material effects.[26]

Since I started this project, I find dystopian fantasies are everywhere, as I first realized at the New York Film Festival in fall 2011, shortly after *Contagion* was released. If, in 1922, Freud warned against prophecies, it seems film directors were not listening.[27] Films were divided between dystopian futurist imaginaries (*Melancholia, 4.44*) and profound nostalgia (*My Week with Marilyn, Pina, The Artist*). Alluding to the prevalence of the disaster theme *New York Times* film critic Stephen Holden, trying to make a bad joke, asked, "Will the World End before or after the Festival Does?" More movies of both types have continued to emerge (for example, *Take Shelter, Hugo*). The *New York Times*'s report on Sundance on December 1, 2011,

"Quirk Meets Bleak at Sundance," describes the grim view of America in many of the new films: "This time," Brooks Barnes notes, "filmmakers appear intensely focused on a rotting America."

Many of these films, like Lars von Trier's *Melancholia* (2012), were uncannily anticipatory. On February 15, 2013, a meteor exploded over Siberia. While it was not the clash of two planets as figured in *Melancholia*, the event was labeled unusual because the scale of the explosion was rare for a meteor that astronomers had not known about. The front-page headline in the February 16, 2013, *New York Times* read "Meteor Explodes, Injuring over 1,000 in Siberia," and the report described the damage, noting that the scenes in Siberia "offer a glimpse of an apocalyptic scenario that many have walked through mentally, and Hollywood has popularized."

An inside story discussed the relationship of this event to science fiction. The report by John Williams begins, "Life is scariest when it imitates science fiction." Williams observes that even those "with long experience imagining catastrophic events" were unnerved. Later in the article, he states that more than a decade before Tunguska, the 1908 event of a low-passing asteroid in Siberia, H. G. Wells predicted such an event in his fiction. Williams also mentions the many Hollywood films that deal with apocalypse from the perspective of relationships, such as *Melancholia* and *Seeking a Friend for the End of the World* do. Discussing 9/11 in 2001, Slavoj Žižek also pointed out that *Independence Day* (1996) seemed to anticipate that very disaster.[28]

How are we to understand such media anticipation? For Žižek, the pre-science spells conspiracy. The media prefigure what the U.S. government makes sure will happen. Sociologists, however, have less explicitly political theories. In his research on catastrophes, Richard Grusin calls such fiction a kind of "premediation." Grusin explains the phenomenon of premediation (in my case, films about future disasters) in terms of a society preparing for the worst by relying on new technologies or scientific predictions. Media, in Grusin's words, "works to prevent citizens of the global mediasphere from experiencing again the kind of systemic or traumatic shock produced by the events of 9/11 by perpetuating an almost constant, low level of anxiety or fear about another terrorist attack."[29] My argument is somewhat similar, although I see anxiety about a future attack as—at least for some people and in some cultural groups—approaching the phenomena of pretrauma.

In the chapter "Apocalypse at the Gates," Žižek outlines three versions of "apocalypticism," which he describes as Christian fundamentalist, New

Age, and techno-digital-post-human.[30] The discussion of techno-digital-post-human strategies includes a useful critique of digital-human fantasies. It applies to Stephen Valentine's aim to build a "cryonic castle," a timeship that would house fifty thousand people who have been frozen in the hope that they can be brought back in the future.[31] Valentine's award-winning book, *Timeship: The Architecture of Immortality*, argues that after space exploration, "practical immortality" is the next great human adventure. The British TV series *Cold Lazarus* (1996), invented by Dennis Potter as he was dying of pancreatic cancer, anticipates such efforts at "practical immortality" in imagining a cryogenic London institute where a writer's brain has been frozen and is now being mined by scientists.[32] These fantasies seem intriguing, if desperate, attempts by humans to make sense of and find ways around the global catastrophes already in process—ones that the pretraumatic cinema addresses and arguably warns against.

In conceptualizing pretrauma, I focus on temporality, which is often lacking in trauma studies.[33] Awareness of a traumatic past is figured in many of the films in the genre, as this past is understood to have shaped the future (i.e., the narrative present), a fictional future that we should avoid. But we also need to consider how these imaginaries of the future in turn shape constructions of the present and the past.[34] If always implicit, temporality needs to be made explicit so we can move beyond focusing only on the memory of past wounds.

And what about the politics of catastrophic images? What cultural work do they perform? My interest in futurist dystopian images and language arises from their function as cultural phenomena that signal both unconscious fantasies informing today's imaginary as it dominates the public sphere and a deliberate creation of a culture of fear by some in power. Narratives of a destroyed planet, inhospitable to life in all forms, emerge at the intersection of scientific predictions about global warming (finally seeping into public media) and corporate businesses, determined to resist costly changes to their practices. Hollywood, HBO, and Showtime, as well as the Internet and other media, gauge the sociopolitical moment and hope to capture audiences who are now sensitized to dangers without taking things so far as to alienate audiences or the conservatives.

While the long tradition of utopian thought—so long that it seems built into the human DNA—has gained new life in the new millennium, scholars rarely deal with utopia's underside, dystopia, which is central to my project.

I find this interesting, especially given the *American Heritage Dictionary*'s linking of the terms *utopia* and *dystopia*. Etymologically, the *u* of *utopia* is replaced by *dys*, making it a part of Utopia, not a concept in its own right: the dictionary presents it as "dys + (U)topia." (If you look up *dystopia*, you are generally referred to *utopia* for the same reason.)[35] Although critics such as Fredric Jameson favor using *utopia* (and *anti-Utopia* for negative worlds), I want to emphasize the negative side of utopia by working with *dystopia*.[36] One definition for *dystopia* calls it "an imaginary place where the conditions and quality of life are unpleasant. The opposite of Utopia. See also Utopia."[37] The *American Heritage Dictionary* defines it as "an imaginary place or state in which the condition of life is extremely bad, as from deprivation, oppression, or terror." In between is a concept such as Jameson describes in the introduction to *Archaeologies of the Future*: "For those mindful of the very real political function of the idea and the program of Utopia in our time, the slogan of anti-anti-Utopianism might well offer the best working strategy."[38] But this concept still does not address the kind of utter negativity of worlds in at least one of my generic subdivisions—namely, the pretraumatic disaster film.

What I appreciate about dystopia as a concept is its very close relation to utopia while seeming to be its opposite. Margaret Atwood grasps this interrelation well when she says that while "dystopias are usually described as the opposite of utopias . . . scratch the surface a little . . . you see something more like a yin and yang pattern; within each utopia, a concealed dystopia; within each dystopia, a hidden utopia." She invents the term "ustopia" to indicate a middle ground. The films in this book form a genre partly because of the way they show an oscillation between dystopia and utopia—an oscillation inherent in their very etymology—and which Freud understood long ago.[39]

It is because of the inherent instability embodied in the term *dystopia* that, for my purposes here, I prefer it to *apocalypse.* The first and most common definition of *apocalypse* in the online Oxford English Dictionary is "the complete final destruction of the world, as described in the biblical book of Revelation [or] the end of the world as described in the Bible." Neither of these is useful for my project, which is about slow decline rather than an abrupt ending. But other definitions from the same online Oxford dictionary site *do* work for my purposes: "a situation causing very serious damage and destruction, [or] an event involving destruction or damage on a catastrophic scale." The strong connotations of a sudden happening or utopian break of a religious kind that the word *apocalypse* carries work against the atmosphere of most of my films, however.[40]

The worlds of pretrauma cinema might best be described as post-apocalyptic, although again, this term assumes some sudden event takes place to bring on the end. The subgenre involves a morbid but ongoing destroyed world. If there is an implied or stated sudden event that starts the decline, the world of the film is one where humans have to endure extremely harsh conditions of slow deterioration and increasing desperation over many years. As Žižek puts it, in imagining how a real world (not filmic) catastrophe might come about: "No big bang," he says, "just a small-scale interruption with devastating global consequences."[41] He provides the example of the inexplicable and very serious massive dying of bees, which are essential for the pollination of plants humans need for food.[42] Meanwhile, in *Slow Violence and the Environmentalism of the Poor*, a remarkable book devoted to "calamities that are slow and long lasting," Rob Nixon asks, "How can we convert into image and narrative the disasters that are slow moving and long in the making, disasters that are anonymous and that star nobody?"[43] Given the gradual and subtle shifts in ecosystems damaged by humans, rather than a Big Bang sort of event, *dystopia* seems best to convey what this genre depicts.

Far less scholarly energy has been devoted to dystopia than to utopia, perhaps for obvious reasons. Scholars interested in the future for humanity have traditionally been drawn to thinking about worlds that would be an improvement on the world in which the scholar lives. Liberals and leftists (and more recently feminists and minority authors) are the ones usually writing about utopian possibilities for humankind. Scholars generally don't want to spend time with "a place where everything is as bad as it can be" (to cite another definition of dystopia). George Orwell is perhaps an exception—but even his work, as Fredric Jameson points out, is really better described as anti-Utopian, because it "is informed by a central passion to warn against Utopian programs in the political realm."[44]

Utopians are a very mixed lot, and there is perhaps even less definitional clarity about the concept than ever. Ernst Bloch's extensive analysis of utopian thought, starting in the 1930s and continuing into the 1970s, is a topic unto itself. In the era prefiguring the death throes of socialism and communism, Bloch looks for hope in practices of art as an unraveling of meanings; he believed the process itself would lead humans toward "a society without oppression."[45] Ruth Levitas's 1990 history, *The Concept of Utopia*, tracking the idea through the 1980s, is an exhaustive reference for any scholar in this field. Meanwhile, Sally Kitch's clear-eyed look at feminist utopias in her volume, *Higher Ground*, covers important territory as well, and her conclusions have inspired me. But as Russell Jacoby notes in his critique of liberal anti-utopians, "inasmuch as history saturates utopian thought, no single definition can fix its essence."[46]

The work of Tom Moylan and Raffaella Baccolini, with its also exhaustive and compelling analyses of dystopia/utopia has nevertheless begun to clear the field. Their discussion of "critical dystopia," which builds on research by Constance Penley and Peter Fitting among others, applies in some measure to some of my films. Penley, Moylan notes, argues that certain sci-fi films "challenge the systemic 'atrophy of the utopian imagination' by examining the socioeconomic operations that not only produce the present reality but also silence the utopian opposition to it as all serious alternatives are apparently crushed."[47] Moylan and Baccolini later define critical dystopia as distinct from dystopia *tout court*. For them, dystopias are "a bleak, depressing genre with little space for hope within the story." Such dystopias only suggest utopian hope outside their pages, for "it is only if we consider dystopia as a warning that we as readers can hope to escape its pessimistic future." Critical dystopias, they argue, "maintain a utopian impulse [and] allow both readers and protagonists to hope by resisting closure."[48] This conceptualization of dystopia certainly applies to some of my films—although one difference between the 1980s works discussed by these critics and the 1990s and post-9/11 films involved here is that there is much less, if any, analysis of the specific operations that have produced the post-traumatic worlds for characters, and there is little sense of positive, secure human possibilities in the often very uncertain glimmer of hope for the future.

Moylan usefully returns to Baccolini's research on gender, genre, and feminist dystopias of the 1990s to illuminate the importance of memory and language in literary dystopias. "With the past suppressed and the present reduced to the empirica [*sic*] of daily life, dystopian subjects," Moylan writes, "usually lose all recollection of the way things were before the new order, but by regaining language they also recover the ability to draw on the alternative truths of the past and 'speak back' to hegemonic power." Moylan goes on to quote Baccolini, who has written that "memory plays a key role in the dystopian opposition and locates at least one utopian node not in what could be but in what once was." I will explore how far this insight applies to the dystopian worlds in pretraumatic cinema. Moylan notes further that "the dystopian protagonist often reclaims a suppressed and subterranean memory that is forward looking in its enabling force, liberating in its deconstruction of the official story and in its reaffirmation of alternative ways of knowing and living in the world."[49] This relationship to memory applies to some of the dystopian political thrillers discussed in the following chapters, such as *Soylent Green, The Handmaid's Tale,* and even *Blindness;* whether memory is ultimately enabling or disabling is a major focus of Chapter 4.

While I restrict my focus to cinema in this project, it is clear that many other media venues offer disaster scenarios. In 2011, Fox launched a dystopian series, *Terra Nova,* set 138 years in the future, while the TV zombie and *Survivors* series continue.[50] Wikipedia lists fifty or more titles under the category of "dystopian shows," several of which fit the futurist political thriller scenario or a combination of dystopian futurist political thriller and post-trauma cinema. See, for example, *Cold Lazarus,* a precursor for later shows, *The Powerpuff Girls, Dark Angel, Five Years Gone.* Hardly any of the listed titles fit the other subgenre I study, the narrower class of pretraumatic scenarios, although *Survivors* and *Island City* (also a precursor) exhibit many of the genre's characteristics. *Jericho* belongs in the nuclear disaster genre. The *New York Times* gave front-page billing, including a huge, ghastly image of a zombie, to announce the return of *The Walking Dead* on AMC in the fall of 2011.[51] David Itskoff's article ran with the headline "It's Never Really Dead in Zombieland: After Off-Screen Turmoil, 'The Walking Dead' Returns to Fight for Civilization." YouTube and the Internet are important venues but, I would argue, are less likely to affect largely young users deeply as they flip through the Internet from site to site.[52]

Video games are a major venue, and perhaps the fact that the player actually enters the scenario, is situated within the catastrophe, and has to deal with it personally allows more psychological agency than is required to sit through a two-hour film or a half-hour TV show. Video games with disaster scenarios have long been available, but are on the rise.[53] A "Spring/Break Art Show" opened in March 2012 in Soho, New York, with the theme "Apocalist: A Brief History of the End." The installation *Desi Monster* by Desi Santiago got much attention, but no one commented on what such a sculpture says about young people's view of their future.[54] I was reminded of a *New York* magazine article, "Coming of Age in Post-Hope America," written by Noreen Malone for the October 4, 2011, issue. The front cover shows a depressed-looking young person with "Sucks to Be Us" blazoned across her image in bright red. A series of images inside the magazine show glum or impassive faces, and the captions reflect some of the young people's concerns.

Dystopian novels abound, including those addressed to young people. Whether these fit their hopeless sense of the future or are intended to prepare them for such a future is not for me to say.[55] Marie Lu's novel *Legend*, reviewed by Ridley Pearson in the *New York Times*, follows the by now standard dystopian imaginary: the world is a future Los Angeles, "reduced, post-apocalyptic style (by an environmental disaster? We're not told) . . . and those living with the resultant plague find their homes marked with a large red X by the military."[56]

If cinema may no longer be said to be the most public medium in the digital era, it nevertheless retains its power as a special kind of public experience. While films can be viewed on numerous small devices, there is something unique about sharing the experience with others in a darkened room facing a huge screen with loud sound. The spectator enters the filmic world in a total way impossible with a small device. Film is also public in the ongoing sense of widely advertised disaster movies, blaring out at us from movie houses as we walk the streets, from huge newspaper ads, or from previews on DVDs. I focus on cinema in the context of interest in the future-selves viewers become in the public screening situation—selves that I go on to argue change our ways of being in the world. The focus is justified by the proliferation of futurist disaster movies in the wake of 9/11, even though other media also include more disaster scenarios since that catastrophe.[57]

Having established the various subsets of the futurist dystopian pretrauma genre, in the following seven chapters I develop my theoretical frameworks through analysis of the selected films. In Chapter 1, I provide a frame for the theoretical field for the book. I first take the opportunity to revisit trauma theory and meditate on what such theory has been able to achieve and what some of its limits are. I attend to criticisms from scholars in other disciplines. Next, I propose an extension of trauma theory, which takes into account the future time of the narratives as well as memories of traumatic histories. Drawing on research by Adam D. Brown and other clinical psychologists who have worked with combat veterans on autobiographical memory, PTSD, and future thinking, I theorize what it means for

viewers (as opposed to characters within dystopian fantasies) to identify
with future selves in imaginary scenarios of catastrophic devastation. Anxiety about the future incited by such fantasies may produce traumatic emotions similar to those of PTSD and a disabling uncertainty about one's own
future. But engaging in such fantasies may, on the contrary, offer what I call
"memory *for* the future," less a disabling anxiety than a productive warning to bring about needed change. Finally, I define the sci-fi subgenre that is
the primary object of the book and situate it against genres such as nuclear
holocaust cinema, though that is in many ways close to pretrauma cinema.

While the culture of fear lumps all possible catastrophes together, in the
chapters that follow I work with two kinds of catastrophic imaginings. The
division reflects the different ways that directors focus on futurist dystopian
worlds. In Chapter 2, I begin by looking at pretraumatic climate dystopias,
defining the concept of pretrauma and exploring in what ways films in this
genre offer viewers a pretrauma experience linked to catastrophic climate
change. Jeff Nichols's *Take Shelter* (2011) and M. Night Shyamalan's *The
Happening* (2009) show the world as we know it interrupted suddenly by
a catastrophic natural event, while John Hillcoat's *The Road* (2012) tracks
what happens in the wake of such a climate disaster. The pretraumatic scenario in *The Road* imagines total environmental collapse. Humans struggle
to survive in a death world devoid of institutions and civil society—a world
reduced to the chaos and lawlessness of the Wild West but now with few
heroes as such and few possible saviors. In these worlds, there is little or no
hope for any future.

The Road invites us to consider humans now as a "geologic force" as they
enter the Anthropocene.[58] Through my analysis of *The Road*, the complex
relationship between the collapse of the natural world and the disinte-
gration of the social contract emerges clearly. *The Road* raises interesting
questions about the future for human memory in a situation where the
world, as well as the human species, is dying. Viewers are again invited to
identify with future selves struggling to survive and to witness a future we
should be provoked to avoid. If both novel and film foreground a moving
relationship between a father and son, this cannot in the end hide what
I consider the *real* story of the film, namely, the fact that human impact has
turned nature into a violent presence as it surges and storms in its graphic
collapse. Yet the novel's author, Cormac McCarthy, and cinematographer
John Hillcoat (who directed the film) cannot allow the scenario to end

without a sliver of hope—utopia circles up once more, although there's in fact little on which to base any future for the characters.

In Chapter 3, I address pretrauma political dystopias, a relatively old subset of the sci-fi genre that has taken on new life and cinematic style in the wake of 9/11. Terrorism and political revenge haunt these films. Action heroes battle fascist dictators who rule dwindling social worlds. Such worlds offer bleak political possibilities very much in tune with the scenarios described by Agamben in "What Is an Apparatus?" and Žižek in *Living in the End Times*. These are worlds devoid of political subjects as such—the bourgeoisie, the workers, civil rights proponents, feminist movements—a world where all are reduced to passivity and a common bland identity, if not a terrifying subhuman existence.[59]

The films in this subset are important both in offering a pretraumatic vision of political dystopian worlds ruled by authoritarian leaders and, like the pretrauma disaster film, in raising questions about human life on the edge of extinction. Time and memory are rarely addressed by critics of these films, but I show that such concepts are central to their meanings. I situate Alfonso Cuarón's *Children of Men* (the central text in this cohort) in the context of two precursors: Richard Fleischer's *Soylent Green* (1973) and Volker Schlöndorff's *The Handmaid's Tale* (1995), made from Margaret Atwood's 1985 novel. The three films form a sort of trilogy in dealing with time and memory; they raise diverse questions about a future for memory even as they offer viewers memory for the future. In *Children of Men*, the dystopian world circles up to the utopian hope embodied in the borderless, moving ship (aptly named the *Tomorrow*), but there is no assurance that the cycle won't start over, with utopia spiraling down again.

In these films, memory takes the form of nostalgia for old, lost pleasures (such as fresh food and wine, showers, a comfortable space to live). I reserve for Chapter 4 a detailed discussion of memory in the Hughes brothers' *The Book of Eli* and Hillcoat's *The Road*. I consider the degree to which memory in the genre functions for characters more often as enabling or disabling. In some cases, memory of a political or at least a functional past inspires characters living on the edge of catastrophe to move toward redress and renewal; but memory for other characters is disabling because of the huge contrast between what was and what is now, and because traumatic loss overwhelms the subject. Writing as an indigenous poet, Simon Ortiz asks the profound question "What is memory?" from his real-life perspective in the American

West. I adapt Ortiz's question to illuminate the futurist world of dystopian fictions and to analyze the concept of memory for the future.[60] I see futurist fictions as partly displacements from the past and present, but I also look at them as constructions of the future that in turn shape the present and past. I argue that, while memory in *The Book of Eli* is enabling in a normative way, in *The Road* it is shown to be crippling, disabling of any forward movement.

In Chapter 5, I continue the focus on pretrauma political scenarios, only the spotlight is more explicitly on affect and the body in destroyed worlds. I begin by exploring issues raised in Fernando Meirelles's challenging film *Blindness*, made from José Saramago's powerful experimental novel. The film is not so much an allegory as it is the description of what happens to the body and affect in a society where resources are scarce and the social contract deteriorates. Locked in an old asylum with overflowing toilets, no water, and dwindling food and resources, the characters resort to primitive capitalism and worse. I include brief reference to *The Book of Eli*, focusing now on the film as a commercial Hollywood product. My aim is to consider what we can learn from transnational approaches to futurist worlds. I ask what happens to empathy, morality, and caring as humans enter the Anthropocene and confront the collapse of infrastructures needed to sustain human life. What happens to bodies as resources decline? Each film offers a look at the ways a primitive capitalism resurfaces in the most deprived conditions, confirming Freud's pessimistic view of human nature in *Civilization and Its Discontents*. But the overall vision of human futures differs greatly. If *The Book of Eli* focuses on the need to rebuild monuments of (largely) Western civilization in its hopelessly utopian ending, Meirelles doesn't want to leave us in a dystopian world. His conception of transformation has to do, not with artworks and high (white, male) culture, however, but with the recognition of the need for community, empathy, and caring. Both films invite the viewers to identify with future selves, but the characters in Meirelles's film are far more complex than those in *The Book of Eli* and give us much more to think about. Memory for the future plays a key role in *Blindness* as viewers watch the deterioration of bodies, relationships, humanity—but an inconclusive ending leaves the future for memory in doubt, even though the immediate scourge of blindness has passed. One fears again that utopia will spiral down to a dystopian reality.[61]

In Chapter 6, I address constructions of catastrophes that are ongoing in the new millennium. One has to look to genres other than the commercial to find the ethical witnessing of the planet's future catastrophe that I am interested in. Documentaries such as Mathieu Roy and Harold Crooks's *Surviving Progress* (2011), Michael Madsen's *Into Eternity* (2010), or Jennifer Baichwal's films *Manufactured Landscapes* (2006), and *Payback* (2012), bear witness to a probable catastrophic future that has not yet taken place—rather than to past atrocities, the typical object of trauma studies. In such films, we encounter *what must never take place*, just as, in art about the Holocaust or other genocides, we confront *what must never happen again*. As such, we are perhaps inspired to think through what needs to change in order for us to survive into the future, much as witnessing historical genocides that didn't happen to us motivates us to prevent them in the future. The two documentaries I study in depth—*Into Eternity*, Madsen's intriguing experimental film about nuclear waste, and *Manufactured Landscapes*, Baichwal's astounding reinscription of Edward Burtynsky's photographs of huge corporate intrusions into nature—capture the viewer in ways that are linked intriguingly to their position in the fictions studied earlier. In constructing the viewer as a future human being, Madsen self-consciously extends the viewer position noted in the fiction films, so that we take on a new body and imagine a future self more explicitly than before. It is an effective mechanism for asking the public not only to witness but to experience virtually a probable catastrophic future. It is a form of pretrauma linked to that in the commercial films—dramatic in a less sensational way but more disturbing in its relation to an ongoing historical project to safeguard Finland's nuclear waste.

Finally, I argue that Baichwal addresses the traumatic underside of Burtynsky's work as she travels with him to Chinese locations where projects on a monstrous scale are being undertaken without any regard for ecological destruction, human/animal devastation, or vast global implications. Without a narrative that impels a certain structure and the investment of viewers in idealized relationships, these films demand that we think about what we are seeing. Viewers cannot avoid what they are being told and shown. That the films are also constructions—presenting real events through specific lenses—goes without saying, but we have little choice about taking notice. Either way, we have to think. These films are neither dystopias nor utopias, categories that belong to most stories yet which do not serve humanity well.

The book's afterword, Chapter 7, returns to the question as to whom pretrauma cinema is addressed and also to thinking through explanations for these narratives' addressing a large (often blockbuster) audience. I return to the research categories that have concerned me from the start of this project. The devastation to come will impact everyone, but (as noted above) far from equally. Women and minorities will be affected first and suffer the most.[62] Indeed, such groups are already undergoing loss of water and agricultural land.[63] How is it then that most of the films in the pretrauma genre (both the pretrauma political thrillers and the environmental collapse films) are made by male directors about (largely) male protagonists? Of the eight feature films I deal with in some depth, all are made by male directors (two films, however, are adapted from novels by women), and all but two feature male protagonists. I consider the extent to which Susannah Radstone's concept of nostalgic masculine melancholy might be pertinent to these films, although the context and loss being mourned are not exactly the same as Radstone deals with.[64] I meditate on what I have shown about the way gender and race emerge in the genre—how minorities and women are represented and why. Finally, I take up once more the question of why the dystopia/utopia binary is so pervasive and why I think humans need to move beyond it.

1 · TRAUMA STUDIES MOVING FORWARD
Genre and Pretrauma Cinema

"Narratives and images are indexes to the still unfolding traumas of a history—the history of modernity—that has become synonymous with trauma and shocks."

—E. Ann Kaplan and Ban Wang, *Trauma and Cinema*

As should be clear by now, trauma studies as a discipline is alive and well today, and its reach is expanding as scholars in more fields find its lens illuminating for understanding art about catastrophe. Partly because global disasters dominate our mediated worlds as never before, such art is more visible than in the past. And along with such art, scholars continue to analyze not only its impact on audiences but also the ethical imperative to create witnesses to disaster through art. Years ago, Dori Laub insisted on the importance of bearing witness to catastrophe, where before there was no witness. In recent years, artists have responded by making works about global disasters.[1]

Which kind of art best offers the position of the ethical witness is central to my project and will be addressed in due course.[2] I am first interested in the interdisciplinary debates regarding theories dealing with collective or cultural trauma incited by sociologists such as Wulf Kansteiner and Jeffrey Alexander, themselves sometimes inspired by reading humanities trauma studies.[3] I will then address my new concern to move trauma studies forward—that is, into the future—by defining the genre of pretrauma cinema as it relates to a specific kind of witnessing. In this genre, viewers witness probable futurist dystopian worlds as they are imagined on film *before* they happen in reality. Media images proliferating through a society create what I have called "cultural trauma," when people live in fear of imminent disaster and fears of future threat dominate consciousness.[4] But other films offer a position of being witness *avant la lettre* to the challenges that face humans worldwide in regard to disastrous human impact on the planet and the collapse of infrastructure.

Witnessing in the ethical sense has to address not just the individual but the social collectivity as well. Such witnessing involves taking responsibility for injustices in the past and preventing future human-based catastrophe. It is a position in which one acts as a member of a collectivity or culture. Understanding this kind of cultural witnessing and its implications requires theorizing how cultural trauma functions and how we can generalize for a collectivity. Humanists have had trouble defining collective trauma. From a Freudian and specifically clinical point of view, trauma can only be known by its belated return in symptoms such as nightmares, phobias, hallucinations, panic attacks. No event, then, is inherently traumatic; it only becomes so in its later symptomatic return. Yet we talk of events themselves as being traumatic. Focusing heavily on a specific event as the origin of trauma phenomena runs the danger of rejecting the psychoanalytic understanding of memory "as the outcome of a complex process of revision"—as Susannah Radstone puts it, following Freud—in favor of a linear registration of events as they happen.[5]

Nevertheless, to abandon *trauma* is to lose the resonance and aura, if you like, that the word carries. We know we are talking about something atrocious, almost beyond understanding, if we call an event "traumatic." When I use the term *trauma culture*, I mean a culture in which discourses, and especially images, about catastrophic events proliferate, often managed by government. These discourses overtake public discussion of other things, dominating the social atmosphere. Like Jeffrey Alexander, a sociologist, I understand that trauma "is not something naturally existing; it is something constructed by society"—and, I would add, especially constructed through the media.[6] When I refer to people being "vicariously traumatized" by the proliferation of catastrophe discourse, I mean that people suffer effects similar to those from trauma, caused by watching or experiencing the trauma of others. So I use the term *trauma culture* loosely but (I'd argue) effectively. Other words do not communicate as much as the term *trauma* does.

However, the leap from describing traumatic symptoms—clarified in clinical research with individual subjects in therapy—to applying such symptoms to national discourse has long plagued humanists. While we may be intuitively right about nations "forgetting" for generations events that were too traumatic to confront directly, making a viable argument (or at least one that scholars in other disciplines will accept) has not been easy. Ross Poole, a sociologist, reminds us, "Memory requires a bearer: If there are social or cultural memories . . . there must be groups, that is collective subjects, to which the memories belong."[7] Here Freud, whose trauma theories appear to work against moving from the individual to the collective, might paradoxically be an ally. Freud starts his 1922 volume *Group Psychology and the Analysis of the Ego* by noting that, "while Individual Psychology is concerned with the individual man [*sic*] and explores the paths by which he seeks to find satisfaction for his instincts . . . only rarely . . . is Individual Psychology in a position to disregard the relations of individuals to others."[8] However, Freud's focus on the self-contained individual leads him to focus less on a cultural unconscious than on a critique of individuals losing their distinctiveness.[9] Michael Roth's extensive study of Freud provides more support from *Interpretation of Dreams* for the phenomenon of a "group mind," including a cultural unconscious.[10] He finds the concept of group repression of ideas too uncomfortable to confront. These ideas include ethnic genocide and other historical events in which a population is complicit. Carl Jung argued that myths and folktales, as well as the frequency of similar dreams that come up in psychoanalysis, provide data that suggest a group unconscious. He noted that "the collective unconscious . . . appears to consist of mythological motifs or primordial images, for which reason the myths of all nations are its real exponents."[11] But Freud went further in theorizing a motivated unconscious.

Building out from Freud, then, I suggest that, just as dreams reflect unconscious thoughts the dreamer perhaps cannot face, so group practices may be based on similar unconscious memories that a society cannot address because they are too shameful or morally unacceptable within that society's norms. More recently, cognitive psychologists offer support from experiments to test theories of a "group mind." In their studies Alin Coman, Adam D. Brown, Jonathan Koppel and William Hirst conclude that, "just as social contagion shapes individual and group attitudes and behavior by providing individuals and groups with new memories, we posit that induced forgetting shapes individual and group attitudes and behavior through the opposite means."[12]

Teresa Brennan, heavily influenced by Freud and psychoanalytic theory, offers a related but somewhat different hypothesis regarding groups. Her theory builds out from her interesting work on what she calls "the transmission of affect." Brennan argues, "To understand how the transmission of affect takes place, metapsychology has to begin again, and from the standpoint that individuals are not self-contained." What she calls "the foundational fantasy" fosters the illusion of self-containment, that is, the mother is situated as the "passive repository of the child's unwanted raging affects" while the infant is "the true fountain of energy and life."[13] For Brennan, affects are social and predate the individual. The subject is born into a world of affects that then become his or her own. This readiness to receive the affects of the other as well as of the culture and be changed by them—a kind of emotional contagion that Hirst and Koppel also theorized—explains in part the impact on viewers of dystopian fantasies in the films I study. Transmission of affect takes place as readily between viewer and cinematic emotions as between individuals in life.

Humanists can benefit from Freud, especially as Roth interprets him, as well as from Brennan and cognitive psychology. But there remains a need to better clarify the difference between a national public discourse, creating a "group mind" through pronouncements by prominent officials (the president, governors, elected officials) and circulated broadly via various media, and minority discourses produced by small collectives whose knowledge does not get widely disseminated.[14] Humanists need to better differentiate between perpetrators and victims. Criminal acts performed in the name of the nation-state are often the ones that elected officials work to render absent, forgotten in public discourse. This is an effort that the majority of the people (those not affected by the crimes) might concede to, either because they are partly implicated in those crimes or, as humanities scholars might argue, because they themselves are vicariously traumatized by what the nation has done.[15]

Traumatic memory, in its belatedness, involves a kind of forgetting. Victim collectives may also forget, through the same process of traumatic amnesia experienced by the perpetrators. Meanwhile, the discourse of those who do remember is stifled, until the time arrives when the nation-state can no longer suppress its crimes. As Poole notes, when rediscovered knowledge of organized brutality is addressed to us as citizens of the state, this knowledge falls within "the 'horizon' of our collective memory and it places the events described on our moral agenda."[16] Poole's comments capture what humanities scholars have in mind when they talk about nations' also showing effects similar to traumatic symptoms in individuals.

In examining the impact of imaginary worlds and the humanities' critical work on society, let me suggest the following: works enter the cultural sphere, where they are shown and reviewed and discussed in widely circulating blogs, Internet sites, television entertainment channels, journals, and newspapers. In these ways, these works seep into public consciousness. We may turn to the popularity of films and literature about trauma as partial evidence for impact. As Alexander has argued, certain events get circulated in symbolic form and thus come into public consciousness. He gives the example of the Holocaust and pervasive emotionally moving literature, such as Anne Frank's diary, or the increasing Holocaust cinema in the last decade or so.[17]

In a work on the global impact of catastrophic memories, Michael Rothberg discusses one result of such public consciousness. A group that has suffered a traumatic event might come to recognize the event's meanings when, through visual media or written texts, it learns about another catastrophe. As people come to view their particular tragedy through the lens of, say, the Holocaust, they may initiate less a competitive memory and more solidarity and understanding across cultures in regard to trauma.[18] Further, new neuroscience research demonstrates not only that fictions stimulate the brain but also that, as Annie Murphy Paul puts it, they may "even change how we act in life." Paul notes that "the brain, it seems, does not make much of a distinction between reading about an experience and encountering it in real life." This is obviously debatable, but it seems that humanists may not be so far out of line. We can show that humanists contribute to knowledge using their aesthetic (literary, film) data and draw on social processes linked to that data.[19]

But we do more than that, because we also use frameworks such as psychoanalysis that is not typically very visible in sociological studies. Alexander, for example, argues that the failure to recognize collective traumas results not from the intrinsic nature of the original suffering (which humanists usually focus on) but from the failure to carry through on the gap between the event and its representation, what he calls "the trauma process."[20] This process has several stages, but at each stage—from defining painful injury to the collectivity to distributing ideal and material consequences—the signifying chains of language, sound, and images (that is, representation) are the medium, and this not only in the aesthetic realm but also in the legal, scientific, mass media, and state bureaucratic worlds.

Humanists' objects of study differ from those of sociologists to the extent that our specific data is at one remove from lived reality, namely, the worlds of literature, film or digital media, and other arts. We come close to the sociological object, however, because they emerge from the society and culture that are studied by sociologists, such imaginary worlds are closely linked to it. Humanists' focus on the cultural role of genre, and its importance is often overlooked by sociologists. Through genres, literature and the arts showcase symptoms of social processes, cultural energies, and cultural change. They provide us with a barometer of what's going on in any particular society. In the case of trauma studies, humanist scholars produce new knowledge concerning trauma and its cultural ramifications by studying the contribution of art about atrocity in the processes of memory (past, present, and future), and by witnessing, healing, and the working through of both national and international catastrophes.

However, such approaches in trauma studies now need complementing by exploring the trauma of the future—what I call *pretrauma*. The genre of pretrauma cinema, like others, offers "a powerful dynamic of repetition and expectation" that is the ground, as Christine Gledhill puts it, of "all our imaginings and thinkings."[21] Thinking about the role of society and trauma, one can conclude that genre analysis tells us not just about kinds of films but also about the cultural work of producing and knowing them.[22] By definition, genres change as the social context changes. In this case, part of the critic's job is to lay bare such dual contexts of society and genre. The pretrauma genre emerges as Eurocentric cultures become newly aware of the uncertainty of human futurity. Genres shape how we think about our lived worlds by establishing certain kinds of story, certain repeated narratives and situations, that lead to well-defined expectations. It is just such work of genres that I hope to show—first, by further defining the new pretraumatic film and then, in the chapters that follow, by presenting analyses of films in the genre.

The pretrauma dystopian genre addressed in this book is a subset of the familiar science-fiction film, itself notoriously difficult to define.[23] The worlds in the future-tense subset function both to further a culture of fear about social collapse and to work against the exploitation of catastrophe through subtle critique (for example, by offering a position for the viewer as witness to the damage being done). I began to study such futurist fictions as partly displacements from the past and present, but I have come to see them also as constructions of the future, which in turn shape the present and the past.

There are two genres related to the new dystopian futurist subset, namely, classic science fiction (with its long literary and film tradition) and nuclear disaster cinema.[24] What is it that distinguishes the new pretrauma genre? As regards classic sci-fi, Ronald Emmerich's popular *Independence Day* (1996) serves as a useful placeholder to differentiate the disaster films I am interested in. As a classic example of sci-fi, *Independence Day* starts with an enormous spaceship already almost on top of planet Earth. What ensues is the desperate attempt of scientists, the military, and presidential teams to destroy the monstrous ship, after they realize that its passengers are not, after all, friendly. The patriotic fervor is perhaps more exaggerated than in many films, but still, patriotism is often involved. America and its mighty power save the major cities being targeted worldwide.[25] The film's images of New York's huge skyscrapers being demolished look uncannily like images seared in our minds from 9/11, so an allegorical reading of the film as anticipating powerful foreign attacks makes sense.

The new films focus on human and natural causes of social collapse and don't displace cultural anxieties into allegories of aliens invading planet Earth, as in standard sci-fi such as, for example, Spielberg's *War of the Worlds* (2005), a remake of the 1953 classic based on H. G. Wells's novel, which may be read as an allegory for the Holocaust. Terry Eagleton also reads sci-fi as using an "elsewhere as a reflection on where you are."[26]

As regards nuclear disaster, there are enough American films to constitute another subset of the disaster genre, and these more closely approach the pretrauma genre than those in regular science-fiction cinema. There are significant differences between nuclear-disaster films and future-tense trauma cinema. First, in contrast to the future-tense genre, this subset relates to a specific technology that is a real threat to human life and to a specific political context, that is, the Cold War between the United States and the Soviet Union. *On the Beach* (1959) and *Fail-Safe* (1964) are classics of this subset. While Susan Sontag saw fear of nuclear war as a central anxiety in 1950s films generally, these films address the fear head-on.[27]

Some films—such as the B movie *The World, the Flesh and the Devil* (1959), the controversial TV drama *The Day After* (1983), and the powerful British film *Threads* (1984)—actually anticipate one subset of the genre, namely, the pretrauma climate dystopias, in which an apparently secure world of characters going about their daily lives is suddenly interrupted by a catastrophic climate event. Tragically, in a similar way as we saw with *Independence Day*, some of these nuclear-disaster films anticipated the 2011 Japanese catastrophe, when a tsunami suddenly broke through the levees protecting a nuclear power plant in Fukushima Daiichi and created an abrupt hell for the people living in the area.

Beyond my scope here, but crucial to mention, is the riveting new attention to nuclear disaster in the wake of this catastrophe. There has been a flood of films, literature, and journalism following the meltdown and its horrifying impact on Japan and other nations globally.[28] The area was almost instantly turned into what looks like an historical equivalent of the traumatic scenarios depicted in the films I am studying. A major difference between the pretrauma genre about destroyed worlds and the nuclear-disaster genre is that the pretrauma genre worlds are often ones that have long suffered deprivation—worlds that have slowly been declining over a long time.

A third related genre, theorized by Claire King, overlaps somewhat with the pretrauma genre, but just in relation to select films. King's research differs from my current project because she views post-traumatic films as allegories (or screen memories, in Freud's sense) that displace into disaster narratives unpleasant realities about U.S. culture's destructive and violent actions. King usefully and cogently demonstrates how popular culture has seized on trauma discourse as a way to reinstate the status quo. According to King, the films posit an a priori coherent male subject, who then suffers a fracturing traumatic shock and, through heroic sacrificial acts often leading to his death, returns his culture (and himself) to wholeness, security, a fantasized plenitude. King argues that trauma culture in this sense is a disservice, because it blinds publics to the reality of their dangerous situation.[29] My project, by contrast, tries to move trauma theory forward by analyzing at least one set of films—not as allegories but, as Margaret Atwood also claims, probable future worlds.[30]

Novels like Aldous Huxley's *Brave New World* and George Orwell's *1984* portray a dehumanized negative utopia, but significantly, *social systems, even if repressive, remain in place.* At least one subset of the post-9/11 futurist disaster genre (including Margaret Atwood's *Year of the Flood*), however, does not allay fears (as Sontag suggests) or simply reflect on today (as Eagleton notes) but, rather, produces a deeper shock through imaging the total collapse of systems of meaning and social life altogether.[31] As Mark Bould and Sherryl Vint point out in their excellent *Routledge Concise History of Science Fiction*, "Since the end of the Cold War, many feel that it is easier to imagine the end of the world than the end of capitalism." They mention Kim Stanley Robinson's *Science in the Capital* trilogy, which follows models of global warming derived from climate-change science to imagine worlds "in which humanity barely and only provisionally, survives." Their conclusion from this and other examples is that "the only imaginable end of capitalism lies in the approach to the end of the world itself." As I also show in the pretrauma political thriller subset, we are witnessing, in Giorgio Agamben's words, "the eclipse of politics, which used to presuppose the existence of subjects and real identities (the workers' movement, the bourgeoisie)."[32] With the "state of exception," Agamben defines the world of pretrauma cinema. It is a matter no longer only of dictatorial control but now also of democratic process, in which people allow themselves to be controlled, that is, they do not revolt when leaders declare a state of exception as a necessity, supposedly for the people's own protection.[33] Discussing contemporary politics, Agamben argues that as an increasingly "dominant paradigm of government in contemporary politics . . . the state of exception appears as a threshold of indeterminacy between democracy and absolutism."[34]

Second, and equally important, in the new films the devastation of the world is the premise for narratives however different, requiring that the films be set in the future—albeit a future still recognizable. This future may be just a few decades away, unlike completely futurist technological cinema such as *The Matrix* (1999), the *Terminator* series (1984–2015), or even *Transformers: Dark of the Moon* (2011). If classic sci-fi plots set in the directors' contemporary time are about preventing the world (or locality) from being destroyed by usually hostile aliens coming from afar, most of the new disaster films are set in a future near to the director's time.

Margaret Atwood agrees with such a distinction between classical science fiction and the related futurist genre—pretrauma imaginaries (my term); speculative fiction (Atwood's term). By "speculative fiction," she means "plots that descend from Jules Verne's books about . . . things that really could happen but just hadn't completely happened. . . . I would place my own book in this second category: No Martians."[35] Atwood coins the term "ustopia" for her own first dystopia in *The Handmaid's Tale* and describes the worlds she creates as what human beings have already done or are likely to do under certain circumstances.[36] As Joyce Carol Oates puts it, echoing Atwood, "there is no reliance on 'other worlds' in the conventional SF sense of alien infiltration. If there is species destruction, it will be interspecies."[37]

The nearness of the new futurist disaster genre to the director's time justifies the term *pretrauma*, because the traumatic scenario is one already seemingly possible given scientific projections (for example, of the devastating impact of climate change). These films then are not allegories. They insist on the probability of the worlds shown or, to refer again to Timothy Morton, the possibility of these worlds already being here.[38] The obsession with dates, numbers, time, and futurist elements in many titles emphasizes the probability of the trauma—it already has a date! Such titles include *28 Days Later, 2012,* and *The Day after Tomorrow.* Other films feature numbers, such as *12 Monkeys, Nine,* and *District 9,* or the date is noted early in the film, as in *Children of Men,* when 2027 is prominently displayed. Most of these films set in the future start with the world already destroyed, with all systems and coherent life gone, or the world is destroyed very early in the film. The plot is about how usually white males survive the destruction while saving a woman or child. The difference between films set in highly improbable futures and those in the pretraumatic genre I isolate says much about the sociocultural shape of deepening imaginaries of disaster.[39]

The subgenre of dystopian films is a genre, then, which serves as a future-oriented memory for audiences watching: we are invited to live for two hours in desolated environments, experiencing desperate humans who seek to survive the total collapse of infrastructures on which we humans depend. This offers spectators a way to remember what we have now and what we should not lose. The invitation aims to mitigate future tragedies, but there is the question of how identifying with such future traumatic selves may impact the viewer's psyche.

It turns out that research by Adam D. Brown and his colleagues usefully addresses the question of such impact. The concept of pretrauma benefits here from research in cognitive psychology on future selves. While most of this research does not dwell on future selves in the context of climate catastrophe, my work dovetails with that of Brown and his team working with combat victims. Although I explore pretraumatic stress and Brown examines future selves in the context of Post-Traumatic Stress Syndrome, there is nevertheless synergy. Brown explores the impact of PTSD on subjects' future imagined or "possible" selves in ways productive for this book.[40] In 2011, Brown's team found that "individuals with PTSD viewed their . . . pretrauma self more favorably than their current or anticipated future self."[41] Meanwhile, Hazel Markus and Paula Nurius have found that "the pool of possible selves derives from the categories made salient by the individual's particular sociocultural and historical context and from the models, images and symbols provided by the media and by the individual's immediate social experiences." They go on to argue that "possible selves . . . reflect the extent to which the self is socially determined and constrained." Further, they suggest that "possible selves are important because they function as incentives for future behavior (i.e. they are selves to be approached or avoided) and second, because they provide an evaluative and interpretive context for the current view of self."[42]

This latter idea is important for the future selves that viewers encounter in pretraumatic cinema. In connection with textual representation, the impact of these future selves is suggested by theorizing spectator experiences of viewing traumatized subjects in futurist fictional worlds. Although our methodologies are different (the psychologists conduct experiments with student subjects, while I theorize traumatized selves in fictional context), the projects' connection is revealing. While Brown's work is unidimensional, mine involves two levels: first, inferring spectator reaction to futurist traumatic fictions and what the reaction says about memory for the future (and the future for memory) on both the individual and the social level; second, studying the depiction of memory in relation to a future self on the part of characters within the dystopian narrative as such.

The central question here is, What is the impact on the viewers watching a pretraumatic futurist scenario in regard to their sense of their own future self? If the veterans' traumatic war experience, lived as PTSD upon their return to the United States, is shown to change how the veterans view their future, what about these pretraumatic visions of the viewers' future? Brown's research, then, raises several questions for me: In what ways do these identifications also alter the subject's idea of a future as a human being facing possible catastrophes? And how does the situation of living in uncertain times change people? In the following chapters, I explore the images of future selves in pretraumatic worlds figuring forth catastrophic social collapse. I discuss the politics of how those selves are imaged as dealing with such collapse, along with theorizing the impact of the future selves on the viewer.

2 · PRETRAUMA CLIMATE SCENARIOS

Take Shelter, The Happening, and The Road

"It is the end of the world because I can see past the lip of the horizon of human worlding. Global warming reaches into 'my world' and forces me to use LED's instead of bulbs with filaments."

—Timothy Morton, *Hyperobjects*

The worlds in all the films discussed in this project offer pretrauma scenarios in the sense that they all figure forth destroyed worlds and devastated humans in catastrophic situations that have not yet happened, or the situations may have happened to certain ethnic or marginalized humans but the dominant white middle class does not yet know it.[1] Viewers are invited to engage with pretrauma narratives by identifying with a probable traumatic future. As in Michael Madsen's documentary about nuclear waste (see Chapter 6), the viewer is addressed as a potential virtual future human.

I start with discussion of Jeff Nichols's *Take Shelter*, the only film in this group whose *protagonist*, as against its viewers, is traumatized by something that has not yet happened. The protagonist, Curtis LaForche, suffers quite classic symptoms of PTSD (violent nightmares, hallucinations, flashbacks) even though the events that trouble him have not yet come about. PTSD is often marked by unheralded intrusions of past traumas into one's present experience. In this case, something in the present triggers memories of a traumatic event. In *Take Shelter*, Curtis appears to experience future events directly, until the film's viewers realize he is having nightmares or hallucinations. The film thus depicts an example of the phenomenon I am calling pretraumatic stress. It also offers spectators a view of their own position as spectators of pretrauma films, that is, Curtis is in a similar position to that of the pretrauma film's viewers: his fantasies of catastrophic climate change are similar to the fantasies viewers watch in the genre.

However, there is a difference in positioning vis-à-vis the traumatic events: viewers rarely suffer pretraumatic symptoms as directly as Curtis or to the same degree from watching such scenarios. Rather, they occupy the vicarious (or secondary) trauma position and, following a screening, may express only minor or no symptoms, depending on personal difference.[2] Anticipatory anxiety perhaps best expresses what viewers endure in watching this genre of films. Two of the three films considered here, *Take Shelter* and *The Happening*, start in the present of a Western society (the United States or, for a moment, Paris), but things very quickly become terrifying for varied reasons. The pretrauma climate distress for viewers is in each film a central part of the affect generated.

All the films discussed in this chapter invite us to reconsider the symbiosis of nature and humans in a future where the natural world is either undergoing disturbing dramatic changes, as in *Take Shelter* or *The Happening*, or it is all but destroyed, as in *The Road*. But the futurist pretrauma disturbances envisaged in the films emerge because of changes already at work in the cultural discourses that the film directors are responding to. I am thinking especially of the ways in which discussions that used to be about "nature" have gradually been replaced with discussions of "climate." In a sense, the change from *nature* to *climate* parallels another change I have discussed elsewhere, namely, the change from *world* to *planet*.[3] This shift requires a longer discussion than I can give it here, but suffice it to say that I understand the move to be reflecting a change in Western cultural discourse from a focus on the social and the aesthetic to a focus on science and danger.[4]

Dipesh Chakrabarty stresses that, by becoming geological agents, humans have disturbed the essential conditions (such as the planet's temperature zone) they need to survive on Earth. In his words, we have destabilized "the parametric conditions needed for our own existence."[5] Humans have arrived at this juncture through their drive toward what was seen as "progress" (we now view it differently) ever since the Industrial Revolution and the widespread introduction of fossil fuels.[6] The competitive drive that brought humanity to its current plight endures in all the works considered here in the form of competition for survival, rendering each futurist world a travesty of the utopian ideals humans strove for in earlier periods. As Jane Elliott points out, neoliberalism encourages such competitive drive rather than offering other models for survival.[7]

What's at stake in these pretrauma scenarios is a new orientation to the ages-long assumption about the closeness of humans to the natural world. The film fantasies stimulate us to move toward such thinking and toward remembering about a relationship that has been taken for granted as crucial to the human. In his comparative international history of attitudes toward the environment, *Environmentalism: A Global History*, Ramachandra Guha notes that, in early indigenous cultures such as that of Australian Aborigines, the intensely fused human-ecology relationship goes back millennia; in later indigenous cultures, it goes back thousands of years and in Asia for a very long time (e.g., Chinese traditional landscape painting renders nature as a regenerative, wild refuge). Guha does the important work of describing historical non-Western environmental movements in India and elsewhere.[8] In Western antiquity, as Lyn White Jr. has shown, spirits were believed to inhabit everything in nature, and these had to be placated before any cutting could happen. But when they destroyed paganism, Christians made exploiting nature permissible. The Romantic Movement revived reverence for nature, and for centuries poets and philosophers in all cultures have written at length about nature, assumed the importance of the natural landscape to humans, and drawn inspiration from it.[9]

Perhaps the most familiar Western voice on the subject of human nature and the natural world is William Wordsworth's. His intuition of the natural world's moral influence on humans (found particularly in *The Prelude* and *Tintern Abbey*) charts an extreme position even for his own time, but American Transcendentalists such as Ralph Waldo Emerson and Henry David Thoreau later posited similar relationships to nature.[10] If poetry and fiction have long explored this terrain, perhaps it is most obvious in the history of Western landscape painting and in theories of the sublime deriving from German philosophy.

These various traditions established a Western view of the sublime or impressive natural landscape. In his introduction to *Landscape and Film*,

Martin Lefebvre argues that the legacy of five hundred years of Western landscape imagery is that people in the natural environment "find a view by creating or shaping it through framing." Ordinarily, he says, "we look at the natural environment *as if it* were framed. . . . The form of landscape is thus first of all the form of a view, of a particular gaze that requires a frame." Further, "with that frame nature turns into culture, land into landscape."[11] With her research into colonial adventurers, Mary Louise Pratt has shown the process whereby foreign nature was transformed into European, Victorian-style vistas. Analyzing Richard Burton's travel writing on Central African lake regions in 1860, Pratt observes that "first, and most obvious, the landscape is *estheticized* [*sic*]. The sight is seen as a painting, and the description ordered in terms of background, foreground, symmetries . . . and so forth."[12] Ann Bermingham's research on eighteenth- and nineteenth-century English rustic painting in *Landscape and Ideology* illustrates the traditions on which Pratt's travelers drew, including the idealization of nature, to provide sustaining myths for urban culture in the long modernity of Western industrialism. In this period, the natural world was plundered, its resources were exploited, and the security of the natural environment and its endless riches were taken for granted—all in the name of a triumphal concept of progress that spoke to the times. The horrific result of this process is tragically depicted in Jennifer Baichwal's film *Manufactured Landscapes* (discussed in greater detail later on). The film overturns the earlier idea of industrialism as a primary benefit to human society just as recent nuclear power disasters have tempered utopian views of atomic research.[13]

Some critics now question not only earlier "nature writers" and their sentimentality about nature's beauty but newer eco-critics who tend to idealize nature.[14] Even before the current influence of eco-criticism in the academy, Joyce Carol Oates meditated on the long Western tradition in regard to nature. Her distinction between "Nature-in-Itself" and "Nature-As-Experience" makes sense, but her statement that, contrary to what many eco-critics believe, "Nature has no instructions for mankind" is ironic in that nature now is offering instruction to humankind by its very violent intrusions into human civilizations, flooding where we build, ripping out power lines, piling up ever more snow, producing more tornados, and so on.[15]

In his fascinating thought experiment, Alan Weisman wonders, "How would nature undo our monumental cities and public works?" and imagines it taking revenge on humans once we have allowed our own extinction.

"After we're gone, nature's revenge for our smug, mechanized superiority arrives waterborne," and he goes on in graphic, painful detail to describe how water seeps into our houses, pulling them apart essentially.[16] Meanwhile Kate Soper's masterful *What Is Nature?* explores and illuminates debates between ecological advocacy of nature by some, aimed at conserving it, and post-structuralist critics who argue for the cultural construction of nature that now pervades the academy. As early as 1995, Soper aimed to resolve tensions between two dominant groups—termed by her, "nature-endorsing" and "nature-skeptical" approaches.

In addition, the Virtual Age that followed fast on the heels of global industrial modernization has already begun to drastically alter human relationship to nature in a different sense than that of industrialization. People, and especially children, spend more time on the computer than outside, so that some academics see a need to reintroduce a sensitivity to nature to college students. While discussions of the impact of the Internet on humans and the environment often involve New Age sentimentalism and idealism in their critiques of domestic life in the Digital Age, new programs in environmental humanities and the arts are developing in tandem with scholarly research on the role of literature and film in attending to dangers of environmental degradation.[17] Some of these programs mark a strange, belated return to Wordsworthian impulses, now out of desperation for what humans are doing to nature. In aiming to newly sensitize young students living in their digital virtual worlds to "caring" for nature, programs bring students out of their digital comfort in order to examine marine life. (See, for example, the University of California at Santa Barbara's Carsey-Wolf Center project "Figuring Sea Level Rise," which aims to increase students' awareness of water and its importance.)[18]

In a more explicit return to an idea of nature as essential for healthy human development (this time via Emerson and Thoreau), Richard Louv critiques the focus on pathology and human disasters in research on nature and human health. Articles proliferate today about the danger to young children of what *New York Times* columnist Nicholas Kristof has called "toxic stress" (uncontrolled pollutants in the air they breathe and the food they eat), and environmentalists are right to pay detailed attention to corporate disasters that create health hazards wherever these disasters impact natural worlds. But given new discoveries in and the pervasiveness of neuroscience, it makes sense to ask whether there is evidence that the natural environment has a role in shaping the architecture of the brain. Again, it seems, little research has been undertaken to show any shaping of the natural world on both emotions and morality, or on affect more generally, leaving authors little else to do but return to the traditional wilderness ideology being critiqued by many humanist environmentalists. As Louv notes, research studies are hard to find, because scientists immediately ask, "How do you define nature?" It seems that for this group, anything molecular is "nature," rendering moot the question of the natural environment.[19]

Timothy Morton, working within multiple discourses, including those of science, philosophy, psychology, literature, and the arts, takes such issues to a fascinating and terrifying extreme. For Morton, as indicated in his subtitle to *Hyberobjects*, which reads "Philosophy and Ecology after the End of the World," nature no longer exists. As he puts it, "The aesthetics of Nature impedes ecology and a good argument for why ecology must be without nature." The end of the world is already here. "The spooky thing is," Morton says, "we discover global warming precisely when it's already here."[20] For Morton, global warming is one of a number of what he calls "hyperobjects"—objects so large and all-encompassing that we can't see or think them. Nevertheless, they dominate our lives. "Global warming," he says (in his characteristic way of bringing things down to earth through his own body), "reaches into 'my world' and forces me to use LED's instead of bulbs with filaments."[21]

In some of the pretraumatic futurist scenarios discussed below the natural environment has long been polluted almost out of existence. Protagonists of the dystopian environmental subgenre have no time or leisure to find a position from which to gaze at the natural world becoming "landscape." The films offer a world opposite to that of the Romantic tradition. While indeed humans and the natural world are symbiotic, they are now negatively so. Instead of the idea of nature as a positive moral guide, it is now imaged as dying, and taking humans along with it.[22] Nature discourse does not even return to the shapelessness and incoherence it had in antiquity or to its pre-Renaissance subordination to religion. It is now not even what humans can rely on for sustenance, since nature, having been stripped of all life, no longer bears any fruit or flowers, leaves or nuts. No longer a passive object of the human gaze, nature in its dying is now active, a negative force, a violent presence, oftentimes an actor in its own right.

As a supreme example of PreTSS, *Take Shelter* is situated at the cusp of the cultural unconscious and the uncanny. Curtis, the protagonist,

FIG. 2–1 POV shot of Curtis at his front door apparently looking at a terrible storm approaching.

represents the cultural unconscious about global warming. He represents those humans who are anticipating climate catastrophe and who are traumatized by anticipatory visions before they have even happened. In a very interesting way, through editing, the narrative from the filmic present slides into Curtis's futurist climate fantasies in such a way that at first we are not sure if the violent storms and accompanying zombie figures and monstrous dogs are part of the film's narrative present, as in other zombie works.

As the film opens, Curtis, standing outside his modest house, sees the trees begin to shake wildly. He pauses to check what looks like a very threatening sky. The over-the-shoulder shot captures huge black clouds curling in very strange ways; thunder and lightning dominate the soundtrack, and rain (or what seems to be rain) pours down. It is a so-called establishing scene, common to classical cinema. We are given our protagonist, standing outside his house, and we are shown the landscape that he sees. But even if only unconsciously, viewers sense that something is not right. In fact, things feel uncanny already, as the title sequence unfolds given the Tinker-Bell-like music on the soundtrack. The repeated bell sound suggests something eerie, off-balance. Likewise, in the opening shot of trees with leaves shaken by a wind, the viewer may notice that the speed is slightly slower than normal, giving things an uncanny feeling. The light is not quite balanced, being either too sharp or too dark. As the shot continues, a loud bass instrument complementing the bell sound is mixed with the noise of thunder. Shots of uncanny dark clouds add to the strangeness, and yet the viewer tries to accept that what he or she is seeing is a normal

FIG. 2–2 Curtis in close-up winces at what's pouring from the sky.

stormy landscape. Curtis's gaze seems intense as he looks upward at the rain falling.

We cut to Curtis's hand in extreme close-up and discover that what's falling is not rain but brown oil. As Curtis looks at the sky again, water pouring on his head, the film cuts to Curtis in the shower. The viewers realize that Curtis must have had a hallucination of such a climate catastrophe and may feel as if they've been played with. But they are also fascinated. The director has captured their attention.

This powerful and shocking opening sequence sets the stage for what will follow in terms of one narrative strand of the film, namely, Curtis's pretrauma dreams and hallucinations of catastrophic climate change. This strand is intertwined with the main world of the film, that of Curtis's family life and his middle-class midwestern culture. The cut from the shower to a close-up of a pan of scrambled eggs brings reality upfront. As Curtis enters the room, looking tense, we have shots of his wife, Samantha, and (as we soon learn) hearing-impaired daughter, Hannah, who is petting the dog as she feeds him. Everything in the shot looks utterly normal, a family having breakfast, and the parents' talk is about daily issues.

A skilled worker, Curtis nevertheless faces big problems in his personal life. His hearing-impaired daughter requires expensive surgery; Samantha, amiable and accommodating, has long been hankering for a seaside cottage. She earns extra money by making and selling handmade silk items at the local weekend market. Loving moments between the couple happen periodically, while tensions arise increasingly over Curtis's behavior, which disconcerts Samantha. Curtis's relationship with Dewart, his mate on the

FIG. 2–3 This close-up shows it's oil, not rain.

FIG. 2–4 Dewart is skeptical of Curtis's plans to build an elaborate tornado shelter.

construction site where he works, is equally complex and Dewart is disturbed by Curtis's strange moods.

The local white Christian community that Curtis and his wife belong to and their daily lives are nicely detailed. Curtis and his friends, however, are all seen living their middle-class life on the edge (in that sense as well, the film hits a contemporary note). This only adds to Curtis's psychic stress.[23]

Jeff Nichols clearly wants viewers to keep a dual focus throughout—on the one hand, that of an uncanny and uncertain environment and an unsettled, unpredictable hero, and on the other, that of a typical white middle-class family living their daily lives under the same kind of economic and social stresses as are endured by many couples. Nichols subtly indicates the uncertainty about the natural world, which is intertwined with his portrayal of daily work and family life. For example, as Curtis leaves his house after the opening sequence and goes toward his car, the camera cuts away from him and slowly moves up into the blue sky, where it pauses a moment. We then have a close-up of green grasses shaking in a breeze, before the camera settles on a flat square of concrete. A loud drilling noise enters the soundtrack along with a close-up of a large drilling machine. Curtis is at work on the construction site with his mate, Dewart.

Nichols thus keeps our awareness of something uncanny at work through periodically inserting shots of nature that do not further the narrative, and by including at such times the unnerving bell- or single-note sound on the track. In doing this, he unsettles viewers' expectations as regards conventions of classic Hollywood cinema, which demand that every shot has a narrative purpose. Viewers are thus put on edge as to what kind of a world we are involved in, as Nichols blurs the distinction between what is diegetically "real," and what is illusory. This enhances the PreTSS aspect of the film by bringing viewers into Curtis's own uncertainty.

One day while working with Dewart on the construction site, Curtis pauses to look at the sky. The soundtrack changes as we have a shot counter-shot, followed by another point-of-view shot. We see what Curtis now sees, namely, the sky eerily filled with huge swarms of birds gathering in wild formations, swooping in rapid motion almost down to earth and back again. Dewart has not seen anything, while Curtis (and the viewers) try to take in the strange event. Later in the film, Curtis has another hallucination about birds, only this time it's far more brutal with birds dropping by the dozen to fall dead on the road. As often in these episodes, Hannah is in danger. Indeed, Curtis's anxiety about Hannah is a central part of nearly all the pretraumatic hallucinations. More than just showing Curtis's love for his child, which is important in developing his character as a complex postfeminist masculine figure, depicting a child in such tremendous danger hits right at the heart of unconscious anticipatory anxiety about climate change. If they think at all about the dangers of climate change, most parents realize that their children, rather than themselves, will suffer the worst consequences of what their generation is allowing to happen. Even if they don't consciously think about such dangers, unconsciously they know. In figuring Hannah in these hallucinations, then, Nichols manages to disturb audiences even more.

FIG. 2–5 Another POV shot, as Curtis stops work to stare at the strange behavior of the birds.

FIG. 2–6 Curtis holds Hannah tight as another hallucination starts.

Curtis's reactions to his hallucinations jeopardize his family life. He is late for important social events. A very abrupt cut from Curtis and his family at a meeting at Hannah's special school (everyone is learning sign language) shows another huge storm in process. Since viewers have witnessed such a storm earlier on, when Samantha taught Hannah the sign for "storm," we think it's just another regular climate event. Curtis is at home as the storm starts. He gets in the car and looks at Hannah with him in the front seat. As he wipes his face, once again it seems oil is raining down, not water. As he drives, things get very blurry; a figure in a raincoat can be dimly seen. Everything goes black as Curtis is knocked out as the car crashes. When he recovers, zombie-like figures break into the car and seize him; one reaches in and carries Hannah off, just as Curtis is being strangled by another zombie. When it would seem that the viewers can not take any more, the film cuts once more to a shot of Curtis waking up screaming from another nightmare. We realize that Nichols has been playing with us again, continuing to unsettle our sense of the filmic world. We cannot rely on its being dependable.

Curtis's pretraumatic hallucinations and nightmares increase in their ferocity and their terrifying climate-change effects. Curtis is losing his sense of what's real and what's hallucination or dream. As our hero loses touch with reality, so we are also made uncertain about the status of what we are seeing. As we watch Curtis jeopardize his own and, in the end, his work mate's jobs, we become increasingly unsettled and anxious for these decent people caught up in something very strange.

After finding Hannah playing with a dangerous piece of wood from a trash pile in the yard, Samantha tells Curtis he needs to clear the pile out since it could hurt Hannah. We cut to what we assume is the next day with Curtis dealing with the trash, when suddenly he looks at the sky. We cut to a point-of-view shot of Curtis facing a sky full of dark threatening clouds that fill half the screen and almost consume Curtis. The dog barks frantically, and the noise of thunder grows ever louder on the soundtrack. Suddenly there's a cut to Hannah (whom we didn't know was outside) standing by her playhouse—and a cut back to the same shot of Curtis looking at the sky, only now it's more threatening than ever. A shot of Curtis holding Hannah's hand cuts to a close-up of the dog becoming ever more frantic now. The dog suddenly breaks loose and savagely attacks Curtis, his teeth buried in Curtis's arm. If we partly believed the events were actually taking place, the cut from Curtis screaming in pain (we have a close-up of Curtis's mouth open wide, making blood-curdling cries) to Curtis awakening from what seems to have been a nightmare, settles the point. The edit brings us to Curtis waking up screaming and holding his arm as if it hurts.

The next sequence shows Curtis sitting at the breakfast table and brooding. There is an unsettling high-pitched note on the soundtrack, unusually loud and unpleasant. Again, Nichols is breaking cinematic convention in inserting the sound from one strand of the film—Curtis's hallucinations— over a "normal" family scene, confusing the viewer. There's a cut to Hannah calmly stroking the quiet dog who was so wild in the hallucination.

FIG. 2−7 His nightmare is so real, Curtis hugs his painful arm.

This dream follows Curtis for days afterward. We see him at work stroking his arm, apparently still unable to believe that what happened was only a dream. It is clear that his worry about the environment and about the violent events that go with terrifying climate events are hindering his ability to undertake his work responsibilities. He continues to worry about his arm, which suggests that he is suffering from what trauma theorists have called classic post-traumatic stress symptoms. But, importantly, in this case the symptoms come from *anticipation* of a climate catastrophe, not in the wake of the disaster experience.

Because Hannah was in the dream with the violent dog, Curtis decides to build a doghouse; he buys materials he cannot afford and locks the dog up outside, against the objections of Samantha.[24] Samantha cannot understand why Curtis is doing this, and she questions him one evening while they are watching TV. It happens that the story is about a chlorine spill that badly harmed people and trapped them in their homes with the fumes. We see how badly disturbed Curtis is by the news program. Nichols is making a quick reference here to the potentially traumatic impact of terrifying media stories for those who are susceptible to them.

And indeed, the sequence is followed by Curtis having another, even more catastrophic hallucination of an even more monstrous storm, now with zombies not only glimpsed outside, through the window, but rattling the door handles and threatening to come in. There's noise of snarling from what sounds like huge animals. It all begins quietly with Curtis in the house in the evening. As always, we do not know at first that this is a hallucination. Curtis sees Hannah at the window watching it rain, much as she had been shown earlier in the scene with Samantha, which enables us to trust what we are seeing. He looks quietly at her. Then suddenly the rain gets extremely heavy, a storm rages, and the zombies appear. In addition, now there seems to be a sort of wind, sucking up objects in the room. Curtis hides out, holding Hannah tight and seemingly almost suctioned himself. Finally, incredibly, the force of this alien intrusion lifts not only small objects but all the living room furniture up in the air. At this point, we know that this is an hallucination, but we are so caught up in the drama we no longer really care. We are feeling pure terror.[25]

Significant here is that weather events do not only disturb the atmosphere and embody extreme climate change, they also disturb human nature, turning normal beings into zombies, monsters. What does this mean? Zombies (or zombie-like humans) have long figured in many plague- or radiation-disaster movies, from George A. Romero's *Night of the Living Dead* (1968) to Boris Sagal's *Omega Man* (1971), which was remade as Francis Lawrence's *I am Legend* (2007). But what's unusual and significant is that, in *Take Shelter*, the zombies are linked directly to changes in the weather. Is this a dramatic reversal of ideas discussed earlier in relation to traditional Western conceptions of the links between humans and the natural environment? That is, nature, instead of creating moral humans as in Wordsworth, now creates monstrous zombies corresponding to the damage humans have wrought upon the planet. It would seem that Nichols is making this point, creating what Sarah Lauro has called the "eco-zombie," a subcategory of the "Natural zombie." Obliquely, Lauro notes, "these narratives convey that the destruction of humanity is in the long-term interest of the planet."[26]

Waking from the nightmare of zombies trying to enter the house and the furniture being suctioned to the ceiling, Curtis finds to his embarrassment that, given the terror his pretraumatic dream caused, he has wet the bed. He shields the episode from his wife but asks her for their doctor's name, for the violence of the last dream suggests to Curtis that he needs help. This time, aware that something is extreme in these dreams, he gets books about mental illness from the library (Nichols makes sure we catch the title of one of them, *Understanding Mental Illness: Research and Clinical Practice*).

We see him reading these books late at night in the storm shelter he has begun to clean up and stock with food. He fears his PreTSS is part of a mental illness and goes to see the family doctor. Here the film arrives at a third

FIG. 2–8 Nichols closes in on the book so that we see the title clearly.

narrative strand and enables Nichols to play with his audience in a new way. The doctor recommends a sedative and a psychiatrist and, apparently making some connection we viewers don't yet know about, asks Curtis if he's seen his mother lately. We later learn that Curtis's familiarity with mental illness, not something his friends and family would normally know about, arises from his mother's having been diagnosed as schizophrenic when Curtis was a child.

Curtis's dreams and hallucinations are so real, so powerful, that he acts on the basis of them, showing the degree of his PreTSS. We saw that after one dream he built a doghouse. Even more dramatically (and costly in terms of his job and credibility with his friends and family), after the hallucination in which the storm produces zombies who snatch his daughter away, Curtis decides to enhance his tornado shelter, making it into a fully equipped space for his family to live in. He has to take out a loan he can't afford in order to do this, and more seriously, he jeopardizes both his and Dewart's jobs through illegally using their construction equipment for building the shelter.

Another climate change hallucination takes place again while Curtis is at work, only this time the director, Jeff Nichols, lets us see for sure as it's happening that Curtis is involved in fantasy. It starts with Curtis hearing thunder while his mate, Dewart, does not. Dewart sees Curtis's strange behavior, and this is the first time another character is present as the pretraumatic event takes place. We hear the thunder as Curtis does, but Dewart hears nothing and is disturbed by Curtis's behavior. Curtis rushes out and vomits. Meanwhile rushing away in his car, he cannot breathe and nearly crashes. Anxious about himself, and wanting to find out more about his mother's symptoms, Curtis goes to visit her in the facility where she has long been staying as a result of her schizophrenia. He learns his mother has panic attacks and is paranoid, symptoms somewhat similar to his problems, although she doesn't have PreTSS.

Following the visit, unable to afford the psychiatrist in Columbus, Curtis decides to go for counseling locally, again without confiding in his wife. The social workers he can afford and who mean well can't really deal with him. He continues to suffer horrible nightmares, and now he starts having clear paranoid episodes (see below). When the next tornado storm alert comes, Curtis takes his family down into the shelter. He insists his wife and child put on uncomfortable gas masks, and he settles them in as if for a long time. After a day or so, Samantha insists that he open up the shelter to see what's going on outside.

Once again, viewers are uncertain as to what the reality is. We have not been given any shots of the tornado outside, so we are also held in suspense as to the reality of the catastrophe. There is a protracted struggle between the couple about going out. Samantha finally coaxes Curtis into unlocking the shelter, and as he warily goes up the ladder, the audience too does not know what to expect. We really are viewers-as-future-humans at this point, participating in what seems like a catastrophic climate event.

As it turns out, to his disbelief, Curtis finds that all is perfectly normal aboveground. It was a tornado: trees are down, and objects have been hurled around, but his and neighboring houses are all standing. People are smiling as they clean up the mess. Curtis simply cannot believe it. He stands in shocked relief, staring around, and trying to come to terms with the fact that he was evidently wrong about a major catastrophic climate event.

On the basis of this experience of the tornado not leading to the catastrophe he imagined and was traumatized by in advance, Curtis now goes, taking Samantha with him, for advanced psychoanalytic help, certain that he is schizophrenic (or psychotic), like his mother. The doctor, understanding the family history and the likely genetic component to Curtis's problems, seems to agree. Advised to take a couple of weeks' vacation, Curtis rents the cottage on the beach as his wife has long wanted him to do. He agrees that, on his return, he will engage in serious psychoanalytic help within an institution.

FIG. 2–9 Curtis and Hannah happily playing on the beach.

The family members are next seen at the beach cottage. And it is in this concluding sequence that Nichols turns the wheel once again for a last twist of the viewers' perception of "reality." I don't think it's stretching things too far to read this sequence as an example of Lacan's "the Real," since (as will become clear) Curtis and his family apparently fall into the abyss; all pretraumatic visions of the catastrophe finally come to pass.

The sequence begins with a shot of the beach and gulls flying down. A shot of a plastic sand bucket pulls back to reveal Curtis, his back to the sea, happily making sand castles with Hannah on the beach. Several shots back and forth establish the loving play between father and daughter.

There's a cut to Samantha in the cottage kitchen cooking dinner. Outside again, we see Curtis and Hannah finishing the sand castle with a moat around it; but a close-up of Hannah shows her with a concerned face. Curtis looks up, sees it, and gradually turns around. So far viewers have not been given a counter-shot as to what Hannah and Curtis are seeing. But Curtis looks awestruck and grabs Hannah as they stare out together.

It is not until there is a counter-shot to show Samantha coming out of the cottage that viewers see the sky with angry clouds and tornado formations, not directly (interestingly) but reflected in the glass doors and large windows of the cottage.

Samantha moves forward in shock, very much as Curtis moved at the film's opening, as the music on the soundtrack increases in volume and speed. There are a few shots back and forth as Curtis and his wife share shocked looks revealing their implicit understanding that after all Curtis's pretraumatic hallucinations have come about in reality. As Curtis rushes to join Samantha

FIG. 2–10 Looking directly at the camera, Curtis's and Hannah's faces show horror.

FIG. 2–11 Samantha stares out in shock, while images of the monstrous storm are reflected in the glass panes of the cottage.

at the cottage door, there's a close-up of Samantha's hand on the deck rail. She opens it, much as Curtis had done in the first scene, to reveal that instead of rain, oil is pouring down. We cut to a point-of-view shot of Samantha, left of the screen, the back of her head, as she looks at a terrifying series of tornadoes coming toward her from across a wide expanse of sky and sea.

There's the sound of fierce cracks of thunder, getting ever louder. We cut to a shot of the family in front of their cottage, the tornado-ridden sky again reflected in the windows, as a huge crack of thunder explodes and the screen goes black. The thunder continues as the credits roll, merging into a soulful song related to the last scene, presumably written especially for the film.[27]

FIG. 2–12 A close-up of the back of Samantha's head and what she's seeing, namely, the storm Curtis had pre-imagined.

In order for Nichols to make sure the audience knows that this is not another of Curtis's hallucinations (which we had just about become accustomed to) but a genuine climate catastrophe, he shows the event first through Hannah's point of view, and then through Samantha's. We realize that this event is the very thing that has pretraumatized Curtis all along. The final twist, then, is that Curtis—diagnosed as schizophrenic, which stabilizes his condition—is happily on vacation when his deep knowledge of the coming of a genuine end-of-the-world storm turns out to be true.

The uncanny aspect of the film arises from the very fact that Curtis from the beginning has apparently known on some deep level that the catastrophic climate event really is in the offing. His climate trauma anticipates reality. As he tells Samantha, once he is able to confide in her after a particularly horrible dream: "It's more than a dream; it's a feeling. I am afraid something might be coming." As Samantha looks on, hurt and astounded, Curtis continues his predictions. And he tells his church friends, after an outburst at a gathering: "There's a storm coming and not a one of you is prepared for it. . . . Sleep well in your beds because if this comes true, there ain't going to be anything anymore." His community, believing he's crazy, ignores what he says. They believe he was ridiculous to spend so much on building such a fully equipped tornado shelter.

Take Shelter thus addresses the reality of a sudden and catastrophic climate event, along with the reality of nature as potentially dangerous. The narrative deals with the psychic state of a human being who is traumatized by imagining future climate catastrophe. That the film essentially plays a trick on us—the hero turns out to have been correct in anticipating climate catastrophe—does not take away from the fact that he is traumatized *before* that reality comes about.

In regard to debates about climate change, however, Nichols, like most of the directors of films in the pretraumatic cinema genre, avoid claiming that human activities have caused a catastrophic weather event. As we will see, catastrophe is often said to have been caused by a sudden flash or a devastating uncontrollable fire destroying the world. *Snowpiercer*, a 2014 film by a Korean director, comes closest to insisting that it is human intervention that causes a crisis.

M. Night Shyamalan's *The Happening* (2008) anticipates *Take Shelter* in terms of unsettling the viewers as regards the reliability of the environment. But in a sense, despite being made earlier than *Take Shelter*, it starts where *Take Shelter* ends—that is, with nature turning catastrophic. The film adopts the trope of a sudden event that changes the world. In this case, the characters are traumatized as the event happens in the filmic present. Viewers, however, are once more in the position of witnessing an event that has not yet happened—experiencing, as virtual future humans, a kind of pretrauma or anticipatory anxiety. Lefebvre has argued that there have been three main categories for nature in cinema: (a) landscape, (b) setting, and (c) territory.[28] None of these terms applies to the view of the natural world in *The Happening*. As the film opens, people are enjoying an afternoon in Central Park, New York City, when nature suddenly quivers. Humans stop in their tracks and then mysteriously start to commit suicide.[29] A girl stabs herself in the neck with her hair pin; men get out of cars and fall onto the road; police shoot themselves; and finally, as if a haunting of 9/11, workers are seen in long shot falling through the air from high up on construction sites to land on the ground.

Here nature takes on a role similar to that found in *Take Shelter* but it is more pervasive. Instead of apparent isolated periods of disturbance, as with Curtis's periodic pretrauma episodes, nature now takes on an ongoing distinct and uncanny presence. It has become an entity in evil communication with humans, far from the aesthetic framing of the Western landscape tradition. It is also far from being merely the background to narrative action or a territory that characters possess or fight over, as in a war. In *The Happening*, wary protagonists watch nature for signs of its disturbing trembling, which signals danger to humans. They learn to flee from plants, trees, and grass, all of which are apparently dispersing a dangerous chemical that incites humans to sudden suicidal actions.

Unlike the other films discussed, *The Happening* includes arguments, via several narrative devices, to the effect that humans are the cause of the sudden eerie change in nature which makes humans destroy themselves. For example, in the opening scene, we find a math teacher (played by Mark Wahlberg) asking his students why they think bees are fast disappearing. His apathetic students slowly come up with possible causes, including global warming, pollution, or a virus, so that viewers are primed to consider such causes when word of the bizarre goings-on in the outside world reaches the classroom. Panicked people suggest that terrorists or a nuclear leak are the cause of the crisis, but gradually our hero, the math teacher, figures out that people seem to be setting off the plants, resulting in the idea of going about in small groups. This suggests that Shyamalan is thinking allegorically such that humans' making nature do weird things stands in for a much broader argument—that humans are now a geologic force that is destroying the very elements we need to survive. A later scene with a plant supplier, who generously gives the protagonists a ride when all others have spurned them, reveals his close relationship to his plants. He suggests that plants do give out chemicals and that they need humans to relate to them. Plants can communicate with other plants, the man says, so why not with humans?[30] But this leaves unresolved the question as to why nature is now relating negatively, rather than positively, to humans—a point that later news reporting tries to clarify.

The math teacher, leading one of the groups trying to escape, begins to scan nature rather than admire or aestheticize it. The group watches the natural environment suspiciously, waiting for the quivering that happens when humans incite the production of the chemical. Toward the end of the film, when the danger seems to have subsided, Shyamalan constructs TV interviews in which scientists suggest that human pollution could well have caused nature to react in this way. A Dr. William Ross, the expert brought in by the TV station, claims that the phenomenon "is a preamble to global warming, the first spot of a rash. We've become a threat to this planet, and this is a warning." He continues, "Most people believe it's the government because it happened in one place; if it had happened in any other place, it would have been a different story."

The expert turns out to be prescient. *The Happening* does not have the utopian ending that at first seems will be the case. Very much like *Take Shelter*, the last scene unsettles us and leaves us with uncertainty. There's a cut to the Luxembourg Gardens in Paris, where people are again, as at the opening shot in Central Park, New York, enjoying a quiet afternoon. Suddenly two men walking together come to an abrupt stop, stare forward, and remain motionless. In the eerie silence, we understand that the bizarre natural phenomenon is happening all over again.

I find it interesting that, in both *Take Shelter* and *The Happening*, climate change is envisaged as uncanny—in some way beyond rationality or understanding. While in *The Happening* there is at least some argument about cause, in *Take Shelter* there is no indication at all that humans are the cause of changes in the climate. The catastrophe is simply there. What we previously thought of as untroubled, aestheticized nature is now suddenly monstrous, violent, punishing. It is true that including in the narrative proper any discussion of human activities' producing global warming would interfere with the forward movement of the story, thus deviating from the related horror genre adapted by many of these films. But there is a question about the cultural work performed by such ways of presenting climate change. It could be that, even without addressing causes, the films act as that wake-up call I've theorized. But equally, such devices may make it seem that global warming is beyond our control. It is just happening or already here, and like Curtis we just wait to be doomed.

I want to conclude with a brief reference to John Hillcoat's *The Road*, set in a pretraumatic catastrophic world quite different from the worlds in *The Happening* and *Take Shelter*. I will return to *The Road* later in relation to temporality and memory, but I include it here also because of its links to the pretrauma nature scenarios in the films just discussed. Whereas in those films, the world is normal and people are going about their lives as usual before the sudden climate-change event takes place, by contrast *The Road* opens with the futurist environment already devastated. Although it is still dimly recognizable as having been (or, à la Morton, *being*) our contemporary world, the world is in shards—destroyed, depleted, crushed, emptied out.[31]

Adapted from Cormac McCarthy's powerful novel of the same name, *The Road* comes close to envisaging the world without us (to reference Alan Weisman's provocative 2007 book with that title).[32] The destroyed world in

The Road looks very much like the world Weisman describes as one of the stages in the long ruining of what man has built during two thousand years. And a terrifying vision it is. For interesting reasons, the vision has different qualities in novel and in film: McCarthy's refined, careful use of language and his haunting deployment of metaphor enable him at once to depict a death world beyond recognition (and yet, paradoxically, still recognizable, unlike traditional depictions of hell or techno-futurist sci-fi worlds) and to distract or amaze us with how he depicts this world. What keeps us reading is less fear for the protagonists, as in the film, than the haunting, almost hypnotic quality of the language. Through McCarthy's use of metaphor and the power of his language, the novel is able to convey more closely than the film the negative symbiosis between humans and the natural world. McCarthy's language suggests the tragic degradation of humanity that works in tandem with the loss of harmony with nature. At the same time, he engages readers in mourning for nature (memory for the future) and for its suffering on a different level than happens in the film.

A couple of brief examples: metaphors open up associations and levels of meaning within the following short sentences, in which the protagonist sums up the death world that includes him: "He walked out in the gray light and stood and he saw for a brief moment the absolute truth of the world. The cold relentless circling of the intestate earth. Darkness implacable. The blind dogs of the sun in their running. The crushing black vacuum of the universe. And somewhere two hunted animals trembling like ground-foxes in their cover. Borrowed time and borrowed world and borrowed eyes with which to sorrow it."[33]

While the concrete translation to meaning is not immediate, we grasp numerous sensations via the language and experience humans symbiotically dying with nature. Elsewhere, McCarthy creates texture and mourning for nature with metaphors. For example, he writes, "In the draws the smoke coming off the ground like mist and the thin black trees burning on the slopes like stands of heathen candles." Or, again, "The small wad of burning paper drew down to a wisp of flame and then died out leaving a faint pattern just for a moment in the incandescence like the shape of a flower, a molten rose. Then all was dark again."[34] These metaphors have power because they at once recall natural beauty that once was, and its tragic loss. It is beautiful in its dying, in a sense. Here McCarthy calls upon a long history of such linking of beauty and loss (I am thinking for now of John Keats's sonnets, but any Shakespeare play would offer the same). In the film, such sensations and reflective gesture toward a long literary tradition are impossible, as we will see.

One can understand why the novel is often described as biblical (think of the Book of Job or, as Elaine Pagels might argue, the Book of Revelations) or an allegory of human determination to survive.[35] But my reading of both the film and the novel favors Margaret Atwood's understanding that fictions like these should be read as offering "probable worlds" or, as Morton would say, as showing us the end of the world that is, rather than standing for abstract meanings.[36]

Ultimately, because of the visuality of cinema, the depiction of nature in Hillcoat's adaptation of *The Road* is more graphic, overwhelming, and physiological for viewers than what we get from words. Political geographers Sean Carter and Derek McCormack argue that film has a particular role "as an affective assemblage through which geopolitical sensibilities emerge and are amplified."[37] *The Road* offers a good example of this. Music and sounds convey what's happening to nature, which, hostile and dangerous to the couple, provides as many dangers and difficulties for them as do other surviving humans. The film thus offers a political intervention in terms of effects to do with nature's death through human impact.[38] The story of nature's fall assumes importance partly through the way cinema's visuality forces us to identify in an almost physical manner with the futurist depleted, destroyed, suffering landscape of the film. Put out there in front of our eyes on the large screen, the images inevitably capture our gaze and sensations (see Chapter 5). We experience the agony of nature in its fall through the story of the death of the world; nature literally dies as Man and Boy battle on with huge trees falling around them; fires burning what remains; thunder, rain, snow, and hail beating down without end. The powerful effects of nature's violence appear to punish humans for not caring about the environment, much as Wordsworth's looming mountain haunted him throughout his life. Far from being "part of the problem" in inoculating us, as Morton argues, this film instead forces the viewer-as-future-human to recognize the hyperobjects we are living with.

3 · PRETRAUMA POLITICAL THRILLERS

Children of Men—with Reference to Soylent Green and The Handmaid's Tale

"What our planet and species need saving from is a slow-motion environmental catastrophe. Mr. Nolan drops us quietly into what looks like a fairly ordinary reality . . . a land of battered Pick-up trucks, dusty blue jeans and wind burned farmers scanning the horizon for signs of a storm."

—A. O. Scott on Christopher Nolan's film, *Interstellar*

If the powerful effects of nature's violence in the pretrauma climate scenarios seemed to offer a political intervention in terms of paying attention to global warming, other dystopian futurist films engage with politics more directly. The films and fiction studied here—by Richard Fleischer, Margaret Atwood (Volker Schlöndorff made the film of her novel), and Alfonso Cuarón—all raise questions about human life on the edge of extinction, either because of infertility (*The Handmaid's Tale, Children of Men*) or because of overpopulation (*Soylent Green*). But more than the pretrauma films discussed in the last chapter, as political thrillers they address the dangers that are inherent in the corporate capitalism of the twentieth and twenty-first centuries, capitalism that is directly related to environmental degeneration. These dangers come into play as each director creates a scenario for the future. Historical memory of the European fascist regimes that gave rise to World War II haunts all three films, while Cuarón's in addition signals more recent ominous directions that capitalism has taken in the digital age as outlined by Giorgio Agamben and Slavoj Žižek. The films are political thrillers, and at the same time they offer pretraumatic worlds on the brink of disaster caused through human inattention to environmental change.

The continuum of past, present, and future seems built into our DNA (quite literally, if we are to believe evolutionary psychologists, who offer some evidence that, not having a basis for planning, the future can be traumatic).[1] It seems traumatic—sometimes more traumatic than annihilation—for humans to be left without the sequence of past, present, and future.[2] (That's why Alzheimer's disease is so horrifying.) But trauma time is itself ambiguous. First, trauma's temporality indeed collapses past, present, and future into one horrifying and paralyzing zone of fear. Second, this collapsing of time zones leaves humans living in a present that is characterized by trauma, creating the "trauma culture" I discussed in my 2005 monograph. In what follows, I argue that Cuarón is able in the first half of the film to demonstrate the ambiguity of trauma time as a collapsing of temporality into one timeless present and is then able, later, to indicate the historical moment as indeed that of pervasive trauma.

I focus on the film by Mexican director Alfonso Cuarón as the most complex work of the three, but I want to situate his film in the context of two other texts—Richard Fleischer's 1973 Soylent Green, based on Harry Harrison's 1966 short story "Make Room! Make Room!" and Atwood's 1985 novel, The Handmaid's Tale, which Volker Schlöndorff made into a film in 1995. Similar themes and the similar mix of political and environmental concerns render these films a sort of accidental trilogy. All three deal with the problem of time and memory in a futurist dystopian world in which humanity's future is in doubt. All three look back to earlier periods when things were different and offer us what I call "memory for the future"—that is, images of a possible pretraumatic future, unless we remember history and what humans are losing through abdicating power to corporate interests.[3]

Revisiting the two texts that prefigure Children of Men indicates how much more seriously we take the end of humanity, in the millennium, and also shows how Fleischer and Atwood/Schlöndorff's grim warning has quickly been eclipsed in following decades. Speaking of Harry Harrison's work, Sabine Höhler notes that "the book's argument about extreme population growth, environmental degradation, scarcity, mass uprising, and mass mortality is quite common for its time and had been the topic of many texts of the era."[4] But the full gravity of these issues, as we know, did not enter public consciousness or get governmental attention until only recently. The world of *Soylent Green*, with its depleted infrastructure, is close to what Alfonso Cuarón imagines in *Children of Men*. Electricity rarely works (Sol, played by Edward G. Robinson, uses his bicycle as a generator), food is limited to crackers supposedly made from plankton, water is scarce, people have no place to stay and crowd the staircases of apartment houses, children are rarely seen. Meanwhile, the world of Atwood's novel (as well as of Schlöndorff's adaptation) anticipates that of *Children* in showing how pollution and depletion of the environment entail general infertility, with only a few women still able to give birth. The rich in both precursory films live in protected communities, savoring the hoarded food, water, and electricity resources, as is also the case in *Children of Men*.

One difference between Fleischer's and Cuarón's films is not so much that the disasters of overpopulation, environmental degradation, and depletion of Earth's resources were not understood in the 1960s or before (Höhler lists the warning of dangers from before and after World War II) as that the rapidity with which disaster would happen was not yet known. Fleischer's film is set in 2022, at that time fifty years in the future. *Children of Men* is set in 2027, only twenty-one years in the future. (Many dystopian films, such as *2012*, are already out of date.) As Höhler indicates, in light of the worries about overpopulation, the creative imagination of economists like Kenneth Boulding, biologists like Paul Ehrlich, or geniuses like Richard Buckminster Fuller turned to conceptualizing a "Spaceship Earth," linking an idea of "the technical 'life-support system' of the space-capsule and the biospheric system of the earth."[5] If these are not ideas in the mainstream in 2014, there are comparable if more realistic efforts ongoing to find adaptation if not solutions to current environmental challenges.[6] In 2014, the urgency of increasingly dramatic climate change is gaining ground among the public, if still resisted by politicians and corporate leaders.[7]

Fleischer's film, *Soylent Green*, building on Harrison's story, does address concerns including overpopulation that are still pertinent today even if somewhat eclipsed in public discourse by sensational climate events, which the media gravitate to.[8] And like Cuarón's film, it combines the plot of a political thriller with the issues of overpopulation and the depletion of food resources on Earth. Indeed, like *Children*, there are two stories in *Soylent Green*, the thriller plot and the background pretraumatic environmental disaster scenario, and once again the background story is the real one. The significance of the story of Earth's exhaustion is made evident in the eye-catching collage of images from around 1860 to the present that opens the film, focusing on the impact of increasingly rapid technological advancement on the environment and on social life. The thriller plot is a simple one: Thorn (played by Charlton Heston) is a detective called in to investigate the murder of a senior official of the Soylent Corporation, Simonsen, who lives in luxury in an apartment fitted out with what, for the 1970s, were futuristic design accoutrements and even video games. Also included is the "living furniture" given to the rich, in the form of classically sexy women. Thorn lives with his colleague Sol (played by Edward G. Robinson in his last movie role), who remembers and loves books and is able to help Thorn by getting access to secret archives jealously guarded by a council of wise elderly women. Aside from this council (perhaps Fleischer's nod to the women's liberation movement of the time), the gender politics in the film follows that of the subgenre and remains stubbornly masculinist. The real love relationship in the film is the homosocial bond between Thorn and Sol, who declare their love for one another specifically as Sol is dying at the end of the film. Thorn also has a close relationship with the black lieutenant who is his boss. They have been on the job for many years and have worked out a mutually beneficial way of working the system. The other black character is the priest, turned mad through what he has had to experience and by the revelation of the cannibalism during Simonsen's confession.

As in Cuarón's film, the issue of time and memory haunts the background story in *Soylent Green*, especially through Sol's character. Sol is one of the few people still able to remember the world as it was before the overcrowding and the depletion of resources. In one of the first sequences in the small apartment they share, Thorn prepares the breakfast of Soylent crackers. Sol recalls the time when food was food, before the soil was polluted and plant life decimated, before everything burned up because of the greenhouse effect. "How can anything survive in a climate like this?" Sol asks. Thorn shrugs. He has no knowledge of what Sol recalls, such as eggs, meat, fresh vegetables.

FIG. 3–1 In *Soylent Green,* crowds of people dressed alike wait for food.

In a second sequence in the flat, Thorn returns with exactly such foods, stolen from Simonsen's rich apartment after his murder. Sol is ecstatic to have fresh lettuce, apples, and the prize is a big hunk of meat, together with whiskey, all reminding him of the past. The scene where Sol savors this food carries enormous emotional power due to Robinson's performance. His is a future self that is easy for viewers to identify with. The memory of what has been lost—connoting much more than just the food—is effectively conveyed through Sol's ecstatic savoring of every bite. Nearly every film I discuss uses the image of food from the past, long lost to those living in the future world, as it is discovered and savored. The powerful affects linked to food are the reason for this repeated trope. Viewers are invited to think deeply about what is being lost—much more than just food—through our cathexis to delicious kinds of food. Those of us watching are able to experience, once again, memory for the future. Just as Sol remembers what he's lost, those of us watching come to anticipate (part of the pretrauma process) what we will lose if we don't mobilize our communities to change. If at the moment we still have what Sol lacks, we are invited to consider what losing fresh food would mean.

Thorn's investigation of the murder masks the real purpose of the movie, which is not only to expose the corruption and seizure of power by the few, which is central to all the dystopian political thrillers, but to show what happens to humans and social life when resources for food, water, and power run out. There are many scenes showing crowds of shoving people, all dressed in the same plain clothing, standing in endless lines waiting for their coupon or cash allowance for water or for the precious new food, soylent green.

When supplies run out, the people riot. The state brings in the guards and (a creative flourish on Fleischer's part) huge vehicles reminiscent of garbage trucks with enormous buckets to scoop up the protesters and dump them in the back.⁹ The plot takes Thorn into a church, where we see (as in Fernando Meilleres's film *Blindness*) the sick and orphaned once again piled up, to be tended by a priest who has gone crazy from exhaustion and disgust. Such scenes of mounds of bodies being swept up and dumped inevitably calls up images of the Holocaust. In fact, the depleted, starving humans common across the genre recall concentration camp victims and suggest that imaginaries of futurist catastrophe in these dystopian films unconsciously take the form of a catastrophe Western cultures have known but often repress.

I reference this issue of genocide because an interesting feature of several films in the subgenre is that they show not only the violence that results from scarce resources (to be expected) but also the image of humans becoming monstrous (often now in the form of zombies, as we have already seen in *Take Shelter* and will find in other films). The degree of monstrosity varies in each film, but cannibalism is often a subtext even if it is not directly involved, as in this film.¹⁰ *Soylent Green* shows less violence among the commoners than other films (the rich, as usual, stop at nothing to keep their place at the top), but the film ends with detailing the lengths to which humans go when food runs out.

Early on, viewers learn that a monopoly, Soylent Corp., produced what hitherto was a choice between Soylent Red and Soylent Yellow. A new product, Soylent Green, is being introduced, supposedly also made from the plankton fields of the world. Thorn, however, stumbles upon the truth when he rushes to attend Sol's chosen going "home" (really euthanasia, similar to the "quietus" in P. D. James's novel *The Children of Men*—an element Cuarón chose to reference only indirectly). There is an elaborate, sentimental, and for Fleischer clearly hypocritical or manipulative procedure through which older people are encouraged to die.¹¹ Sol is hoisted on a platform, allowed to select his favorite music and is given wraparound images—memories of how life used to be on Earth—accompanied by the soaring sounds of Beethoven's symphonies as the euthanasia takes place. The powerful and beautifully orchestrated sequence, despite its touristic sentimentality, acts as memory for the future for those of us watching. Lush tourist-style images of flowers, blossoms, Rocky Mountain streams

FIG. 3–2 In *Soylent Green,* Sol is given images of a natural world long lost.

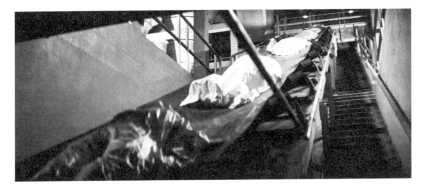

FIG. 3–3 Thorn sees dead bodies being processed for the new "soylent green" food.

gushing down, splendid animals, and mountain vistas remind us of the richness of the planet that has been lost to Sol—and that we could easily lose as well.

After forcing his way in to say good-bye to his friend, Thorn chases after the coffin that carries Sol away. He finds himself in a gigantic factory where Soylent Green is produced from dead bodies arriving from the Euthanasia Center. It is a ghastly, dystopian ending, projecting what is essentially cannibalism as a way for the species to survive. But this is a cannibalism from which the capitalists of the Soylent Corp. derive their profit in order to continue to live in luxury.

The question of what the future holds for Thorn and the ordinary people who remain after Sol dies is left open at the end of the film. Once Thorn has gotten word out about the cannibalism, will authorities have to end it? If they do, does that mean the end for humans? Or will the rich be compelled to think of alternatives more complex than cannibalism and far more costly? The film leaves us to ponder such concerns. As Roger Ebert, reviewing the film in 1973 puts it, "*Soylent Green*'s real achievement is to create a 21st Century world that's convincing as reality; we somehow don't feel we're in a s-f picture." He continues to note that Fleischer assumes "a basic (depressing) probability: that by the year 2022, New York will look essentially as it does now, only 49 years older and more run down."[12]

Atwood's *The Handmaid's Tale* as well as Volker Schlöndorff's 1995 film adaptation also leave us with much to think about. This is another narrative haunted by memory, only this time the traumatic nature of memory is in the foreground. The female protagonist, Offred is self-consciously recording her story and addressing a future audience (readers only find out about the narration being recorded in the "Historical Notes" at the end of the novel, however). She suffers from PTSD. She is haunted by nightmares and daydreams of her traumatic separation from her daughter and husband when fascist authorities seized control of North America. In the frequent flashbacks triggered by something in the present, she is running away with her child, the police catch up with her and force the child out of her arms, and then she is herself captured.

As in *Children of Men*, pollution and depleted resources are envisaged as endangering human fertility. (I say "human," but in the novel, as is generally the case, sexism of the societies envisaged ensures that women are blamed when births dwindle, not men.) The text spends nearly as much time on Offred's flashback memories of her life before her family's arrest as it does on her present life as a surrogate for the Commander's wife, Serena, who is barren. Handmaids like Offred are given to men in authority in order to ensure the continuity of the human race but also to enable the authorities to gain control over the newborn children. These children will join the fascist fundamentalist leadership now in control of North America, leaving the rebels (childless) to die out if they are not caught and publically hanged.

Offred is a formidable protagonist, with feminist hunches that she barely understands. She outwardly resisted her mother's 1960s feminism, but she now vividly experiences her own oppression. Atwood has created a heroine who is obsessively vigilant and observant, and who is clever with language, as she puns and plays with words—a punning that leads to new insights.[13] Offred is filled with feminist rage at being confined, with nothing to do except wait for the next sexual "ceremony" with the Commander and his wife. Offred imagines stealing objects in the house or killing the Commander. Her sad memories of her friend Moira, who did attempt murdering her so-called trainers, inspire her. Recording and formulating a narrative through memory partly enables Offred to work through her trauma. As Yun-Chu Tsai argues, Offred moves from being a melancholic subject, attached to her loss and unable to grieve, to gradually opening up her memory.[14] The rage that follows suggests a healthy resistance to her plight. Her split subjectivity is effectively elicited through her narration. On the one hand, outwardly she is the meek puritanical female demanded by the regime, her face hidden in huge cloth folds, her eyes only directed downward; on the other hand, inside is a woman seething with rage and agonizing over the traumatic loss of her child.[15]

This is a novel very much of its historical moment, when female liberation was on the rise. Her mother is frequently part of Offred's memories as she slowly comes to appreciate what her mother did, often at a cost to her daughter. Those memories of the 1960s and 1970s—like the ones we will see in Jasper's house in *Children of Men*—are presented as a world now lost, remaining alive only in Offred's memory. The novel and later film both warn that pervasive religious fundamentalism, if allowed to gain control, will sweep away all the gains of the women's movement.[16] Yet, in a canny move, Atwood allows the barren wife and the fertile young surrogate to devise a risky plan together to enable each to get what she needs and to thwart male dominance. They conspire to make Offred pregnant by setting her up with Nick, the Commander's driver—and it works. However, soon a van appears to pick up Offred. As Offred's narration ends, she tells the reader that she does not know "whether this is my end or a new beginning." Her last words are mysterious: "And so I step up, into the darkness within; or else the light."[17]

Per Freud's and Atwood's understanding of the dystopia/utopia synergy, *The Handmaid's Tale* is a "ustopia" (recall Atwood's remark that within every dystopia there hides a sliver of utopia). The novel ends with an academic meeting, attesting to the fact that the world did survive. We don't know much about this new world, except that there are still pompous professors in it—is Atwood commenting wryly on her own attitude toward the academy? The professors in the last section of the novel, "Historical Notes," attempt in 2195 (Offred's narration dates to 150 years earlier, 2045) to understand Offred's narration. Readers now learn that the text was found by them on old 1990s-style cassette tapes in a U.S. military locker. They offer elaborate theories about what might have happened to Offred, including an escape through Canada to England, but the novel ends in uncertainty.

What's most interesting from my point of view is the discussion about the reasons the nation was plunged into infertility. Professor Pieixoto suggests as causes the R-strain syphilis, the AIDS epidemic, nuclear plant accidents, and leakages from chemical and biological warfare stockpiles, as well as toxic-waste disposal sites and the uncontrolled use of chemical insecticides. These reasons for infertility, spelled out nicely in Atwood's story, would seem to pertain to the 2027 world of *Children of Men*, to which we now turn.

Cuarón is able to achieve a very complex film partly because of his mixture of genres in earlier projects.[18] *Children of Men* is unusual for the sci-fi genre. It is a crossover film in a technical sense, that is, it mixes documentary style and leftist politics with Hollywood action conventions. Universal Pictures, evidently nervous about *Children*, did not invest in elaborate marketing, and at first the film mainly played in the United Kingdom. It then got a big boost from the DVD, partly because of Žižek's commentary. In adapting the elegant 1992 novel by P. D. James, Cuarón retained infertility as the central component of the narrative, although he also provided a political framing, a critique of capitalism that is absent in James's work. Coming from Mexico, where there is an overproduction of babies, Cuarón is fully aware that in the more prosperous United States, there is already an underproduction of children.[19]

The main action in *Children* involves the protagonist Theo Faron, who saves the rare pregnant Afro-Caribbean Kee and brings her safely to the ship, which is aptly (and perhaps ironically) named the *Tomorrow*. In this film, as in *Soylent Green* and *The Handmaid's Tale*, there is a background story that is actually the real meaning of the film—only in this case it contains an explicitly political theme, namely, a critique of the post-9/11 Western capitalist response to that tragedy. This critique is visible in the images heavily oriented to UK, US, and global political crises—9/11, Iraq, Abu Ghraib, and Guantánamo—to say nothing of the July 2005 bombings in London and Madrid.[20] In interviews, Cuarón mentions other global catastrophes he had in mind (Northern Ireland, the Balkans, Chernobyl) and admits that his "iconography mostly came out of the media."[21]

Both Žižek and Cuarón in interviews and commentaries suggest that there are two stories in the film—that of the foregrounded, action-hero, Hollywood-style story in which the white male hero saves the black woman, the first female to become pregnant in eighteen years, and that of the background story that offers a critique of capitalism as we know it. The latter is, at least for Žižek, the real story of the film. As Žižek puts it in his DVD commentary, "The true focus of the film is there in the background, and it's crucial to leave it as a background." He further adds (correctly, I think) that the film "gives the best diagnosis of the ideological despair of late capitalism."²²

That Cuarón shares much of this politics is clear not only in his online interviews and commentaries but in the short film he made with Naomi Klein showcasing her thesis about "the shock doctrine," which is readily available on YouTube. He also made a documentary, *Possibility of Hope*, featuring Žižek and more leftist scholars theorizing the end of capitalism.²³ This politics is suggested (if not followed through) in the carefully depicted visual and political context for *Children of Men*. Most societies globally have already fallen apart due to infertility, and environmental disaster is in full view.²⁴ But as the TV announcer tells us near the start of the film, "Britain soldiers on." Immigrants by the millions seek entry into Britain because there is still a semblance of society there. There is still food and shelter and a degree of order, and a nation which is theoretically a democracy but in fact (Cuarón's point) essentially a dictatorship. Illegal immigrants are captured on arrival and imprisoned in camps without rights or recourse.

But issues of time/history are less discussed than such political, cultural, and philosophical themes in regard to the film. These issues are implicit in Freud's study of trauma and the death drive, along with his concept of the pleasure principle, linked to hope. Pretrauma worlds such as these produce not only horrifying images of humans' future, with possible traumatic effects in audiences, but also the trauma of not having a future at all, or of there being only a temporary one. It is perhaps this fear of the future that binds dystopia to utopia as a powerful aspect of human thought, repeated from generation to generation, and the binary of utopia/dystopia is a way of thinking that constantly leads Western culture astray.²⁵

There are three broad concepts of time in the film, each inspiring various corresponding emotions. The first time is a dystopian futureless present (2027), a time reflecting affects of loss, depression, anomie, cynicism,

FIG. 3–4 Theo Faron is almost killed by a terrorist bomb.

very much as found in *Soylent Green*. The second time is a melancholic, nostalgic looking-back to the utopian 1960s (when for a moment activists thought they could build a better society) and to a recent past in which infertility was normal (in essence this is the world of *The Handmaid's Tale*). The third is a utopian, indeed messianic future, figured in the character of the Afro-Caribbean refugee (the "foogie," as the film calls her), Kee, whose miraculous pregnancy drives the action (and action-hero) aspect of the plot mandated by Hollywood. This messianic future offered in the film renders it the most utopian of the trilogy I address here. Each set of affects is brilliantly expressed not only through Cuarón's much-cited innovative technical feats but also through the powerful musical score, which focuses especially on British composer John Tavener's haunting commissioned musical fragments. These emerge in counterpoint to bursts of rock or pop tracks from the Beatles to Test Dept., Aphex Twin, and Radiohead, among others.[26]

The very real, concrete, and horrifying future 2027 present is evoked at the start of the film by the death of the last child (eighteen years old but still imagined as Baby Diego) to be born and the mourning that follows. The explosion that nearly kills the film's hero, Theo, powerfully evokes raw documentary footage from the wars in Iraq or Afghanistan, which the film's audiences are familiar with from contemporary TV news reporting—footage that dominates the film's style throughout.[27] The resemblance of the footage to reportage

FIG. 3–5 Refugees in cages line the station platform as Theo gets off the train.

is stunning, and Cuarón uses *cinema verité* techniques with the handheld camera to provide many of the shots with an uncannily realistic feel, which brings the spectator into the film. Such footage—reflecting appalling environmental conditions and immigrants in cages—is seen in shots of Theo, suffering from the shock of the explosion, on his way to visit his friend Jasper from the 1970s, an erstwhile leftist activist.

The sequence with Jasper represents the second time zone, a nostalgic looking back to the past, which the film itself constructs as memory—for a possible hopeful future through Theo's mission. Memories are similar to those that Offred records about her mother's liberation activities in *The Handmaid's Tale.* Jasper lives in a 1970s time capsule, where he smokes pot, plays sixties music, and keeps memories of his own activist past—together with that of Janice, his now-brain-dead wife—displayed on his wall. As the camera slowly pans this interior wall, Cuarón efficiently packs in information about his main characters' utopian revolutionary past when they tried to influence the government by legal means.

By contrast, the 2027 violent subversive rebels (the Fishes, now headed by Theo's ex-wife, Julian) eschew regular political channels, working as underground terrorists. Julian finally embroils Theo in the Fishes' project to bring Kee and her baby safely to the coast where the (mysterious) Human Project will, they hope, keep her and the baby safe. Now powerless, Jasper and Theo can only reminisce. Janice, formerly a reporter before being

FIG. 3–6 Shots of children's faded drawings on the walls of the abandoned school tell the story of loss and trauma.

tortured by MI5, sits by seeing nothing. Janice in her blindness symbolizes both the inability to see the future and the blindness of the 1970s activists toward the ferocious power they were up against.

A second stunning nostalgic scene—perhaps one of the scenes producing the most emotion for viewers—is where Theo, the nurse looking after Kee (Miriam), and Kee, on their journey, stop at a derelict elementary school. The evocation of a past where children learned, drew pictures, played on swings, all now falling into ruin—a lost place emphasized by the reindeer who surprises Theo as he enters the school—is so vivid as to confirm Cuarón's concern with history, time, and the passage from hope to death. We almost hear the lost children's voices—voices we will in fact hear as the long series of credits roll at the end of the film. At this point in the film, Miriam's sad recounting of her gradual realization that infertility was rampant adds to the scene's dystopian force.

In addition, there is a third, temporary kind of time, reserved for the elite group. This group is frequently represented in the futurist political dystopian genre when catastrophe has led to fascism or to a police state, as in both *Soylent Green* and *The Handmaid's Tale*. In *Children*, the palace where the Minister of Art resides represents the collapsing of history into one flat endless present—a kind of pastiche theorized as postmodern.[28] In this masterful sequence, as Theo enters the Palace, he is confronted with a huge

FIG. 3–7 The Minister of Culture hoards all the great international artworks in his elaborate postmodern palace.

statue of Michelangelo's *David* followed by Picasso's *Guernica* spread along a wall where the meal is served, and by Pink Floyd's 1976 helium-filled balloon of a pig hanging outside the window (originally designed to hang over the Battersea Power Station, which this scene replicates).[29]

Later Theo and the Minister stroll along a corridor where pictures by Rembrandt and other earlier artists hang, a sequence that is a kind of temporary step into a postmodern time zone. Here the film complicates the overarching dystopia/utopia binary by introducing other time zones—nostalgia for the past, a collapsing of time in the postmodern zone of the palace, and the futurist search for safety. In fact, through contrast, the sequence highlights the polarized dystopian/utopian movement by temporarily arresting it.

Utopian present-tense time and its hopeful future orientation (in contrast to the dystopian affects studied already) are represented near the start of the film in the forward-moving journey that brings Kee to the Human Project's vast ship, aptly named the *Tomorrow*. In a provocative scene (it is hard to interpret Cuarón's intentions here), Kee reveals her pregnancy to Theo.

If Theo's story images the despair and cynicism of the white male (perhaps symbolizing the subject with most to lose in the collapse of the environment, the social sphere, democracy, the market, and whatever held meaning for him, and his class and race), then Kee is meant to represent

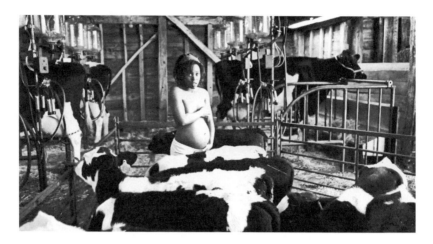

FIG. 3–8 In an overdetermined scene in a cowshed, Kee reveals her pregnancy to a shocked Theo.

hopes for humankind's future—hopes that finally transform Theo into the positive active hero required by the genre.[30] Cuarón has stated that his choice of an actress with Afro-Caribbean heritage was meant to honor Africa as the birthplace of humanity, and we can appreciate that humanity's future arrives in the form of a baby girl with African heritage. But still, despite a degree of agency sometimes ignored, there are problems with Kee's messianic role. If Cuarón may be said to be progressive in imaging the world's future embodied in a black woman, the sexual politics, as Heather Latimer and Sayantani DasGupta have argued, require analysis. These scholars have unraveled the film's problematic treatment of gender, race, and reproductive politics.

In addition, there is a strange absence of sex in the film, which reflects its social conservatism. By contrast, both *Soylent Green* and *The Handmaid's Tale* involve plenty of sex. In *Soylent*, as one would expect in 1973, the sex is sexist, as it were, but Atwood is in tune with female liberation and her heroine has plenty of sexual fantasies of varied kinds, as well as nostalgic memories of sex with her husband, Luke—memories that get played out once she and the Commander's driver, Nick, become lovers. In *Children*, a brief possibility for sex arises when the former couple Julian and Theo are bringing pregnant Kee to the coast.[31] The cowshed scene with Kee at first suggests sex but changes quickly to the declaration of a miraculous pregnancy. In

FIG. 3–9 Stunned by the sound of a baby's cry, the soldiers hold their fire.

the end Theo and Kee are made to re-create the normative family as, along with the new baby (named after Julian and Theo's dead son, Dylan), they travel to the coast and onto the ship *Tomorrow*.[32]

Cuarón seems to accept a literalist view of reproduction—a view contested by Lee Edelman because it represents what he calls "reproductive futurism." By this, Edelman means the notion that politics and public consciousness are inevitably located in the symbolic child of the heteronormative family as the only possible vision for the future. Edelman wants, with reason, to queer this politics and to say no to reproductive futurism. The only problem is that, in saying no to this particular futurist politics, he is also affirming negativity—the death drive, not looking to any future at all, something we also find in pretrauma climate fictions. Edelman's gesture of resistance to sentimentality about the child seems also to exclude women, even though he *includes* women in his definition of the queers already excluded.[33] To a degree, Cuarón resists the affirmation of negativity and the death drive, but in so doing he leaves us with a problematic utopian ending, embodying reproductive futurism and a return to the heteronormative family—as if that were the only family possible.

For my purposes here, however, Kee's image is problematic for other reasons, having to do with her ambiguous role representing the utopian future time that parallels (or seems necessarily to go along with) the negative dystopian death-leaning time. The cowshed scene is where Kee reveals

FIG. 3–10 Utopian hope sidles up again, as so often in the genre.

her pregnancy to Theo, and the scene seems so overdetermined as to have an ironic aspect. The stories of Jesus' birth in the homely manger and of Kee as the new Virgin Mary seem to be deliberately invoked by Cuarón, who is Catholic, while at the same time the association is too obvious to be taken seriously. The same may be said of the very effective and affecting final scene, in which Kee, her baby, and Theo bring the violent cross fire between the revolutionary Fishes and the Dictator's army to a sudden halt as the baby's cry awes and silences everyone. Perhaps in this case, the haunting music that accompanies the action allows the film to transcend what might have been an uncharacteristically sentimental sequence. The film ends with history moving again, as Kee is brought by a dying Theo to the Human Project in their never-grounded ship, the *Tomorrow*.

As if to complete the circle, Kee names the baby girl Dylan, and the heteronormative family is reinstated. Latimer and DasGupta have argued that the world of the film reveals the new post-sovereign biopower as what cultures globally confront. But Cuarón allows his humans to escape (or control) this biopower in the much debated—potentially utopian—ending, in which time moves again because of the future child.[34]

Cuarón's film is more hopeful about the future than either *Soylent Green* or *The Handmaid's Tale*. *Soylent* ends with no solution to the problem of food except an unacceptable cannibalism; Atwood's novel does suggest that humans were able to continue on Earth, but the academics studying the era of Gilead seem stiff and cold. It's interesting that Latin American directors are the ones drawn to hopeful endings. Is this perhaps because the nation formation in many of these nations is relatively young? Or does the interest in futurist scenarios suggest a special vulnerability of Latin American nations to future catastrophe?

At any rate, utopian endings, evident in Cuarón's film, often confuse the difference between absence and loss. As Dominick LaCapra shows, Earth never was a paradise, so it can't be lost or regained. Paradise is simply absent. But if *historical loss* can be worked through, LaCapra argues, it still cannot be *restored* as utopian endings often hope for.[35] Nevertheless, as a futurist political thriller, *Children* makes a much stronger and more specific political critique of Western bourgeois capitalism than does either *Soylent Green* or *The Handmaid's Tale*. The film is arguably in tune with Naomi Klein's shock doctrine and with the short film Cuarón made with Klein. In that film, the image of shock is shown via terrifying footage from both 1950s psychiatric hospitals where shock treatment was routinely given and from the CIA's handbook, which apparently mimics such terrifying strategies.[36] The analogy between individuals being given electric shock treatment to control them and politicians shocking the public following a traumatic crisis in order to control them is in itself shocking. *Children of Men* offers an urgent message for humans to guard against the new police state that often follows catastrophe because, as Klein's *The Shock Doctrine* shows, governments take advantage of people's vulnerability at such times. *Children of Men* fits also with Klein's 2011 integration into her politics of realities of climate change being exploited by governments. As she put it in *The Guardian*, those protesting have "to insist that we can afford to build a decent, inclusive society—while at the same time respect the real limits to what the earth can take [in terms of] trashing the natural world."[37] Cuarón tries to show that the real global traumas of destruction of the environment, racial conflict, immigration, and terrorism can be exploited by government and politicians creating, in the process, a trauma culture. So, as against others studied here, the film includes a dimension—an explicit critique of capitalism—that trauma theorists may underplay.

But what about the pretrauma aspect of the film? Arguably, Cuarón (like Fleischer, Atwood, and Schlöndorff) wants to shock people through creating an imaginary world, his fantasy, embodying trauma future tense. His film is a wake-up call to audiences to attend to what their actions are doing to the species and the Earth—to the real dangers of climate change and other global economic and social conditions.[38] This effort to invite viewers and readers to meditate on probable future catastrophes makes all three films important as showing how the realm of fiction can contribute to changing social consciousness.[39]

4 · MEMORY AND FUTURE SELVES IN PRETRAUMA FANTASIES

The Road and *The Book of Eli*

"Yet what has happened so far during the epoch of the Anthropocene has been the gradual realization by humans that they are not running the show, at the very moment of their more powerful technical mastery on a planetary scale."

—Timothy Morton, *Hyperobjects*

The subgenre of pretrauma films, as we have seen, is a genre that serves as memory for the future for audiences watching. We are invited to live for two hours in desolated environments where desperate humans are seeking to survive. This offers spectators a way to remember what we have now—and may already be losing. The invitation may incite viewers to do what they can to avoid such future tragedies or, at least, attend to our desperate reality. To this end, perhaps, the narratives raise crucial questions about the future for memory once humans have allowed disaster to strike. If "memory for the future" involves remembering past happiness as a way to forewarn against future catastrophe, the future for memory itself is also at stake in the fictional dystopian worlds of these films. Memory of past ecological as well as personal happiness may serve at first to sustain energy for a protagonist to move forward, but what happens when he or she gives up on the past? What happens when, as Simon J. Ortiz put it in a powerful essay co-written with

Gabriele Schwab, "Sometimes you even think memory is a useless and point-less utility. Sometimes you even dare to think: What is memory good for anyway?"[1] This provocation leads to rethinking the overall function of mem-ory in sustaining a possible future self in situations of climate catastrophe.

Rafaella Baccolini's suggestion that "memory plays a key role in the dystopian opposition and locates at least one utopian node not in what could be but in what once was" is a useful place to start, along with Tom Moylan's expansion of the thought. Moylan notes that "the dystopian pro-tagonist often reclaims a suppressed and subterranean memory that is for-ward looking in its enabling force, liberating in its deconstruction of the official story, and in its reaffirmation of alternative ways of knowing and living in the world."[2] I would like to put this concept to the test and dis-cuss temporality in select films in the subgenre under study here. I argue that the concept of memory for the future is a better way of understanding how the past is used in these films. The more complex idea of the future for memory may be linked to Moylan and Baccolini's formulation in some cases, but in others, the question asked by Ortiz may be even more pertinent in regard to what memory is good for in situations of collapse. Reflecting on "the day the river died" in his indigenous community, Ortiz notes how difficult it is to keep track of all the changes leading up to this disaster. "Memory is critically affected since it is the most intimate part of the human psyche that any ongoing human culture has in its substance, structure, and function."[3]

The Hughes brothers' film *The Book of Eli* comes closest to what Moylan and Baccolini have in mind in terms of a "subterranean memory that is for-ward looking in its enabling force"—at least within the film's own terms. The entire project of the protagonist, Eli (played by Denzel Washington, a rare African American hero in the genre), is based on his having memorized a large holy book (not specified as the Bible but implicitly such).[4] Memory is foregrounded here, in Eli's remarkable retaining of the entire Bible in his mind during his thirty years of travel. His mission is to bring himself and his memory to the West Coast where a white-haired professor is diligently collecting by whatever means all the essential lost books, music, and cul-tural objects, mainly from Western history (Shakespeare, Mozart, Wag-ner) or rewriting them, as in the case of Eli and his memorized Bible. The assumption is that re-creating the history of Western culture and all its art, science, and knowledge will enable life on Earth to be renewed. Humans

FIG. 4–1 Having reached the West Coast finally, Eli recites his book as the Professor writes down every word.

will start afresh on the basis of memories of their past culture. In my terms, this conceit offers an example of there being a future for memory. "This is where we are going to start again," the Professor says. "We are going to teach people about the world they lost." The labor of the process is detailed in the time-lapse scenes at the end of the film, scenes of Eli recounting what he has remembered as the Professor writes down every word.

In the film's improbable and sentimental ending, we find Eli finally dying of exhaustion after the Professor has recorded the last lines of the book Eli has remembered. The Hughes brothers bow to political correctness in having the camera zoom in on a shelf where the Bible is placed next to the Torah, the Quran, and the *Saints on the Seas* volumes. Yet the entire project seems closer to another Great Western Books collection than any possible attempt to recoup the extensive multicultural Western heritage that has (in the film's narrative) been lost. As against Moylan and Bacconlini's idea of such subterranean knowledge offering alternatives to the normative story, here it is normative knowledge itself that is being re-created. The future for memory here, then, is conservative, if productive. But as one of the most hopeful films in the genre, a utopian note is established and (however, in fact, unlikely) a future for human society suggested.[5]

The Book of Eli, like other films studied here, provides scenes that function for viewers as memory for the future, that is, asking us to remember (through images of a kind of "bare" life) what humans now have and what we have lost or are in danger of losing. The cinematic techniques used in the tense opening sequence (for me the high point of the film) put viewers into

FIG. 4–2 The Professor adds the book to his shelf of great works.

a lost and depleted world, offering a terrifying future scenario. Before the credits, the camera pans slowly at ground level along a forest with bare trees, a few final leaves floating down. Viewers identify with the camera's gaze. Everything is bathed in an eerie green light as the camera catches a dead man. As it pans the body, there's a screech of some kind, and a weird animal comes into the frame and starts to eat the body. As the camera continues to move, the sound of heavy breathing pervades the soundtrack. The camera now pans to a huge heavily coated figure lying on the ground propped up, his breathing heavy because of his gas mask. A quick cut takes us back to the animal. The man takes a shot at it, and with the camera slowed down, viewers see the implement slicing through the forest to plunge into the animal. It's a shocking but effective sequence, with enough emotional power to make viewers jump.

There follow equally effective scenes of a destroyed world. Eli finds a truck with a skeleton in it. There's nothing to scavenge, but he soon comes upon an abandoned house. Here at least he finds shoes on a man who hanged himself. With his remaining oil, Eli is able to cook the animal he shot. He can even use his old iPod. Music from about the 1960s floods the soundtrack, giving viewers a taste of pleasure—memory of a strangely nostalgic kind, inserted as it is into a weirdly contrasting context. By morning, the battery has run out. For Eli, as for us, memory of the world conjured by the music provides only momentary comfort. He will enter a shantytown later on, partly with the hope of getting his iPod battery recharged.

Eli continues his journey, and the Hughes brothers give us powerful wide-angle images of roads blocked with wrecked, abandoned cars, and a

FIG. 4–3 As in many pretrauma films, roads are littered with abandoned and wrecked cars, in a generally desolate and lost landscape.

desert landscape burned by the raging sun (everyone has to wear strong sunglasses to protect their eyes). Inevitably, Eli gets embroiled, as all other protagonists in this genre, in deadly encounters with vile men ready to rape, steal, and kill for whatever anyone else has. These encounters are particularly nasty, since twice a woman is used as a decoy to halt Eli on his journey, distract him, and leave him prey to the killers. In more than one case throughout the film, female rape (or near rape) is involved. Eli regularly saves the day.

But at least in regard to ecological politics, the Hughes brothers insert a few scenes that offer some explanation for the destroyed universe and memory of the world before. In Eli's discussion with Solara, a woman he bonds with while trapped in the shantytown by the local warlord and who follows Eli when he manages to escape, we learn that she was born long after the "flash."[6] Whatever this was (an atomic bomb perhaps?), it evidently killed almost everyone, and Solara has not met many people as old as Eli. She asks what it was like before. "People had more than they needed," Eli says. "We didn't know what was precious, what not. We threw away what people will kill one another for now." Bearing this out (and following a familiar trope in the pretrauma genre), earlier in the shantytown we've seen that shampoo is an incredible luxury when Billy (the crazed leader) bribes his wife, Claudia, with shampoo. Lip balm and lotion too are enough to kill for.[7] Eli has talked about the war and the flash before as having killed most people with the exception of those who managed to hide out.[8] Since he has been walking for thirty years, one understands how very long it is taking the destroyed

FIG. 4–4 Solara sets out with Eli's powerful sword to set the world right.

world to revive. Memory here may function for Solara as enabling—in the sense of providing the determination to survive and to look toward renewal. The film ends after Eli's death with Solara grasping his large black cudgel. Inspired by Eli and all that she has seen at the West Coast retrieval center, she is setting off back east to engage in renewal. The low-angle shot of her about to take off marks an unusual gendered moment—the image of a powerful female protagonist to be.

In his adaptation of McCarthy's *The Road*, John Hillcoat and his screenwriter, Joe Penhall, took up the challenge to capture McCarthy's desperate vision of what is already facing humankind, inviting us to take notice and remember. While the experience of watching the film is completely different from reading the novel because of the contrasting media (vision, sound, and dialogue versus the rich use of words), nevertheless the film effectively stages select scenes from the novel, if not in the same order.[9] As in *The Book of Eli*, within the film protagonists encounter the ghostly remains of the world we know—roads littered with wrecked and abandoned cars, crumbling bridges, but most often a barren landscape devoid of vegetation.

In addition, *The Road* features violent storms and falling trees, wrecked houses torn apart by marauding, starving humans; remains of gas stations, where every last drop of oil is a godsend; roads now covered in ash, burnt by raging fires; the desolate ruins of a consumer society. Here the film touches on the nearness of its world to the contemporary world. For such "ruins" are already visible in the United States if one cares to look. Wastelands offering the remains of a consumer society—the detritus of

FIG. 4–5 In *The Road*, the focus is mainly on a ruined natural world—perhaps the latest stage of the end of civilization.

prior wealth and fecundity—can be found already as one travels around the United States today.[10] Indeed, Hillcoat and Javier Aguirresarobe found precisely such wastelands (what *Variety* terms "scorched-earth vistas") in Louisiana, Pennsylvania, Mount St. Helens, and Oregon to film in. Hillcoat does not offer a political reading of the existence of these vistas far from wealthy metropolitan areas, confirming the lack of class awareness endemic in the genre. But McCarthy himself suggested in one of his interviews on Oprah's TV show that the book was partly inspired by his looking out from his hotel room in El Paso and seeing a landscape such as those noted here.

As in the novel, this is the story of two humans struggling to survive in desperately harsh conditions—conditions all but impossible to imagine outside concentration-camp scenarios (which both texts call to mind at various points). And it is the story also of the death of humanity. If leaders of concentration camps were deliberately producing death of huge numbers, here humans have together brought about the deprived universe, and those commandants, dictators, and presidents are now nowhere to be seen.

Both the novel and the film offer a much darker fantasy than *Eli*. Through his rich use of metaphor, McCarthy implies that there is an inherent link between humans' capacity for ethical memory and humans living in a stable natural environment (which can be within a city as well). Ecological diversity has been shown to coincide with human diversity, and ethical memory depends on humans living alongside other animals, living plants, waterways, and varied species.[11] While such a link is hard to translate in visual terms, Hill-coat is able to show that, without a viable natural environment, most humans become inhumane. They mimic the violence of a dying nature. The film shows a natural environment no longer anything approaching a landscape and reveals a social world more advanced in deterioration than in other films I study. The social contract, which normally controls and orders a community and keeps it functioning, is no longer viable. The situation has grown even worse in this regard than it was in *The Book of Eli*. The natural world too, in tandem with the social deterioration, has become far more violent, hostile to humans, hindering any renewal of human life. The images in the film of trees falling with a loud cracking sound, thunder roaring, and fires lighting up the horizon come perhaps closest to Timothy Morton's conception of hyperobjects—that is, of the nonhumans that surround us now without our full awareness of them, but which overpower us once we recognize them.

As in *The Book of Eli*, beings (here they mimic zombies) who were once human pounce on the protagonists, ready to murder for their meager food and clothing; humane relationships are nowhere to be found, except in the relationship between the protagonists.[12] Since the social world has all but disappeared, there is little room for any action hero. Instead we simply have characters, significantly named just Man and Boy and (in memory of the past where she figures, Woman) to indicate that even being a specific human subject is all but impossible in the completely deprived environment the Man and Boy find themselves in.

I suggest that for McCarthy at least (we'll see how Hillcoat translates the novel in this regard), memory has no future—that is, it disappears or is seen as useless—once the natural world is destroyed and humans have given up on the species' having any future. Temporality in the novel is extremely complex. Memory has several different levels and takes varied forms for the Man and for the Boy. But, even in regard to Man, how he views memory is not consistent. Implicitly, as for Simon Ortiz in his fascinating essay, Man is insistently questioning what uses memory has in his situation. Sometimes he sees memory, far from being "forward looking in its enabling force," as something that he struggles to control and wishes he could do away with. In this view, memory is as dangerous as the siren calls Odysseus confronted on his journey home to Penelope.[13]

For example, early in the novel, following a glowing dream of his wife coming to him "out of a green and leafy canopy," in a dress of gauze and

FIG. 4–6 The film includes loud frightening sequences of trees falling, nature literally collapsing before one's eyes.

her dark hair carried up in combs of ivory, Man says he "mistrusted all of that." And the text continues: "He said the right dreams for a man in peril were dreams of peril and all else was the call of languor and death." He was learning to wake himself up from his dreams of "walking in a flowering wood where birds flew before them he and the child and the sky was aching blue."[14] Again, in a similar dream, we learn that he has "rich dreams now which he was loathe to wake from. Things no longer known in the world. . . . Memory of her crossing the lawn toward the house early in the morning in a thin rose gown that clung to her breasts." But Man's response to his memory is a bit different from before. Now "he thought each memory recalled must do some violence to its origins. . . . So be sparing. What you alter in the remembering has yet a reality, known or not."[15] This memory of his wife is the last reference to her in the novel (the film allows one final dream vision as Man dies), and this implies that there is no future for memory after a certain point of deprivation. But I anticipate.

Sometimes, Man and Boy find remains of the life before, such as when they come upon a destroyed roadside gas station. In the novel, to the Boy's amazement, Man picks up the phone "and dialed the number of his father's house in that long ago." Later they arrive by chance, it seems, at the house where Man grew up. Boy is scared but Man is drawn to his past and enters. In telling detail, McCarthy describes how the Man "felt with his thumb in the painted wood of the mantle the pinholes from the tacks that had held stockings forty years ago." McCarthy continues: "The Boy watched him. Watched shapes claiming him he could not see. We should go, Papa, he said."[16]

This remark pinpoints another aspect of memory in the novel, namely, that Boy only knows the present, destroyed world. He has no memory of his father's world before the catastrophe and thus is often learning from his father's memories. "Sometimes, [we learn,] the child would ask him questions about the world that for him was not a memory. He thought hard how to answer. There is no past. What would you like?" In other words, Man does not want to burden the child with the real past and, rather, leaves the Boy to his own fantasies of "how things would be in the south. Other children." At one point, when Man is checking the dilapidated map he uses as a guide, he shows Boy that the black roads are the ones they follow, the state roads. Boy queries, "Why are they state roads?" He knows nothing of states or roads and asks what happened to them.[17]

From time to time, McCarthy gives us the Man's extended memories of his past in nature, triggered by something in the present. As against his sense that memories of his wife are dangerous and disabling, some of the memories of the natural environment (before the big flash destroyed all) offer a peaceful moment that he can accept. But the long memory about "the perfect day of his childhood" going to collect firewood in the fall is ambiguous. It arises from Man's wanting to protect Boy from seeing the ghastly dried-up corpses they come upon moving through a city. "Just remember," he says, "that the things you put in your head are there forever." The Boy, however, queries, "You forget some things, don't you?" to which Man replies, "Yes. You forget what you want to remember and you remember what you want to forget."[18] The point Man is making arises from his desire to shield Boy from the horrible sights so they won't stay in his mind. But at the same time, he is thinking about what purpose the memories of his own past serve—which of these he does or does not want to remember.

The "perfect" day Man goes on to remember follows directly from his comment to his son. Does he not want to remember this day? On the surface, it offers memory of a nature before the fall that is unsentimental, peaceful, and somewhat Wordsworthian. In this memory, Man and his uncle silently share the calm of the natural world. Similar brief memories of nature in the past emerge from time to time, often prefaced by reference to how long ago it was: "In that long ago, somewhere very near this place he'd watched a falcon fall down the long blue wall of the mountainside and break with the keel of its breastbone the midmost of a flight of cranes."[19]

But the depiction of there being no future for memory once sociality and infrastructure are gone is conveyed powerfully through Hillcoat's cinematic techniques. Increasingly, Man despairs of there being a future for the world, and if there is no such future, then memory too has no future. McCarthy communicates this sense of no future through a haunting metaphor in a section where Man carves a flute for the boy from a piece of roadside cane. He hears the boy playing: "A formless music for the age to come. Or perhaps the last music on earth called up from out of the ashes of its ruin." The passage ends with the chilling metaphor in which Man sees the child with his music as "announcing the arrival of a traveling spectacle in shire and village who does not know that behind him the players have all been carried off by wolves."[20]

The scene that most graphically demonstrates giving up on memory is where Man finally lets go of the picture of his wife that he has carried all this time in his billfold, now reduced to "a sweatblackened piece of leather." He throws the billfold away but sits looking at the picture of his wife. "Then," we are told, "he laid it down in the road also and then he stood and they went on." A bit later on, we learn that "he thought about the picture in the road and he thought he should have tried to keep her in their lives somehow, but he did not know how." Clearly, the photograph itself was not enough to keep his wife in their lives, but implicit here is a giving up on memory because, as Ortiz might say, what use is it?[21]

Such a view is supported by Man's thoughts that suggest indeed no future for memory: "He thought if he lived long enough the world at last would all be lost. Like the dying world the newly blind inhabit, all of it slowly fading from memory." Again, after McCarthy describes the couple plodding toward a distant strand of trees, "skylighted stark and black against the last of the visible world," Man, we are told, "had this feeling . . . beyond the numbness and the dull despair. The world shrinking down around a raw core of parsible entities. The names of things slowly following those things into oblivion. Colors. The names of birds. Things to eat. Finally the names of things one believed to be true."[22]

Both Ortiz and Man in such a situation find a necessity to live in what Ortiz calls "immediate, actual, and intimate experience," which Ortiz at least trusts more than memory.[23] And from about this point in McCarthy's novel, the present takes over. There are effective scenes describing intense details of how Man manages to build something, to discover ways to repair their broken cart, and much more. Once memory is gone, the entire tone of the novel changes. It moves from the philosophical to an increasingly desperate need for Man to muster every last ounce of his energy to survive while saving Boy from harm and getting him to the coast where he might have a chance to stay alive.

Not surprisingly, it is this latter aspect of the novel that Hillcoat could most readily translate into the visual media of film. All of the dramatic scenes in the novel—scenes where marauding men nearly entrap Man and Boy or those where they enter houses and discover starving humans locked in cellars, screaming for Man's help—translated into film have viewers on the edge of their seats. In these scenes the film merges in with Hollywood's zombie and horror genres, making *The Road* generically complex. As in *Take Shelter* and *The Book of Eli*, catastrophic weather events are linked to zombie-like humans—but in this case, the humans who have lost their humanity also devour children.[24] Hillcoat seizes on the relationship between father and son (purportedly based on McCarthy's own relationship with a son born to him in his later years) that is only too easy to sentimentalize in the manner common to Hollywood melodrama.[25] I view this story about the relationship as, in effect, background to the main story, which deals with what it means to live in a destroyed world, raising questions about ethics and memory in such a situation.

Hillcoat makes effective use of cinema's ages-long narrative technique—the flashback—to dramatize Man's memories of his life before the catastrophe. While most of these would fall into the category of "biographical sound flashback," filling in a protagonist's past life, some flashbacks also dramatize Man's traumatic situations.[26] These memories—such as that of the day the clock stopped and a huge flash caught the world on fire; or of the day his son was born in appalling conditions to his resisting wife; or of when his wife, not able to stand how they were living, leaves him and the child and commits suicide—function perhaps as reflecting Man's post-traumatic stress along with narrative background. He is a victim of the psychic "flashback" so common to trauma victims. Even the clearly biographical flashbacks—such as his wife lying out on the lawn, or playing the piano, or at a concert—reflect Man's experience of traumatic loss. But all of these, since they are about concrete events, make powerful movie sequences while having a narrative function.[27]

FIG. 4–7 Man dreams of his beautiful wife lying out on their lush lawn with flowering nature all around.

Hillcoat comes closer to the meditative feel of the novel when he occasionally uses a voice-over narration by Man as in the long beginning sequence. Significantly, this voice-over was kept in the film at the behest of McCarthy himself, as Penhall notes in his piece on his screen adaptation of the novel.[28] The sequence follows opening shots (we later realize these are Man's dreams) of an idyllic summer day with a husband and wife happy together, followed by the sudden contrast of a catastrophe at night, when the flash happens and all goes dead. An abrupt cut brings us to Man's voice-over accompanying shots of Man and Boy moving through a devastated environment.

Viewers witness the destroyed world, the stark deadness of the natural landscape, the cold and wet they are exposed to, the desolation of it all, as Man talks about the past. Man mentions the clock stopping at 1.17, the flash, and then how each day got more and more gray, colder and colder, crops failed, and all the trees began to fall. He describes the refugees on the roads, the gangs, the threat of cannibalism, how food was the constant problem. The context for the plot is thus established, and the following scenes take us into the narrative present, with Man reading to Boy, followed by the next day's search for food in a farmhouse.

The deeper meanings of memory in the novel were all but impossible for Hillcoat to translate into film. There is no way for Hillcoat to introduce Man's thoughts about his dreams and memories, as in the novel, although Hillcoat might have tried using more of the voice-over strategy. It is left to the viewer to make the connection to PTSD noted above, and it's possible that, for many, the sequences just fill in the narrative background.

FIG. 4–8 Man and Boy trudge onward, dragging their cart of meager supplies.

However, there is one scene in regard to memory that Hillcoat makes much more of than McCarthy did in the novel and that marks a powerful change in Man. If the flashbacks indeed have largely been utilized for the plot, still, we understand that Man is haunted by his apparently happy and fulfilled prior life. The scene in question is where he looks at his billfold, at the photo of his wife, and (the film's innovation) takes off his wedding ring. Penhall makes this a pivotal moment for Man, since here we understand via the sequence some of the meanings about memory in the novel.

The scene starts when the Man and Boy find a large truck stuck on a ruined flyover bridge where they seek shelter for the night. Boy comments that he wishes he were with Mom, which Man interprets as Boy wishing he were dead. He tells Boy not to think that way as they prepare to sleep. We cut to Man's dream—the idyllic scene of Man and his wife playing the piano together in his prior life. We just see their hands touching fondly as they play and we hear their soft voices on the soundtrack. Man wakes abruptly to the usual gray dawn. Hillcoat selects total silence for this scene, as he shows Man get out of the truck and look over the edge of the bridge. At this point, Hillcoat makes a dramatic change in his shooting style. Where before the majority of scenes have been close-ups of Man and Boy together or long wide-angle shots of their trekking in desolate, ruined environments, suddenly now we are given an extremely low-angle shot of Man from way down below the bridge. He appears as a mere speck, way up on the concrete ledge. The entire world seems to open up.

There's a cut to Man in medium shot. He takes out his billfold, looks at the photo of his wife for a while—then, again from that low-angle shot,

FIG. 4–9 This shot stands out as dramatically different in style and perspective. The shot opens the world up at the same time that Man's psychic world is closing down.

we see him throw the photo away. Next, from an extreme high-angle shot over the Man we see him take off his ring. We cut to an extreme close-up shot of this ring on the bridge, with Man's fingers gradually pushing the ring to the edge. Hillcoat stops there so we never actually see the ring fall.

What's interesting here is how the film paradoxically opens up to these astounding, contrasting low- and high-angle shots of Man at the very moment that we are being shown how memory is shut out. Are we to infer that Man is freed by the act of disowning memory—a freedom Hillcoat expresses visually by opening up to shots of enormous spatial height and depth? The imagery suggests also a paradoxical freedom for the Man from the social contract—even from morality—to enable him simply to focus on saving his son at all costs. McCarthy suggests (and Hillcoat attempts also to convey) that human caring in the present can be elicited through imagining future catastrophe. Is he also suggesting that catastrophe itself can elicit human caring, even if most people regress? that staying human is possible?

While the film suggests that memory is disabling rather than enabling in Man's context, the question again emerges as to what memory is for. After this sequence, as in the novel, Man lives mainly in the present and focuses on survival and his mission to bring Boy to the coast where things might be better and where he might survive.[29] Living in the present and abandoning everything from his past appear to be the only way to survive the catastrophe.

Just as he now abandons memory, Man has been forced to abandon morality to survive. Critics debate the apparent higher empathic morality on the part of Boy, who always wants to help the wretched people they meet, while the Man—with survival desperately in mind—sees their helping them as dangerous and as hindering his and Boy's chances of surviving. It's a situation many faced in the concentration camps and many no doubt are facing now in refugee camps everywhere. Boy wants to help the old burnt-up man they meet staggering along the road, and a different man (played brilliantly by Robert Duvall) with whom they do share some food at Boy's urging. Such sequences culminate in Boy's shock at his father's excessive punishing of the thief who, toward the end of the film, steals all their stuff while Boy sleeps. Neither can we, as viewers, bear the extreme to which Man goes, as he insists on the thief stripping so as to be left out in the cold naked. Only at Boy's urging does Man return and leave the thief's clothes for him; Boy adds a can of food.[30]

Critics ask how Boy can be moral without memory of a past social contract he never knew. But hasn't Man taught his son this morality by his words, if not his deeds? We learn that at night Man often "told the boy stories. Old stories of courage and justice as he remembered them."[31] Man has also taught Boy a great deal through his love and caring for him, so that Boy transfers the treatment he's received to others in his world.

It is in this caring—and Boy's memory of it over the years they have traveled—that reveals what's most significant about memory and about its uses for creating future selves. Boy exists with a future self that, because he remembers horrific scenes alluded to by his father including men eating children, fears not so much being eaten himself as his and his father's becoming cannibals so as to avoid starvation. A constant refrain from Boy is asking reassurance that he and his father are "the good guys": "We'll never eat anybody, right?" he asks. This suggests another future self for the Boy, namely, being moral. In a sense, Boy tests this future self— a self that cares about others—each time he meets someone struggling to survive. It is the caring connection with his father that he remembers in these situations.

Ortiz offers a similar understanding in his essay, which starts with Ortiz's nephew saying to him: "I remember the day the river died." The nephew's focus on this memory leads to Ortiz's meditation on the uses of memory and his ambivalence about memory. On the one hand, Ortiz finds that "the significance of memory is the actual lived experience itself, not the fact it recurs mentally or intellectually later on" and, further, that he trusts "the

FIG. 4–10 Man is unreasonably harsh on the Thief, as Boy tries to reason with him.

FIG. 4–11 Man reads to Boy as long as the fragile book they've carried for ten years remains intact.

immediate, present moment more than anything else, more than memory, more than memory of the past." Yet on the other hand, he realizes that memory is a way of connecting to others; Ortiz's own future self needs the connections that memories provide. Ortiz and Schwab's piece ends with Ortiz's visiting an old high school friend. In reconnecting with his friend and others there, he realizes that "it is the connection with each other that we have, and it is with memory that we maintain that connection."[32]

Both the film and the novel of *The Road* support the view that what matters about memory is its connecting us to others. This has nothing to do with sentimentality. Boy and Man are linked by memories of their ten-year struggle to survive in desperate circumstances and by Man's conveying to Boy values from the past, even if it is difficult to activate those values in their present context. The question both film and novel raise for the viewers as "virtual future humans" is how far memories of connections that one no longer has—or memories of lives that one can no longer live—are pertinent or useful. As viewers watch the future selves embodied in Man, Boy, and Woman, identifying with them, becoming them, they might wonder what, if anything, they should do with memories of planet Earth as it was before humans acted on it or before the result of our actions became visible? This question arises dramatically as the credits to *The Road* roll on. Very softly, but nevertheless audibly, sounds of a summer evening in a cozy neighborhood flood the soundtrack (very much as in the closing credits for *Children of Men*). We hear a lawn mower, cars going by, Man's voice asking what someone did all day, other sounds of doors shutting, and so on. We are reminded of the film's opening dream here, although these sounds suggest more activity and more people around than in that early idyllic flashback scene. It is as if Penhall is asking, indeed, what use are such memories when all is destroyed? Are the sounds there to prompt us to take heed of what the family lost in the film, which we might lose too? That both novel and film raise these crucial ideas is part of their importance to us in the context of environmental challenges we are facing as humans.

5 · MICROCOSM

Politics and the Body in Distress in *Blindness* and *The Book of Eli*

> "Fear can cause blindness, said the girl with dark glasses,
> Never a truer word, that could not be truer, we were already
> blind the moment we turned blind, fear struck us blind, fear
> will keep us blind."
>
> —José Saramago, *Blindness*

The world of Fernando Meirelles's film *Blindness*, adapted from José Saramago's novel with the same title, resembles the worlds in other futurist dystopian films, but unlike those films, here the focus is on details regarding the human body in distress in the context of a severely constrained physical space. It is all but impossible not to be reminded, again, of the Nazi concentration camps as well as of the fascist regime Saramago knew in his youth in Portugal. *Blindness* lies between the pretrauma political dystopia and the pretraumatic disaster film. In the worlds of some films studied here (especially *The Road* and *The Book of Eli*), democratic civil society has already broken down, with all systems for sustaining life depleted and lost. *Blindness* on the other hand tracks a society on its way to total decline. We move from a bustling, modernist, glass-and-steel city in an advanced industrial world to that world's loss of infrastructure—as reflected in the microcosm of the asylum where the characters are rapidly incarcerated.

Although sometimes read as an allegory, I view the film as a study of what happens to the body and affect in a society where resources are scarce and the social contract deteriorates. While other films study humans within a larger frame (people are often seen on a journey, struggling to survive environmental challenges in their search for food and shelter), *Blindness* for much of the film shrinks the world to the enclosed asylum space. Viewers are thus invited to focus on what happens to the body in a detailed way that is lacking in other films. At the end of the film, some characters escape and enter a destroyed urban world similar to that in other narratives studied here. As befits Meirelles's socialist hopefulness, perhaps, the end of the film shows a society still with buildings and roads, even though it is badly damaged. There is hope of some kind of renewal, as dystopia spirals up once more to potential utopia.

Combining the two versions, the novel and the film, in my discussion will allow me to draw out the complex meanings of the narrative and the pretraumatic (implicitly) futurist vision that emerges from Saramago's imagination and from Meirelles's reading of it. The novel includes insights about the future of Western civilization that the film simply cannot accommodate, but on the other hand, through its visual, auditory, and editing aesthetic, the film adds much that cannot be portrayed by the written word. Both novel and film significantly depart from prior texts in delivering a narrative in which a female character becomes the leader. Viewers can appreciate the different ways in which a female leader does her job. The woman's resistance to the dominant order as she challenges authorities and ultimately takes control from the oppressors in the asylum differs from the way many male leaders stand in as agents for governmental control in many pretrauma cinema texts.

The novel is quite unique in form and does not fit into any literary genre as such. While it mainly consists of conversations between people, these do not take place as they would in a realist novel. Characters have no names; spoken sentences flow into each other, often without it being clear who is speaking; commas replace periods between speech acts. There is a mysterious, omniscient, self-reflexive narrator who seems to be telling the story of this disaster (traumatic for the characters) but who also adds seemingly extraneous comments or interrupts events to make a judgment, offer advice, or provide philosophical insight. The first sentences of the novel, for example, suggest straightforward realism—until the fourth sentence, which moves quickly from description to comment: "The people who were waiting began to cross the road, stepping on the white stripes painted on a black surface of the asphalt, there is nothing less like a zebra, however, that is what it is called."¹ The reader is surprised by this last statement that does not have anything to do with the forward movement of the story.² In a later example, the narrative flow is suddenly interrupted by the omniscient speaker's didactic message to the reader about people's forgetting what facilities they take for granted: "The possibility had not occurred to the Doctor's wife," we are told, "that not so much as a drop of the precious liquid was coming from taps in the houses, this is the drawback of civilisation, we are so used to the convenience of piped water brought to us into our homes, and forget that for this to happen there have to be people to open and close distribution valves, water towers and pumps that require electrical energy, computers to regulate the deficits and administer the reserves, and all of these operations require the use of one's eyes."³

As is clear from this sample of Saramago's literary style, Meirelles faced an awesome challenge when he decided to make a film of *Blindness*. While an adaptation becomes a work in its own right, not beholden to the original, in this case Meirelles was anxious to please Saramago out of respect for him as an acclaimed Iberian novelist. He wanted to make a film version as close to the original as possible. Many of the reviews that appeared in Portugal stress the film's fidelity to the novel even when the critic takes an overall negative view of the film. Many reviews comment on the film's transnational aspects as part of its value—*Blindness* was shot in Brazil, Guelph, Uruguay, and Canada (especially Toronto) using diverse crews in each place, and it was internationally funded. Although sequences were shot in São Paulo and Montevideo, the city where the action takes place is not named. One critic notes that "the city in which it is set looks both vaguely familiar and effectively otherworldly."⁴ U.S. reviews tended to be negative, perhaps because Meirelles refused to glamorize the horror detailed by Saramago.⁵

Blindness offers viewers a pretraumatic rather than an apocalyptic world because, instead of conjuring the end, obliteration, as in an atomic bomb going off, planet Earth colliding with another planet (as in Lars Von Trier's *Melancholia*), or the world ending as in *4: 44*, it rather shows a world continuing to limp on after a big change. Such a change can be sudden as in *Blindness* or gradual, as in the example of infertility in other films, but it does not end life all at once. Instead, as Robert Nixon has pointed out in his volume, *Slow Violence and the Environmentalism of the Poor*, there is a gradual depletion of resources, a descent into chaos, disorder, and a general degradation of life, what he calls "an attritional violence that is typically not viewed as violence at all."[6] Predictably, once basic infrastructure is gone, greed and aggression take over. Now those who seize power and resources dominate others with violence in its usual normative sense. The world does not have to be totally destroyed for humans to resort to shocking kinds of ugly behavior, as we know from daily news reports from around the globe, but in these fictions such behavior is deliberately magnified.

In this film, the trauma is sudden blindness. In creating a catastrophe resulting from blindness, Saramago introduces a topic that has been used as a rich metaphor in the history of Western civilization. Blindness as punishment for immoral acts is at the root of Western culture from Sophocles and the Bible to Shakespeare and beyond.[7] For this reason, the novel and the film are often hailed as an allegory or metaphor for what is wrong with contemporary life. One could argue that the film offers a microcosm for the destruction of the social order through neglect of obvious looming dangers, taking the literal crisis of blindness as a metaphorical tipping point, very much as is infertility in *Children of Men*. Following Žižek, one might argue that the virus of blindness paradoxically allows people to see behind the illusion, which, as Žižek would say, sustains our idea of reality; it breaks the illusion of a sustainable world that allows us to function as if the abyss were not there.[8] From this perspective, the fact that the blind are quarantined in an old insane asylum suggests not only individual psychological insanity (living in illusion) but that the entire world we live in today is like an insane asylum. The asylum's similarity to a concentration camp deepens the analogy. The camps developed into asylums, only then it was the camp leaders who were mad.

Using such theories does not mean that the film cannot also be understood on other levels. Indeed Louis Althusser's Marxism fittingly illuminates Saramago's meanings in the novel, which Meirelles carries over into the film.[9] Through their blindness, the characters come to see their *real* relations to the means of production. The authorities abruptly disempower people as they become blind, then control and isolate them in what had once been a psychiatric asylum. The authorities seize on the crisis as an excuse to institute the "state of exception" that Giorgio Agamben describes so well in his book of the same title. They shepherd people into the old asylum and implicitly abandon them to "bare life," considering them not worthy of humane treatment. Through their suffering, however, and because even the state seized by the authorities cannot be sustained, some of the characters manage to move beyond the normative ideological structures the authorities place them in. Blindness, then, paradoxically in this view, represents an unveiling of illusions both psychological and political.

But I will read *Blindness* less as metaphor or allegory and, rather, as presenting an image of what we could become (or have already become) if Western civilization does not change.[10] As with other films discussed here, I take Saramago quite literally—as envisioning a catastrophe that, in its effects, is similar to the deadly viruses posited by other pretraumatic films for humans in the future. As in those films, the social order slowly deteriorates as resources diminish.

Written toward the end of his life, *Blindness* perhaps offers one of Saramago's very darkest visions for the future, despite the glimpse of hope at the end. In interviews, he has noted that Western civilization, based on ideas of the Enlightenment, is coming to an end.[11] In his words, "what is really clear is that we have reached the end of civilization."[12] While this rhetoric does not enable us to move forward, it does dramatize a certain limit that has been reached; it certainly suggests the end of a particular era, socially, politically, and culturally as well as in regard to geologic frames.

But neither Saramago nor Meirelles falls into the trap of postmodern artists who reflect what Jameson has called a "windless present." Rather, they attempt, as Jameson puts it, to "jump-start" history through depicting the radical break that the onset of blindness (in this case) has produced. On the didactic level, both Saramago and Meirelles want to show that a society where consumption is rampant is doomed to disaster. Meirelles, it seems, adds a more hopeful note than we find in Saramago in showing that change might happen through people learning the value of a simple life via extreme deprivation and, indeed, social collapse.[13] As we will see, the harmony and new ways of connecting as a community that take place at the end of the film can only happen after the terror and violence are over and the characters reach the Doctor's and Woman's apartment. This is a variation on the dystopian/utopian oscillation featured in many dystopian films, which, I argue, does not serve mankind.

Blindness studies in often unbearably graphic ways the affects, bodily changes, and negative politics generated as humans enter what I call the "contact zone of social collapse," expanding Mary Louise Pratt's original concept of a confrontation between Western colonialists and those they conquered. Here the contact zone is between different sets of blind people—those acting like colonialists by seizing power and those, like the colonized, reduced to victimhood and degradation followed by rebellion. But I anticipate.

The pre-credit opening invites viewers into an aesthetically effective and fearsome world of milky swirls (technically impressive). One has to strain to see the words announcing the film. We cannot see where to press play, for example. In this way, Meirelles hopes to bring us into the fearsome feelings of being blind and helpless. As the credits appear, the scene shifts to a brilliantly edited, almost violent sequence of rapid shots of a very modern cityscape accompanied by terrifying city sounds, cars crowded together and rushing by, horns blaring, blazing traffic lights shown in extreme close-up. The bustling (nameless) glass-and-steel, modern industrial city offers a view of a society that, if advanced, is far from ideal.

No time, date, or place is identified in either novel or film. The time could be a future imagination of disaster or an ominous present—or, indeed, as I argue here, both at the same time. If the sounds of rush-hour traffic are overwhelming, the fast cutting and high-angle shots in turn offer a disturbing look at a world where everyone is in a hurry, cars crowd the highways, and no one stops for a moment. When the Japanese Man (JM) driving a fancy car suddenly goes blind, viewers are invited to see from JM's point of view. Once again milky swirls fill the screen and viewers can barely see the street or the people, just blurry shadows and cars, and experience the sensations of fear and stress. The driver does not at first receive any sympathy for his distress. Meirelles cuts to drivers honking horns loudly and shouting at JM to get out of the way; people trying to cross the street also shout at him, angry at the delay. This is a highly commodified world—people in the busy city are well dressed, driving big cars, and (as we soon see) living in luxurious apartments—but people's sociality and sense of the Other leaves a lot to be desired. What the JM gets instead of empathy is impatience and annoyance. The fast-paced world has no place for infirmity. Even JM's wife (a stylish, professional woman), when she discovers her husband blind and bleeding in their flat, feels less empathy than annoyance as she rushes to get help. Like McCarthy, Saramago chooses not to personalize the characters by giving them first and last names, which adds to the sense of a culture that no longer really cares about individuals—a culture in which (in a sort of Marxist critique) everyone is anonymous, just a cog in the social machine.[14]

FIG. 5–1 The film opens on a sleek, modernist, bustling city.

The person who ultimately offers to help the JM stuck in his car is in fact a new character, the Thief (Don McKellar), who ends up stealing the man's car. The sequence where the Thief calculatedly helps JM is done so as to show him figuring out what he can get from helping. Meirelles's strategy is to alternate shooting from the JM's point of view (when we get those milky swirls again) and from the Thief's position (when the view is, for now, clear). Meirelles will continue this strategy throughout, even once the characters are in the asylum, so as to remind us what it means to be blind.

The following sequences set up the chain of infection, from the moment JM goes to see the eye doctor (Mark Ruffalo). We see the Doctor himself get infected once he is home. Remarkable here (and in anticipation of what happens later) is the empathy the Doctor's wife (played by Julianne Moore, called Woman) shows for him, not fearing getting infected herself. She actually kisses his eyes. And, paradoxically, she is the only one who does not get infected.[15] Everyone in the Doctor's office gets the infection, and these characters make up the core group that the narrative follows.

The opening sequences, aside from setting up the narrative, focus again on the bright modern city, the luxury shops whose windows we see as the Doctor walks home, the bright modern homes the characters live in, and the luxury foods they eat. Meirelles enhances the effect of this super-bright, super-modern city by frequently using shots superimposed on others, so that we see characters imaged in reflections in the glass windows or in mirrors in their homes. The reflections create an impression of overconsumption, overproduction of goods, and hysterical human activity and prepares us for the counterpoint of loss, once characters are inside the asylum. Meanwhile, as people go blind one by one, we are treated to the contrasting milky swirls accompanying their panic and desperate fight to get help. The milky swirls suggest the illusion that blinds characters, while the false truth of their overproduced world on the brink of disaster is shown in bright light.

As the crisis develops, government agents storm the Doctor's office, track all the people he saw that day, arrest them, and lock them up in an abandoned asylum. It is only poetic justice that the Thief arrives in the First Ward in the asylum, which includes the JM and his wife. The Thief's punishment for trying to seduce the Woman with Dark Glasses (WDG, whom we earlier learned is a call girl) is a kick from her stiletto heels, resulting in a wound that gets infected and leads to his death early in the film. Saramago enjoys such loops of moral failure and punishment (the same cycle happens to other characters, such as the Black Man Born Blind and the King of Ward Three, who together engineer a power coup) as part of Saramago's overall wish for a justice he knows is utopian.

After the complex opening section that sets up the context for what follows, the second part of the film begins. It takes place once the blind are shut up in the abandoned asylum. There are haunting images of people arriving at the asylum and trying to find their way. Once again, the milky swirls convey how the world is for the blind. Images of the ward show a place that looks like a prison.

Memories of António de Oliveira Salazar's methods in Portugal are surely behind the scenes of people being arrested and then, once locked up, treated to a repeated government voice conveyed through an old video system, dictating orders and refusing to provide any help. On the other hand, the situation in the asylum offers insight into how capitalism continually recreates itself. In so doing, capitalism destroys the more just world that could have been, resulting in a dystopia.[16] We see this when the Doctor, standing in for liberal humanism, tries to be a rational leader, suggesting a democratic way of organizing the new world the people are suddenly in. Very quickly his leadership is questioned and refused, and he gives up trying. His wife, the Woman (the only person who can see), now takes over, providing an example of caring, mature leadership and also of brave actions. While the Doctor does not object to her leadership as such, his male style backfires.

FIG. 5–2 Meirelles gives viewers a sense of what the characters see with images of hands reaching out in a milky haze.

FIG. 5–3 People sit on mattresses within what amount to wire cages.

For example, he challenges the King, saying, after an ugly exchange, "I don't know how you live with yourself." He also chides the Black Man Born Blind who has the Braille calculator, saying "You, born blind, should at least understand empathy and human decency." But unlike the Woman, the Doctor can't control his temper, and such speeches get him nowhere; in fact, they make the situation worse. As a rare female protagonist in this genre, the Woman embodies Saramago's progressive ideas that include a degree of feminism. She perhaps escapes going blind, as I suggested, because of her empathy, although this is never explicitly suggested.

But the Woman cannot prevent the bodily deterioration that gradually takes place as more people are arrested, less food and water are available, and sanitary conditions become a nightmare. The specificities of what happens to bodies in conditions like those in the asylum are not often dealt with in great detail. In the novel, Saramago refuses to avert his eyes, and therefore ours, from the wretched aspects of bodies in constrained conditions—and blindness exacerbates what would happen to any bodies so situated. Asserting that "no imagination, however fertile and creative in making comparisons, images and metaphors, could aptly describe the filth here," Saramago nevertheless proceeds to try. He describes how some, knowing they could not be seen, simply turned into the corridors to relieve themselves. Others, more sensitive, spend the days restraining themselves, then go at night, "clutching their stomachs or squeezing their legs together, in search of a foot or two of clean ground, as if there was any amidst that endless carpet of trampled excrement." Saramago describes the stench that reaches the wards from the corridors, joined with the already dense fetid smell from the sweaty bodies lying in dirty clothes on unwashed beds where they have defecated.[17] In other words, Saramago has found the language to imagine and convey what happens to bodies driven to such lengths because of impossible incarceration.

Meirelles in turn insists that we watch the bodies degraded and shamefully exposed, but his version is less graphic—perhaps so as not to disgust viewers more than necessary, perhaps through a failure of the visual medium to convey what words can. He softens the horror of bodies in this distress by a series of superimpositions and dissolves, with shots merging into one another, marking the passage of time. Each of these shows things markedly worse, but within a bleached out and distanced perspective. Meirelles shoots characters in medium shot through frames, screens, or architecture, so as to show multiple actions on the part of different people in the shot. The style offers then layers of ongoing activities, the King commanding his gun, while people carry boxes of food; the King's henchmen playing with objects, bored; other people weeping.

Much of the time we watch people sitting in despicable surroundings, lying in trash-laden corridors, or naked, urinating in the corridors. At first, people try to wash themselves, although the bathrooms are overcrowded and it seems all but impossible to get clean. In one scene reminiscent of the novel's details, we see bare feet walking over excrement that covers the floor of the toilets. As time goes on, empty food cartons litter the floors, since the blind cannot see to pick them up and dispose of them. We have shots of bodies weak and expressionless from lack of food, lying on the camp-style beds, in dirty clothes and bare feet. The body seems to simply give out. There are shots of the ward overcrowded with people, bumping into objects, screaming in pain, trying to find space to be. At times, the ward looks like a refugee camp with clothes hanging on lines, all the beds close together. We see the people become dirty, sweaty, and filthy. Although they can't see one another's degradation, they nevertheless are, at least at first, ashamed of how they must look.

These are difficult scenes to watch, but the point for viewers is their need to know what to expect in such a probable future—to observe bodily degradation and to understand not only the shame that results but also our vulnerability. As sociologist Lee Clarke argues, while society must not exploit people's fears of collapse—financial, environmental, or otherwise—neither should people be misled by statistics to ignore what could happen. Clarke's concern is that neither academics nor those in charge of social policy have paid enough attention to how vulnerable we are to worst cases. He argues that we should organize society to come to terms with our vulnerability. So, while some scientists may claim that fears of climate change may be exaggerated or based on faulty science, this is different from requiring populations to be ready for extreme weather or other climate related events. Meanwhile, Karen Cerulo, also a sociologist, shows that tendency to positive thinking makes us resist imagining the worst, and like Clarke, she worries about this. It could be argued both that films in this pretrauma genre help people imagine the worst and that they provide comfort for having imaginatively faced and survived the worst.[18]

In the film, bodies only seem to come alive when there is competition for food (shots of people pushing and grabbing to get their rations reveal perhaps our species's overriding instinct for survival) or when there is a conflict over how to respond to a command from the King of Ward Three. The rape scenes orchestrated by the men in this ward offer perhaps the greatest challenge to viewers, as Roger Ebert has suggested.[19] Humans have reached their zenith in terms of acceptable acts. While this is also true of humans in other films I study, few directors insist that we watch scenes of such pain without sensationalism to distract us (as, for example, in the feats of swordsmanship in *The Book of Eli* as Eli fends off would-be rapists). Like other narratives in the genre, *Blindness* takes us into the worst imaginable zones of human being, so that we might think about what we see, bear witness to the depths to which we can descend. Here, in the microcosm of the asylum, viewers witness in detail ongoing physical deterioration once the infrastructures our bodies need are gone and humans are forced to live like the animals we once were (and remain very close to).

The blind people in Ward Three who reject a rational democratic system increasingly seize power, commandeering the scant food distributed at first by the authorities. The leader (played by Gael García Bernal), who wields power with a gun, claims he is King and terrorizes the others. As less food is given, the King demands payment. Once the little money that people brought with them is gone, the King's cohort ask for jewelry and other worthwhile property, and finally they demand that the women provide sex for food. The violence and brutality that ensue are shocking and traumatize the women. If such scenes are hard to watch, arguably we need to understand how living conditions construct human actions for good or ill.

Meanwhile, outside the asylum, soldiers in a military watchtower (we recall Foucault's description of the panopticon), who are not yet infected, joke about the inmates.[20] They throw food into the courtyard as if throwing food to animals in a zoo.[21] Shots of government authorities, beyond the asylum, trying to deal with a catastrophe they are not prepared for reveal how vulnerable nation-states are to such events—and the automatic way in which the panic-stricken leaders turn to seizing power and locking others up. In other words, the authoritarian world developing inside the asylum mimics what is going on in the world outside.

But what's at stake is not only the world outside the asylum. If these scenes (like the novel) offer memory of the past in Portugal, especially the fascist dictatorship of Salazar, at the same time they warn about a future recurrence of such a violent regime. Here, past traumatic memory and trauma future tense merge effectively into a paradoxical unity of past and future, memory and fantasy. Memory is indeed the past made present, but with a view to provoking thought about the future.

Saramago makes the interesting point that it takes only one person who is not blind to challenge evil. Since the Woman can see, she is finally able to use her advantage to bring down the King (she finds scissors when collecting jewelry for food and uses them to kill the King as he is forcing a woman to have sex). Here Žižek's argument and the allegory it offers partially help: if there is one person who can lift the veil of illusion and face the abyss, change might be possible. (Žižek would agree that it's better not to live an illusory existence, but I doubt he would consider this as opening up the possibility of change.)

Meirelles demonstrates how normative gender roles make life more difficult, in the new situation faced by characters in the asylum. The Doctor's wife, as the only one who can see, is able to wash her husband and keep him relatively clean. However, he feels ashamed and (it seems) feminized by her helping him in these ways, and their relationship grows strained. He tells her that cleaning him and taking care of him makes it hard for him to see her as other than his mother or nurse. He can't think of her anymore as his wife. The helplessness of being blind, then, has a gendered impact on relationships. Not specifically out of revenge for his wife's necessary infantilizing of him but obviously linked to it, the Doctor soon engages in sex with the WDG. It's a spontaneous act, resulting from sexual deprivation, the misery of their situation, and the Doctor's feeling alienated from his wife. The Woman interrupts them mid-act, but instead of being jealous, she understands the context. She realizes that more crucial challenges await them and is able to comfort WDG, who is now guilt-ridden. The Woman's mature ability to rise above this, to forgive them and move on, shows her remarkable empathy—an empathy on which the later transformation of the group arguably relies.

Gender issues emerge again when Ward Three demands sex for food. The men do not want their women to agree to this. The JM in particular objects violently to the idea. The women obviously don't want to be violated either. Once again, it is left to the Woman to turn everyone toward what is necessary for survival. Awful as it is, once she volunteers, other women go along.

The film offers interesting insights into racial connecting that are absent from the novel. There are mixed-race characters in both the main wards in contention—Wards One and Three. The African American actor Danny Glover plays a leading role, and so does John Fort as the Black Man Born Blind (his secret is being normally blind and having a Braille counter with him). Several characters are Latin American or Spanish; there is one

African American boy who is part of the Woman's small group for a while. Other characters are white. But what's interesting is that, while gender continues to be central to the blind, racial difference does not register as it usually does. Skin color not being visible to characters has much to do with this, no doubt. In a short exchange, the African American boy and another man wonder what race the King is. They debate what they can learn from accent or caliber of voice but quickly pass on to other things. However that may be, racial slurs are absent, while gender difference prevails because blindness does not erase sexual desire. The aging Blind Man with Eye Patch, played by Glover, finally bonds, it seems, for the future with the Latin American WDG at the end of the film. It is possible that the openness about race comes from Meirelles, as a Latin American director, having a different cultural heritage in regard to race. The film differs from many others in the subgenre where racial characters are often token figures in only minor roles.

If the film and the novel offer a somewhat predictable picture of what's wrong with capitalism, this is a point that is nevertheless worth repeating. Such scenes offer memory for the future for viewers; within the film, characters can see no future for memory in light of such human degradation. A sense of future selves emerges only at the end, when the group—consisting of eight people (reduced to seven when the African American boy gets lost) who have stayed together once they escaped from the asylum—arrives at the Doctor's and Woman's apartment in the city. Finally fed and washed, they indulge the luxury of thinking about the future, and the WDG and Black Man with Eye Patch decide to live together. Indeed, memory is not a major part of the narrative, as it was in *The Road*. Characters rarely refer to their past, and when they do it is for sentimental nostalgic recourse (see Chapter 3). In fact, in the one scene where memory emerges (the JM tries to engage his wife in a warm memory about visiting a special site in Japan), the memory is abruptly cast aside as the wife says she does not want to listen. The present then becomes all, as dealing with each moment is essential for survival.

After their release, the characters move into a devastated city zone—a zone that looks rather like the worlds in *Soylent Green, The Road,* and *Book of Eli*. With no electricity, water, or power of any kind and dwindling resources, people are forced to compete for what little food remains on the shelves in the wrecked stores. Lodging is even more scarce, since people

FIG. 5–4 The stunned characters stumble out into a destroyed cityscape.

cannot find their own homes and thus sleep in other apartments, which they manage to get into. Our characters arrive belatedly in this world outside the asylum where they were forgotten. As they stagger around, there is a brief renewal moment: a sudden rain shower gives everyone a chance to drink and wash their dirty clothes. Characters smile in relief, hug one another, and for a moment there's a glimpse of the life that once had been. But this soon passes, and the group has to continue to scavenge for food and search for living quarters.

Saramago's novel often reminds me of Nietzsche's nineteenth-century articulation of a binary between the Apollonian and Dionysian aspects of humans. The novel's extreme depiction of humans reduced almost to the level of animals (they defecate anywhere, grab food at whatever cost, copulate anonymously) is Dionysian, while the Woman (and at times the Doctor) represent an ideal of rationality. The Woman in particular represents a utopian ideal of empathy and the ability to transcend her personal emotions for the good of the community. Meirelles does not construct as rigid a binary as Nietzsche does, but as an empathetic director, he maps the philosopher onto spirituality. This is especially obvious in the sequence where the characters are cleansed by the purifying rain.

Critics debate as to whether in the novel Saramago animalizes humans or humanizes animals. Scholars focus on a sequence in the novel where a dog—called "the dog of tears"—comforts the Woman when she finally collapses in distress after she has been attacked by humans because she found some food. The dog comes to her and licks her tears (hence his name). While it is true that the dog shows an empathy totally lacking hitherto in most humans, he is responding to the one human who has shown empathy before—the very Woman whose tears he is licking. I see the dog as a narrative strategy to start the empathic renewal that will happen once the characters reach the Woman's and Doctor's apartment. Also, the dog and the Woman are the only ones who can see, so there is a special link between them.

In the novel, after the dog washes the Woman's tears, she opens her eyes and sees a map of the city. Now she can locate her apartment. In the film, the characters come upon the apartment through their wanderings. Once there, the transformation starts. Everyone is so grateful to have hot water to bathe in, decent food to eat, and wine and coffee (by chance left undisturbed in the apartment) that their mood softens. The Woman acts as a graceful host, sharing everything; the women bathe together and enjoy their now renewed bodies. The men get out of their dirty clothes as well and bathe. The Woman finds new clothes for everyone. And it is in this moment of a turn from capitalism to connectivity that the blindness starts to disappear, more or less in the order in which the people became blind. The JM who went blind in the car at the start is the first to recover his sight. The others follow. The Woman goes to look outside, and as she gazes up at the sky, viewers, following her gaze, encounter white swirls similar to what viewers were given at the outset. We fear that, as the others are now able to see, she will now go blind. However, as she lowers her gaze, the city comes into view, and we realize renewal is possible.

What goes on in the asylum is a slow establishing of a capitalist system that is gradually set up from scratch as more blind people enter the building. Saramago (and Meirelles, in turn) offer a microcosm of how capitalism came about in the first place. Analyzing a vastly different text but one with a similar message (namely, Margaret Atwood's *Oryx and Crake*), Gerry Canavan notes that "the Crakers allegorize the radical transformation of both society and subjectivity that will be necessary in order to save the planet— showing us how very difficult the project will be."[22] Through the contrast between the opening sequences of a highly developed, consumerist society and the devastated asylum world, Meireilles, like Ramachandra Guha, asks us to think about how much we consume and about how much we really need, raising questions about our addiction to continuous growth.[23] In a related move, Katherine Hayles has analyzed the impact on financial trades of digitization of the stock market, resulting in computers working nonstop and making trades according to algorithms traders input. In this world, nothing has meaning except the bottom line. Value, interpretation, and meaning are completely ignored, and the dangers of climate change, if considered at all, are viewed only as a potential stumbling block to producing endless capital.[24] As Naomi Klein puts it, "Climate change detonates the ideological scaffolding on which contemporary conservatism rests. A belief system that vilifies collective action and declares war on all corporate regulation . . . cannot be reconciled with a problem that demands collective action on an unprecedented scale."[25]

Blindness, as a state of being, raises the issue of human connectivity, which is ignored in capitalism. We all need other humans despite our longing to believe we can manage alone. But the blind need other humans desperately. Handling such need is something the suddenly blind have to master. This is a special challenge resulting from the entrenched individualism of Western cultures. As we saw, capitalism relies on individualism and power assertion, not on human caring or connectivity—indeed, these attributes are seen as hindering its advance. The film foregrounds the ways in which people need one another. Hands take on new meanings for the newly blind. At first, they walk alone, splaying their hands out in front of them to avoid bumping into objects and calling to mind images of the blind in classic art that Jacques Derrida discusses.[26]

Soon, people learn that in order not to stray, they need to hold onto one another, and in several scenes we see the blind walking in this way. The danger of losing touch is made clear later on in the film when the group is moving along the desolate streets of the city once the people leave the asylum. The African American boy forgets to hold on and goes in the wrong direction, which offers perhaps a lesson about keeping connected. Among other things, the film focuses on the literal level of the impact that blindness has on the relationships between the people.[27]

In his film Meirelles (like Saramago, in utopian mode) suggests that a post-traumatic world (like the one these characters suffer) may have advantages, namely, a return to human values that have been lost through the overreaching of consumer capitalism. Through the dire straits they have endured, the characters are released from their bonds to material objects, to

FIG. 5–5 Images like these recall images in drawings described by Jacques Derrida in *Memoirs of the Blind*.

their possessions, and to possessiveness. Their aggression has been worked through in what they have experienced, and they discover a gentleness and connectivity that was previously absent in their lives. In his novel, Saramago conveys even more strongly than Meirelles can on film the important change in empathy among the characters once they gain their sight. Starting with the first blind man (JM) gaining his sight, Saramago writes, "At a certain moment, it occurred to the first blind man to say to his wife that they would be going home the next day, But I am still blind, she replied, It doesn't matter, I'll guide you, only those present who heard it with their own ears could grasp how such simple words could contain such different feelings as protection, pride and authority."[28]

Thinking allegorically, the characters recover their sight once their values have shifted. Instead of the film ending in a vague hope for renewal (as in the pregnancy in *Children of Men*; Boy meeting the family in *The Road*; or the busy professor in *The Book of Eli*, re-creating Western culture in his hideout), *Blindness* shows that humans need to live differently and return to values of community and connecting lost in the greed and aggression of capitalism. Is this naïve optimism? Or an impossible utopian gesture, such as has also been claimed of Naomi Klein's work?[29] Perhaps a move related to Meirelles's Liberal heritage in his homeland? And how do we account for the fact that both Latin American directors studied in this project offer a kind of hope for community after the collapse of capitalism that rarely appears in European novels?

In Saramago's case, his ideal leftist optimism is short-lived. The novel that follows hard on the heels of *Blindness*—namely, *Seeing*—demonstrates that the blindness did not teach the corrupt and incompetent Portuguese government anything. It did evidently open the public's eyes to their incompetence, however. Let me briefly explain.

Seeing opens with the public submitting blank ballots in the annual election for governmental officers without any appearance of a conspiracy or other organizational process. As the authorities struggle to deal with the resulting crisis, it gradually dawns on them that the blank votes might have to do with the prior catastrophe of blindness. The JM in the asylum who knew the Woman could see, leaks information to the government about her and the murder of the King of Ward Three. This feeds into the government's imagining that the Woman saw their incompetence during the blindness epidemic and must have conveyed what she knew to everyone, resulting in the blank votes that have so disrupted the president's power. The novel ends with both the Woman and the Doctor, who reappear as characters in *Seeing*, being assassinated. Saramago's pessimism returns here with a vengeance.

The African American Hughes brothers' very American *The Book of Eli* offers an interesting juxtaposition to *Blindness*, which expresses mainly European and Latin American values—this despite the film's international funding and Miramax distribution. *The Book of Eli* also addresses capitalism, overconsumption, and regressive human behavior and addresses memory for the future and the future of memory, only now from a specifically American perspective. But *The Book of Eli* offers a dramatically different kind of dystopian/utopian vision. There is a contrasting main protagonist; an explicit focus on religion, which was muted in Saramago; and a generic style that is decidedly Hollywood. Yet in terms of what happens to humans in a world deprived of resources, as also in regard to the degeneration of politics, there are similarities. Images of how proto-capitalism reemerges in situations of disaster appear over and over again in the futurist dystopian genre. In returning briefly to *The Book of Eli* in what follows, I hope to suggest what can be learned by transnational approaches to futurist worlds.

The Book of Eli looks toward the kind of devastated environmental world discussed in *The Road*, but it shares with *Blindness* images of a destroyed townscape once Eli reaches what (relative to what's available elsewhere) turns out to be a (sinister) oasis. The Hughes brothers decided to give Eli a special (holy) sword and gun powers as part of their interest in his mission to deliver the Bible he has memorized to a utopian project on the West Coast, aiming to restore and gather Western cultural artifacts.[30] Here they follow traditions of impossibly perfect shooters in the Hollywood western genre. Through these formidable powers, with a huge sword and guns, eventually Eli reaches the shantytown where, as also often in the Hollywood western, the mad, evil leader, Billy, has gained control of the community and the resources (in this case, it is water) and wields his power over a woman, Claudia, and her adult child, Solara.

What interested me in this shantytown sequence was less the clichéd authoritarian, power-hungry, and lustful male leader than the regression to the bartering (similar to that in *Blindness*) that presumably would be part of any environmental crisis. For example, when Eli tries to get his old iPod battery charged, the suspicious shop owner (called the Engineer by Billy and played by Tom Waits) points a gun at Eli and asks what he has to offer in exchange. Eli pulls out some gloves, a cigarette lighter, lip balm, a scarf, and other things that finally satisfy the owner. The social world goes back to barter since environmental collapse entails collapse of the financial system. What's left of society regresses to the proto-capitalist trade. Such bartering is repeated when Eli goes into the bar in the town to get some water.

The film develops into a predictable battle between the good guys and the bad guys, with shoot-outs in kung fu style, and then a sentimental, improbable ending, with the white-haired professor, as we saw, diligently collecting all the lost books, music, and cultural objects from Western history, or rewriting them as in the case of Eli and his memorized Bible. In addition, what the film is saying about religion is in general very confused. The Bible as an important part of Western culture is one thing; the trope of Eli being a sort of second coming of Jesus Christ is quite another.

The graphic novel the Hughes brothers include with the DVD, however, suggests a deeper motive for Billy's frantic obsession with the Book.[31] In the story, Billy is fascinated by the evangelical priests he sees on TV. His parents are ugly, violent alcoholics who ignore him as they drink and smoke. Billy sees religion as his salvation but daren't mail the letters he writes to addresses given out on the TV. His father beats him badly for looking at sex magazines. Billy then sets the house alight and disappears. This provides a glimpse as to Billy's vile personality as well as his real interest in Eli's Book.

With this information not provided in the body of the film itself, viewers are left puzzled about Billy's obsession with the Book.

Major Hollywood studio films such as *Eli* rarely deal with values related to building community, nor do they often express explicitly anticapitalist or antinormative views, but as we have seen, these ideas are of interest to Latin Americans. Are Americans unable to move beyond Eurocentrism or dystopic imaginaries predicting the end (*Soylent Green, The Happening*)? Are those Europeans—like Saramago, who lived through the two world wars, including the Holocaust—simply unable anymore to see how capitalism could change or to find alternatives other than the socialist dreams that have failed? There are some documentaries, however, that appeal directly to our need to think in dramatically different ways about the dangers that are facing the human race in the twenty-first century.

6 · GETTING REAL

Traumatic Climate Documentaries *Into Eternity* and *Manufactured Landscapes*

"I am drawn to non-fiction's robust adaptability, imaginative and political, as well as to its information-carrying capacity and its aura of the real."

—Rob Nixon, *Slow Violence*

The fictions of future disaster we have studied so far are different from the documentaries addressed in this chapter in that the documentaries represent disasters that are available in our time to be captured on film and then constructed according to the filmmakers' ends. Even though many of the fictional worlds are probable, they suggest catastrophes on a scale that has not yet taken place—a virus that spreads rapidly and kills all in the world but a few people; apparently permanent infertility that threatens the human species; a planet where food supplies are exhausted, infrastructure gone; floods, fires, and earthquakes that doom the planet, and so on.[1] These fictions, as we have seen repeatedly, only imply that the human race or climate change is the cause of the catastrophe (*Take Shelter* is an exception, in terms of collapse shown as a direct result of climate disaster). Politics and marketing concerns perhaps make directors wary of assigning blame. However, the documentaries make it clear that humans are at fault. They warn us about what is already happening and capture images from around the world that clearly show what our future will be and, indeed, what our present already is. The film directors ask us, in Susanne Moser's words, to "get real," to take notice of what is being revealed about humans and the Anthropocene. We are asked to be witnesses in the ethical sense discussed in Chapter 1.

So here I return to the issue of ethical witnessing that is central in my earlier work in trauma studies. Commercial fictional films offer only limited possibility for the ethical witnessing that is required if humans are to move forward and confront the catastrophes explored in the fictions. Following what Jacques Derrida long ago called "the law of genre" (in work that dove-tails nicely with that of Christine Gledhill and Jane Elliott), the pretrauma film genre repeats the same cycle of dystopia/utopia, which does not serve humans well—not because fictions inoculate us from what is already hap-pening (I have argued that the films in fact function as a wake-up call) but because they insist on implying that there is a way out or that humans can survive despite all.[2] Audiences come to expect a utopian moment as they leave the theater. This is false hope, which is different from inoculation. To have hope for change entails recognizing first that things are wrong. In light of how I define bearing witness, it is clear that the explicit ethical element is missing in the commercial futurist dystopian genre. Films like *Children of Men*, *The Road*, *The Book of Eli*, *Take Shelter* (and others studied here) may give us pause, certainly, but they do not per se inspire us to take the position of responsibility and ethics that witnessing in its true sense involves. The fictions may well prepare viewers for ethical responsibility, but the genre as such cannot provide that position.

Such a witnessing position may be found in select documentaries, like those studied here. Instead of bearing witness to past atrocities as in much of trauma studies, in a film like *Into Eternity* (to take my first example), viewers are asked to bear witness to a specific future catastrophe that has not yet taken place—in this case, the urgent need to find ways to store dangerous nuclear waste. Dangerous nuclear radiation has been released in nuclear power plant disasters (such as Chernobyl and, more recently, Fukushima), but storage of waste from these plants has yet to be fully taken on board in most nations. In *Into Eternity*, we are witnesses to what must never take place—just as, for example, in art about the Holocaust or other genocides, we are witness to what must never happen again. We are perhaps inspired to think through what needs to change in order for humans to survive into the future.

In *Into Eternity*, Danish director Michael Madsen develops a very unusual strategy for producing what I have elsewhere theorized as the "witness position" in avant-garde women's films such as Tracey Moffatt's *Night Cries* or Maya Deren's *Meshes of an Afternoon*.[3] I argued that those films invited viewers to take up the witness position through distancing from the narrative, a process that requires spectators to pay attention to the screen so as to figure out the meanings of what is being shown. Obviously, not all viewers will engage with the witnessing position in films like Moffatt's or Deren's. My point is that Madsen has developed a strategy in *Into Eternity* that makes it impossible for the viewer *not* to take up the witnessing position, by having his narrator do much of the work. Madsen poses questions to the viewer as a virtual future being in a different manner than in the fiction films studied earlier. In this case, the virtual future being may or may not be "human" in any ways we now know.

Madsen's film is remarkable in this and several other ways. Its methods for telling its story are experimental and effective. While its topic, the dangers of nuclear waste, is specific, the warnings about this particular danger apply broadly to other twenty-first-century dangerous uses of resources. The philosophical, ethical, and moral questions raised by the film illuminate much about what humans are doing on the planet today.

Into Eternity, like *Take Shelter*, illuminates my concept of pretrauma, but in a radically different way. *Into Eternity* addresses an ongoing project to deal with nuclear waste, looking toward the future, while *Take Shelter* projects into the future a catastrophic climate event that wipes humans out.[4] If *Into Eternity* follows fairly standard documentary techniques in some sections (such as interviews, monologues, newsreel footage, etc.), the narrator interpellates the viewer of the film in between—not as a present-day spectator (our normal position) but as the future human finding the repository (called in Finnish *Onkalo*, or "hiding place").[5]

The entire mood and atmosphere of the film enacts a pretraumatic scenario, a trauma waiting to happen.[6] The film sets the tone before the credits emerge, through shots of gray rocks laden with ash or snow, lying beneath bare trees with stark leafless branches. In the distance, we see electrical towers and power lines barely visible in a milky white haze. In a sense, the movie enacts a horrific dream, a nightmare from which we long to wake up, while Onkalo resembles a secret place like the unconscious. We cut to the camera moving slowly into a tunnel as the credits emerge. A disembodied voice addresses the viewer: "I am taking you to a place where something is buried to protect you. We are taking great pains to be sure you are protected.

This place should not be disturbed. It is not a place for you to come. Stay away or you will be hurt."

In the process of being addressed as a future human being, the viewer is not only put in the position of witness to a future traumatic event but asked to take responsibility for it. We are asked to deal with many complex philosophical and ethical issues about nuclear waste from the perspective of a hundred thousand years in the future. In interviews, Madsen notes that it was the matter of scale, now in regard to time, that fascinated him. "I thought that first of all these persons, these experts," he says, "will have to be able to relate, to understand, what a hundred thousand years is, which I think is very, very difficult." He continues to say that his "basic question has been, throughout making this film, What does such a facility tell us about our own time and what is its true significance? Perhaps it's something beyond being a storage place for nuclear waste."[7]

The issue of time as it is linked to danger is one of the movie's major themes. And it is through the performance aspects of the work that this theme is developed. In a gesture that will be repeated three times during the documentary, Madsen strikes a long match, holds it up as it burns, and directly addresses the present-day viewer as a future human. The image shows him at shoulder height, in a darkened room, with just his face lit: "Onkalo was begun in the twentieth century before I was born. It will be finished in the twenty-second century when I am dead. Onkalo must last a hundred thousand years. Nothing built by man has lasted that long. If we succeed, it will last forever. If you find it, what will it tell you about us?"

Madsen's performance art here is effective. As these sections perform future-tense disaster, Madsen continues to address the future human directly, through a series of careful questions, gently articulated as if to future ghosts or as though within a dreamscape. The viewer is put in the position of the ghost-like human being addressed. Through Madsen's questions, the viewer as future human confronts the fact of the waste hidden deep in rock in the north of Finland. Performing this being, the viewer has to imagine coming upon the repository. We are the ones who are finding it; we have to decide whether to open it up or not; we have to deal with our impulse to find treasure, with our desire for wealth, our greed for energy, not knowing or not caring to take notice of the dangers that twenty-first-century humans are trying to communicate to us twenty-second-century or later beings. Even in questioning whether the being IS human (and no one

FIG. 6–1 Madsen's performance functions as an alert, with the flame symbolizing human misuse of another kind of "fire."

is sure what kind of human it is or even sure that it would be recognizable to us), we are made to think differently, to worry about leaving this dangerous waste to be misunderstood. But the main point here is how the address directly to this interpellated viewer (that is, the spectator watching the film) pushes him or her to take responsibility for this waste as a kind of pretraumatic virtual being.

Madsen continues the creative strategy of interviewing scientists and philosophers about a number of issues related to nuclear waste. He follows with a shift in tone to questions posed gently to the viewer-as-future-human (VFH).[8] The film is divided into sections, each of which opens with a warning signal as if someone has pushed an alarm button.

The first warning is "Intermediate Storage." After scientists are prompted to discuss how waste is currently being stored and the effort needed to keep the waste safe, Madsen, in his soft voice, gently asks the VFH, "Did the waste get out? Did it happen? Are there forbidden zones with no life in your time?" Some further questions that VFH has to think about include the question of need for so much energy: "Our world depends totally on energy," Madsen says. "Is it the same for you? Does your way of life also depend on unlimited energy?"

The second warning signal is titled "Permanent Storage." Onkalo is an attempt at providing such storage. As the film follows the building of the huge repository deep in the rock, the narrator takes his camera into the tunnel leading down to where it is being constructed. He again addresses the VFH: "You are now in the tunnel; you are in a place where you should never go; what is there is dangerous, repulsive; danger for you, for all of us; nothing here for you. Turn around; go no further." And at this point there are terrifying noises on the soundtrack to emphasize the point. The admonition to the viewer is almost physical. We all but turn around in our seats, so compelling is this unusual strategy for getting the point through to us.

Via a replay of a television news report in this section, we get an idea of the complex ambitious architecture of Onkalo. It will ultimately have many levels and look like a huge underground city. The Beethoven symphony on the soundtrack conveys a sense of the awesome, almost beyond human scale of the venture. There are complementary safety barriers to prevent disaster. Started in 2012, we learn that Onkalo will be completed in 2200 and then sealed for eternity, like Pharaoh's tombs, never to be opened. Accompanying shots of the trees and the bleak wintry landscape, we learn, via the voiceover, of the need for the repository to be back-filled, and for the land to be made available for humans to use again. The voice gently asks: "How about you? How far into the future will your way of life have consequences?"

Striking a second long match, within the same darkened place, Madsen says: "Man mastered fire and conquered the universe," continuing to note that man felt powerful. Now, he says, there is a new fire that can destroy us. It is one that cannot be extinguished; it could burn a land but it is also inside the human, inside his children, his crops. "We need a hiding place for the fire to burn safely into eternity," he concludes.

The following section of the film develops this theme, addressing the worry about "Human Intrusion." Here we see how inevitably scientists and philosophers can only think about the future through lenses of humanity's own past to date—that is, through the lenses of what we know and have experienced. The interviewees compare the situation to current humans finding sites like the pyramids, other tombs, and making archaeological discoveries. The future human may see the site as having religious meaning or as a burial ground with treasure. Madsen asks if there would be anything valuable in the waste and is told that the copper, uranium, and plutonium could indeed be valuable.

The scholars all agree that the site will not be understood in the distant future; they also agree that it is hard to think forward three hundred years, when all seems dark to us. Again, it's interesting to see the speakers vacillate between thinking of the future beings either as far superior to us or as far inferior. They speculate that the future human won't have knowledge of radiation or tools to drill into the rock (one scientist, however, reminds others of how advanced sixteenth-century Swedes were in terms of what they could build).

Madsen pushes further with his strategy of asking questions to a future human. He forces viewers to think within a new time frame instead of relying on frames from our human past. He softly addresses the VHF: "We realized you might find Onkalo. We don't want you to. You may get hurt. Most of all, if opened, it would be available to all. You are the main threat to the safety of Onkalo."

An interesting warning section addresses "The Future" and probes more deeply into the question of communicating to the future being. Prompted by Madsen, the scientists and philosophers talk about how to communicate to the future humans the dreadful danger that the repository represents so as to prevent them from opening it up. The debate—which draws on a 1993 report by the Department of Energy about markers and human intrusion into waste areas—ultimately turns first on whether it is safer to leave markers that present-day humans hope future humans can understand or to simply bury the waste, leave no sign, and just hope that no future beings think of drilling into this particular rock.[9] Models of markers are offered, from a complex monolith with layers of messages, including directions to an archive for more information about radiation, to crude cartoons and the idea of surrounding the site with brutal landscaping of thorns, rocks, and so on. There's even a suggestion of including Edvard Munch's famous painting *The Scream* as universally terrifying.

But none of these ideas seems sufficient. Madsen suggests the best method is for humans to rely on information being passed down from generation to generation. Scientists, however, argue that future beings may be curious and may think there's wealth in the waste. They consider what the future human may do, based on what we have done in the past in our archaeological digs for information about earlier people and their cultures. One speaker mentions a rune left lying down in Finland with warnings not to lift or touch it. But archaeologists raised it anyway. They decide markers are not the answer because either people will not understand what the marker says or they will open the site nevertheless. Since

FIG. 6–2 Munch's *The Scream* was one idea for a "marker" to scare would-be humans from opening the radioactive vault.

markers may provide motivation for opening up the repository despite warnings, some think a better strategy is to leave Onkalo unmarked. This debate has no conclusion. The situation indicates the problem raised by the film about our human inability to provide adequately for an unknown future for which we are nevertheless responsible. Madsen's questions make the point: "We will leave messages for you in different languages: Will you see them? Can you read?"

Part 4 of the film, titled "Human Law," addresses the confusion about different national laws relating to nuclear waste. Some nations require that the waste be safe for five hundred or a million years. In Finland, where the state has taken over responsibility for burying the waste and passing on information, the time is a hundred thousand years.[10] The idea is that each generation will correct the information about radiation in the archive and anticipate new methods for storage. Returning to earlier discussions of the time scale, one speaker reminds us that one hundred thousand years back our ancestors were in Africa and Europe. What would a Neanderthal understand of postmodern technology and radiation? A scientist concludes that senses, appearances, needs, and knowledge of future generations will be different. No humans as we are now will be around. Madsen then wonders if we can trust future generations and, if not, what we can do. The only hope is to set up a repository such that human nature (as we now know it) can't interfere with it; it has to be a place that can function on its own, since we can't predict human nature in the future. As once before, the theme of the transience of culture, society, and the body over a large time scale returns. Empires rise and fall, nations rise and fall. There is no permanence.

The last section, "A Nuclear Remembrance," touches briefly on familiar questions as to whether, knowing all the dangers of nuclear waste, we should still be using nuclear energy. One statistic gives the viewer pause. For China and India to reach the current prosperity in the West, they need to build three new nuclear reactors every day. Also noted is that Onkalo will be only one tiny repository for one nation's nuclear waste. Humans need many more such sites. A scientist cites the principle of decisions made under uncertainty. In addition, scientists are aware that, as it is put, what is most dangerous is "what you don't know that you don't know."

Lighting a third long match, Madsen inserts perhaps the most telling philosophical and ethical question in the film, which, as he asks it, summarizes the journey of the film. Having discovered a dangerous fire, Madsen notes, man put his fire to rest and tried to forget. He knew that only through oblivion would he be free of it. Then he started to worry that his children might find the chamber and awaken it from its deep sleep. So he tried to tell his children to tell their children and so on down the generations, telling them "to remember forever to forget." A very telling paradox, it relates to earlier concerns in the fictional films regarding both memory for the future and the future for memory. Here the future for memory is to forever forget the repository. We must remember to forget it and not open it.

The ending of the film sharpens the point about the potential for disaster. Madsen's last address to the VFH assumes that the future human does open Onkalo. The human does not remember forever to forget, as he hoped: "You have now come deep into the repository; radiation is everywhere; you do not know it, but something is happening to your body; something beyond your senses. You cannot feel it or see or smell it, but a light is in your body, it is shining through you. It is the last glow of the powers we have harvested from the universe." There are grim shots inside the repository, clashing music, and operatic singing about the coming doom. Two ghost-like workers draw back a thick curtain protecting them from the latest explosion inside the repository. There is a sudden silence. They draw back the curtain and then walk off into the dust that was created by the blast, their lights fading as they too disappear into the murky gloom, while credits appear on the blank screen.

The movie's strong impact comes from the unique position it constructs for the viewer as witness to the future. In addition, through the photography, visual techniques, and editing, spectators experience a pretraumatic scenario of a wasted land. The shots of the workers make them look like strange unworldly beings involved in an overwhelming technical task. Even the scientists who talk to us are often shown in freeze frame, as if already dead, or shocked by the seriousness of what they are telling us. There are warm, even humorous moments as well, as the personable interviewees share their expertise. If the overall tone of the film is dark and suggests a doomed human species, Madsen has succeeded through his ingenious cinematic techniques in getting our attention about an issue that is addressed too infrequently. The movie cannot offer solutions to such a complex issue as that of humanity's need for energy combined with the fact that the powers we harness have deadly results. But in situating the viewer as this future-human witness to all the problems raised by nuclear energy, *Into Eternity* insists that viewers take responsibility and work toward new global policies regarding nuclear waste.

As a kind of dreamscape, the film suggests a visual correlative of the unconscious. The stark, gray, foggy landscapes denuded of vegetation and viewed through a slow-tracking camera seem ghostly, surreal, fantasmatic. The figures shot in slow motion likewise seem dreamlike. Onkalo itself, indeed a hidden, secret place, acts as a metaphor for the unconscious, with the dreaded nuclear waste alluding to all that we do not want to know about human aggression and the destructive urges that produced radiation in the first place. The questions are addressed by the superego to the ego, insisting that it take notice, find its moral capacity, take responsibility for what it is intent on hiding, take responsibility for the future. It is as if Madsen is calling upon the ego to take up the witness position that the id and the unconscious resist because of the difficulty of finding solutions, and because of the pleasures of forgetfulness and irresponsibility. To remember to forget requires hard work. Just forgetting is easy.

Manufactured Landscapes, like *Into Eternity* but following a different environmental issue, is often also called "otherwordly" by reviewers. "The hypnotic otherworldiness of science fiction" is how Jim Ridley puts it.[11] Once again, we enter an apparently surreal world that is, in fact, only too real. If

Manufactured Landscapes reminds viewers of science fiction, now the disasters are available in our own time—to be captured on film rather than, as in fictional films, projecting into the future a catastrophic climate event that is wiping humans out. If the future human intrusion into Onkolo in *Into Eternity* was feared because it might unleash destruction, in this case the intrusion into the natural world for the purposes of extracting nature's resources is continuing in the present time on an increasingly massive scale. Unlike *Into Eternity*, where the urgency of the problem of nuclear waste is stated many times and in quite forthright terms, the politics regarding global massive industrial sites documented in *Manufactured Landscapes* is complex. As we will see, the complexity arises partly from the collaboration between the Canadian film director, Jennifer Baichwal, and her (also Canadian) collaborator, photographer Edward Burtynsky. The diverse creative strategies of the two, one working with film, the other with still photography, produce different interpretations of the same phenomena, but the work as a whole demonstrates the drastic environmental and human consequences of mass production (on a hitherto unknown scale) of industrial goods across a whole range of entities. It is as if we are entering a world that only just predates John Hillcoat's *The Road* or the Hughes brothers' *The Book of Eli*. In those fictions, however, there is a deliberate effort to de-aestheticize the world—to make it ugly, destroyed, dangerous. Those are worlds where nature takes revenge on what humans have done to it. By contrast, images in *Manufactured Landscapes*—both photographic and cinematic—are astounding, transformative even, in their scale and problematic aesthetic appeal.

Part of the interest of the film lies in its complex layering of visual media and the artists linked to them. On one level, Jennifer Baichwal's trajectory in *Manufactured Landscapes* follows the work of photographer Edward Burtynsky, who has for many years traveled around the world taking photos (with his special four-by-eight camera) of the sites, equipment, and factories of heavy industry. Baichwal suggested the collaboration after having access to black-and-white footage taken by Jeff Powell on one of Burtynsky's prior trips (that time to Bangladesh) in search of the largest industrial sites that have been his preoccupation. Baichwal saw that this footage needed to be incorporated into something larger and proposed her film.

In their collaboration, the two travel together to sites selected by Burtynsky, where Burtynsky and his crew take photos while Baichwal and her team film on the same location. We move from Burtynsky's huge still photos, seen at the start of the film in a Canadian gallery exhibition, to Baichwal's moving images. In addition, periodically Powell's black-and-white footage is included, which adds yet another dimension and vision. From time to time throughout, cinematographer Peter Mettler zooms in on the original photos or into Powell's footage. Sometimes Mettler and Baichwal are at the site where Burtynsky is shooting but making a moving image instead of still photos. In addition, there is the haunting musical score by Dan Driscoll, which develops Baichwal's politics even as she honors Burtynsky's preference for ambiguity over didacticism. There is, then, a constant awareness of the different media involved—photography, cinema (in color, in black and white), sound—creating the complex, dense, haunting experience of looking at the Chinese industrial sites and huge factories that are the main focus of the film. In approaching the film, I'll show how Baichwal builds an aesthetics of trauma to reveal the loss and suffering that industrial practices on this scale entail. Memory of what has been destroyed and what is in the process of being taken away permeates many of the film's images and sequences.

Manufactured Landscapes is an extraordinary hybrid: a documentary, of course, but one that, like *Into Eternity*, sidles up to science fiction in its otherworldliness. The collaborative project about the ongoing industrial revolution in China, on a scale that few of us have fully realized, entails Westerners' traveling to foreign lands to film the local inhabitants and allows us to contemplate the changes that increased globalization is bringing about. Earlier, such "traveling" might have been viewed as negative ethnography, filmmakers imposing their values, attitudes, and ways of seeing onto those being filmed. But increased worldwide access to the Internet and to social networking may be eroding or reconfiguring such cross-cultural interchange. This is not to deny that viewers of *Manufactured Landscapes* may feel discomfort in scenes where representatives of official Chinese authorities give the required uplifting speeches about the progress that industrial sites and factories illustrate. Because the speeches are not given enough context, the speakers may appear ingratiating. But films now contest and even reverse hierarchical notions of modernity and ethnicity. The issues raised by Baichwal's film about heavy industrial sites, recycling yards, over-mining, and huge dam construction are now global ones. What's important here is that, while activities such as those filmed by Baichwal and Burtynsky can be found worldwide, everyone knows that the United States' carbon footprint is per person much higher than China's—or any other nation's, for that matter.[12]

If a negative approach to the film could perhaps still be made from the perspective of an implicit Western cultural hierarchy (China being situated as the *cause* of global pollution since its carbon footprint is the highest anywhere), I will, on the other hand, argue that precisely through the collaboration of two Western artists, coming to China with differing aims and perspectives, the ethnographic danger is mitigated.[13] Through his ongoing interest in the sites of, and heavy equipment used for, industrial extraction of Earth's resources and in the huge factories where goods are produced from these extracted materials, Burtynsky has long drawn the general public's awareness to the devastating incursion of humans into the natural landscape.[14] But Baichwal is clearly not making a biography of Burtynsky, as she did of Paul Bowles in an earlier project, *The True Meaning of Pictures*. This is not a film that simply, as one critic puts it, "extends the narrative stream of the photographs." Baichwal neither simply "reinforces the spirit of Burtynsky's still pictures," nor, in my view, does she "cede authorship" to him, as this same critic claims.[15] Rather, Baichwal extracts the traumatic underside of the photographs through her cinematography—lighting, movement, editing, camera position, and importantly, Dan Driscoll's sound—revealing in an intimate way the human cost of China's industrial revolution.

While the overall aim of the movie is to study the huge scale of industrial revolution ongoing in China, many of the still photos were produced and exhibited before the film was made. Early in *Manufactured Landscapes* viewers are taken to a gallery where Burtynsky is talking about his images. But when we cut back to the on-site filming, we find that Baichwal not only extends the reach of Burtynsky's discoveries, she has done more, namely, she has reinterpreted Burtynsky's work, partly by drawing attention to his creative process as it differs from hers. More specifically, some questions to consider include Baichwal's interest in creating a position for ethical witnessing in regard to what she and Peter Mettler capture on film. How far does Baichwal avoid the aestheticizing that Burtynsky seems to feel necessary for attracting viewers—or perhaps that for him is a natural aspect of his creativity? How far may aestheticizing in the end be productive for a warning about global warming?

The achievement of the film lies in allowing viewers at once to experience the brilliance and daring of Burtynsky's huge photographs and to have

Baichwal's camera do something else. Burtynsky's photos were secured at great risk and cost to himself as he traveled the globe to track down these sites; we are given their astonishing visual impact and invited to gaze in awe and amazement at what we are shown.[16] Yet the moving camera is able to convey something quite other, simultaneously. As Baichwal moves with her camera into Burtynsky's images, she zooms in on people who are often mere dots in the photograph, while Driscoll's haunting music suggests foreboding, uncertainty, the unknown.

It's tempting to suggest a classic male/female approach to the issue of the representation of the sites—the male taking a distant, abstract, high-angle view, interested in the shapes he finds and constructs through angles, lighting, color, and so on, and their references to sculpture; the female identifying and empathizing with the human cost and implications by coming in close to her subjects. This would not only involve an old-fashioned essentializing, however, but it would be too pat. Burtynsky tells us that he does not do portraits, for example, and in extreme long shot, we look at images taken from his visit to Bangladesh's vast coastal areas, where huge tankers and other cargo ships are brought to be dismantled and broken down for their valuable materials. But in his cool understated way he also draws attention to the difficulty of the work for the very young workers and their low pay.[17] It is perhaps this cool stance, aiming to be as objective as possible, that Baichwal is interested in countering through her own interest in, and implied concern for, the humans involved deeply in the Anthropocene. Hers is a camera that seeks out the individuality of the workers rather than settling for showing them in an anonymous mass. Her interest is microscopic as against Burtynsky's macroscopic view. The two views—and technologies—are complementary and end up together providing a better understanding of what's going on in China than either could have given alone.

Let's take an example from the film's opening, which establishes Baichwal's vision as it complements and contrasts with Burtynsky's. The film begins, before the credits, with a stunning eight-minute panning shot as it tracks through an enormous Chinese factory where several kinds of electronic products are made, from computer components to domestic irons. The shot starts at one end of the factory. With nothing but sounds from the work ongoing in the factory (silence seems to be enforced in these factories), the camera slowly pans along the multiple huge, long worktables with aisles in between.

FIG. 6–3 Baichwal's camera ends its eight-minute tracking shot showing us the scale of the site by closing in on the exhausted boy, showing the human cost of the work.

Each structure has perhaps a hundred workers along it, all dressed alike, each assembling some small component of an object. The workers mostly avoid looking at the camera, although a few males turn to look from time to time. That is as much as we can see in this long panning shot. But having established the scale through movement (a kind of scale that the still image cannot easily catch), Baichwal moves in on one lone worker, left slumped over his table after the others have all gone home. She holds her camera there, as we reflect on the man's exhaustion and the toll that the work takes.

Interestingly, Burtynsky's voice enters into the sequence toward the end, showing right away Burtynsky's ambivalent views. He notes that we should respect nature; if we destroy it, we destroy ourselves. Yet he sees that humans are creating a new landscape with their incursions into nature and declares that he is not trying to condemn it; rather, he wants to show the images to allow viewers to grasp the scale of the incursions and the related industries. As Baichwal's camera catches the factory emptying out, the image slides from the moving camera to Burtynsky's photos (two identical photos, sides by side) capturing the scale of the factory through a high-angle depth shot. It provides a totally different way of experiencing the factory that Baichwal tracked through.

We cut to outside the factory, in the morning, where masses of workers assemble for their morning "criticism/self-criticism" session following

Every time we worked on 7562, if I didn't remind you, ...

FIG. 6–4 Baichwal's camera shooting outside captures the identities of the young workers and details the interchange between supervisor and workers.

standard Maoist practice that is evidently still in play. Baichwal first captures the scene with her moving camera, which closes in on one of the groups being addressed by the supervisor. We learn that he is complaining about the quality of the work, and the workers look ashamed. Baichwal then films Burtynsky striving for another high-angle shot: we see him on a high scaffold manipulating his huge four-by-eight camera. He gives orders to his crew, asks them to bring the workers up to fill the street, complains about the light, but finally takes the shot. This time he captures the assembling process from a long distance so as to emphasize its massive scope.

The image that results shows identically clothed workers in yellow, stretching far into the distance in military-style formations, flanked by the yellow buildings where they work. The image conveys brilliantly the huge scale of Chinese production, but Baichwal, in moving in on the young people in the assembly line, captures some of the anguish in the work and the tight organizational control involved. Viewers see the police on motorbikes making sure there is no trouble of any sort. Burtynsky's macroscopic view, then, in this as in many other examples, complements Baichwal's microscopic and humanizing one.

The viewer is startled by an abrupt cut to Burtynsky talking about his images in a gallery where they are being shown. The strategy involves moving from the live assembling of the workers to the double-photo image

FIG. 6–5 Burtynsky's photo captures the scale and the huge numbers of workers involved as a mass.

Burtynsky had produced now on display. As a man crosses the image of the workers in yellow, viewers realize we are in a totally different space. We see people gazing at the images as Burtynsky lectures—but in filming the scene, Baichwal adds two things. First, she takes her camera directly into the photographs, traveling into an image of a huge quarry in a way that reveals how enormous it is, adding perspectives that the still image cannot show. It is a strategy she will repeat numerous times over the course of the film. Second, Baichwal adds Driscoll's mournful music, the low-tonal swish of the drumsticks, adding an emotional undertow to the images of incursion into nature, a sense of loss, of haunting, of fear of what the images imply. In a sense, Baichwal in this way alludes to the unconscious of Burtynsky's images, the tragedy of human intervention in the life of the planet.

As a man peers into one of the photos, there's another startling cut, as Baichwal's camera returns to look closely at the actual work being done inside the factory. She catches the female workers in close-up so that we see them repeating one single action each second. Her camera focuses first on their hands, revealing the incredible digital dexterity and speed with which the components are tested or assembled, and then provides close-ups of the workers' serious faces concentrating on each action, without looking up or pausing.

As she closes in on these faces of apparently anonymous, identically clothed female workers, we see them laboring intently, expertly testing small

You wouldn't start working until you were told to.

FIG. 6–6 In Burtynsky's image the women are mere dots in the piles of waste, while Baichwal moves in close to the women and we hear them talking about their work.

pieces of equipment on the production line, endlessly repeating the same gesture that requires extreme digital dexterity. In all this, Baichwal reveals their individuality and their subjectivity.[18]

The objects the women are working on in this scene are ordinary irons. Baichwal then cuts from the factory to a photo of the endless recycled waste dumps where discarded irons can be seen. Once again, there's a cut to the moving camera, now in a similar space to that in the photo. We hear noises of metal being turned over, and see women wearing hats, gloves, and masks kneeling down in the trash looking for usable pieces.

The supervisor complains that they have not gathered enough usable pieces and their time is running out. Then Burtynsky's voice is heard commenting on the piles of computer waste, particularly in regard to an old woman he films (a departure for him to capture people) because he is astounded that she is sitting outside her house beside a pile of toxic computer parts. We learn that the place is so toxic that one can smell it kilometers away, and that the watershed is no longer usable because of the toxic runoff into it.

This section of the film continues with more shots of recycled waste, and of women again working on the dumps. We cut back to the factory where the film started and watch the completed irons carried along moving rails, presumably on their way to being sent overseas. After another series

FIG. 6–7 Framed by a black border, Burtynsky's rare portrait of an old lady living next to toxic waste.

of images of other huge factories, the film focuses on dramatic photos and footage of the alternate building and dismantling of enormous ships that haul cargo across vast stretches of the ocean. Where Burtynsky—presenting a photo of a huge tanker at a great distance, apparently situated in endless mud, devoid of anything—mentions that the specks we can see down in the mud are people searching for valuable scraps, dropped as the ship was towed in, Baichwal and Mettler move in with the camera, so that we can actually see the people turning over the mud looking for metals. In repeated shots of these enormous hulks, we learn that Burtynsky's interest in them is their uncanny resemblance to ancient archeological sites, and their likeness to huge sculptures—that is, he is stirred by their aesthetic appeal.

Much later in the film, Baichwal uses another strategy to make her point. Visiting the Three Gorges Dam, the team explores the huge displacements of people (said to be 830 million people) to accommodate the thirty-two generators being installed for electricity. She and Burtynsky discover one old lady who refuses to move, and her old house thus remains standing among the rubble. Baichwal juxtaposes the images of numerous destroyed cities and of people trying to gather bricks and other remains with the upbeat Chinese guides' discourse about the progress that the destruction symbolizes. Looking ahead fifty years, the guide explains how the region will be as big as Shanghai, completely urbanized. However, through judicious editing

FIG. 6–8 Burtynsky captures the discarded hulks of ships now appearing like ancient ruins or huge sculptures.

techniques, cross-cutting, and juxtaposition of shots, Baichwal captures the emptiness of the Chinese guides' utopian enthusiasm for the bright new future, in the form of skyscrapers, that is to arise from the ashes of the past. The related destruction is just too devastating to contemplate—or so her film seems to say.

Once in Shanghai, Baichwal juxtaposes the old streets where a lively communal life goes on with the isolated new Western-style houses. She interviews a real estate agent, who proudly shows the film director her lovely house and large garden, requiring three gardeners every day. This is one of the very few scenes in the film where we see anything green or growing. Nature as we used to understand it is nowhere to be seen. There is a humorous cut from a man cooking on his street oven to the real estate agent's voice-over as she shows the open kitchen in *her* lovely new home. These are strategies not available as such to the photographer, and they make their point by juxtaposition. As we gaze later at Burtynsky's images of the huge skyscrapers being constructed in Shanghai and at the phenomenal ten-track, layered, interconnecting roads swirling around the city, Burtynsky notes toward the end of the film that humans "are changing everything, water, land, the environment; and this is in the world at large, not just China."

The film ends on the darkest note—literally and symbolically. The team finally gets permission to visit the vast coal mines evident in China where

FIG. 6–9 Baichwal captures people living among the ghastly mountains of coal being mined.

burning coal daily sends gallons of fossil fuel into the atmosphere. Ironically, Burtynsky obtains permission through convincing the authorities that his photos always show what he films as beautiful (he has one of his books along with him to prove it). But Baichwal captures people living next to mountains of coal, and the last shot of the film is of neon lights advertising the company in the utter darkness of the black coalfields stretching out for miles.

Let me end with comment on the issue of framing, in a larger sense than that between photography and film, since here we can see how Baichwal and Burtynsky complement one another.[19] If in his discussion of his images in the gallery setting, as in many online interviews, Burtynsky does address the environmental concerns that he believes may surface for some viewers of his photographs, he does it coolly. He notes that "the images are meant as metaphors to the dilemma of our modern existence"; he tells us he is searching "for a dialogue between attraction and repulsion, seduction and fear." Drawn by a desire for a good living, he says, we are somehow aware that "the world is suffering for our success, [resulting in] an uneasy contradiction." But, significantly, he concludes that, for him, "these images function as reflecting pools of our times." Burtynsky clearly does not aim to convey any particular message, and in calling his images "reflecting pools for our time," he suggests a meditative, passive position of thinking about human impact on the planet, rather than an active concern for injustice or a responsibility to bring about change. In relation to this position of deliberate ambiguity, critics mention that Burtynsky's photographs can hang in corporate offices as a celebration of what industry can achieve or they can be used by environmental groups to bemoan what is being done to the planet. For Jim Ridley, commenting on Burtynsky's images, the macroscopic panoramas "show how industry has smashed, scarred, and altered the environment," and yet these same images, he says, through their "lush, awesome, and in a sense beautiful photography, [may] distract us from the appalling heaps of corporate waste and industrial devastation" and lull us into complacency.[20]

This comment captures well the often disturbing ambiguity of Burtynsky's images. As with other photographers of disaster or global practices, more generally (Sebastiano Salgado, for example), the issue is not only how far images are constructed but also what it means to aestheticize horror.[21] An old argument that dates at least to Theodore Adorno's famous comment about the Holocaust and the problem of writing poetry after Auschwitz, the issue has been much discussed over the years. But it perhaps takes on new force in this different context, namely, the intrusion by humans into nature and the human costs this intrusion entails.[22] Burtynsky points out that whereas in earlier times artists like J. W. Turner made paintings (such as his sea series) in which huge storms dwarf humans rocked on tiny ships, now our own creations dwarf us, as we see in the huge mines in Burtynsky's photographs. However, the sublime that Turner offers us is only a temporary unsettlement. We know the storm will pass, the ship will recover (or not), but life will continue as usual. The sublime is often a psychic transformation for the artist and viewer, a lifting up, even a transcendence. It embodies temporary fear and excitement—but not a permanent change in the relationship between humans and the natural world.

The case is far different in regard to human industrial intrusion and violation of the landscape, as nature's resources are extrapolated for profit. John Hillcoat's *The Road* suggests a stage that follows on from humans' intruding too far into nature, dwarfing and hollowing it out. In these scenarios, nature returns in revenge—as if falls—to in turn dwarf us again. Life cannot return to any kind of norm. This damage to nature, if taken too far, is seen by the writers and filmmakers studied in this book to lead to the catastrophic future that artists are now foregrounding already, as in these documentary films.

Nevertheless, if aesthetics attracts viewers and draws them to the disturbing images, "empathic unsettlement" (La Capra) or "pro-social empathy" (Hoffman) may result, moving public awareness further in productive ways.[23] It is true that many viewers are turned off by, and then turn away from, the destroyed worlds in the futurist dystopian films studied in previous chapters. If people can be attracted to the horror, as it were, isn't that better than not looking at all? Through this productive collaboration, then, we get both the macroscopic vision so essential for understanding the incredible scale of these operations and the microscopic humanizing view that Baichwal brings to bear for the viewer.

Baichwal manages to do this without being didactic. She agrees with Burtynsky that giving messages is not necessarily effective. Burtynsky is against didacticism because it limits people to either agreeing or disagreeing with the given point of view. Rather, he wants people to take in what he is showing and to generate their own opinions. He believes not giving a message offers the viewers more space to think, and in the film he talks about our needing "a whole new way of thinking." But what he means by this "new way of thinking" is never articulated as such.

Baichwal arguably moves toward a new way of thinking, which comes close to what I have described as a kind of witnessing. Witnessing in my sense is not passive observation but active engagement like that encouraged in *Into Eternity*—an engagement produced by the work of art itself through its techniques. In other words, Baichwal's engaged concern about the dangers of industrial sites (both as regards the intrusion into and damage to nature and in regard to human impact) emerges in how she directs the film and works with her cinematographer. In different sections of the film, Baichwal offers a series of quick images of Burtynsky's photos, often zooming in or out of the picture; this strategy brings home the scale of the waste and recycled objects in a way that observing the photos in a gallery, one by one, cannot do. Close-up shots of the piles of items discarded in the West that litter the waste sites in China recall the uses the objects once had. The close-up shots of neatly packed squashed cans and steel items seem to embody the roles these objects once served. The toxic piles of motherboards and computer components carry memories of work discarded, gone, torn from bits that previously stored it. There's something mournful and haunting about the largely Eurocentric past embodied by these discarded objects. We get a strong sense of the overconsumption by the wealthy, which Guha and many others have worried about, now brought here to China to be recycled into new objects to send back to the West in an endless cycle of consumption, ejection, and finally, reconstruction through the hard labor of the people we see working on the recycled materials.

That a personal concern underlies Baichwal's direction is supported in several interviews easily available on YouTube. In one of these, Baichwal describes her stance as that of "witness to these places we never knew about." She registers her shock at being in a place where there is not one green thing—"no trees, no birds, yet people are living there"—a view we see many times in the film. In another comment she notes that, whenever she and her crew tried to add dialogue alluding to such observations, it turned out to be didactic in a way she didn't want. Baichwal apparently agrees with Burtynsky's argument that these are "places we are responsible for"— a position I comment on below.

In other comments in online interviews, Baichwal tackles her own fascination with what Burtynsky has uncovered. She wonders if the interest in diverting nature on such an enormous scale is some kind of yearning for humans to be more than they are. Do we "throw things around and completely transform the nature of the planet in our own endeavors," she questions, "as a way of asserting our power? I don't know. I don't know what it is."[24] Baichwal also reveals her concern as she talks about how Burtynsky's images horrify in regard to the huge holes that he shows being cut into nature.

Both Burtynsky and Baichwal state the idea that we are all responsible for these horrendous places—and thus, that taking an oppositional stance to them is disingenuous, if not hypocritical. We are all complicit in desiring "the good life" that depends on extracting materials from nature. Burtynsky's comments in the film describe his unease in driving a car dependent on oil or using camera equipment that requires natural materials. But this position confuses the scales for responsibility. Because I drive a car using up oil reserves or a camera that requires electricity, it does not mean that I am as responsible as the corporate leaders. These leaders benefit from the labor of people extracting the materials, and it is they who damage nature and the planet in the ways they extract the resources. I need these resources (and Hurricane Sandy taught me how devastating it is to be without them, even for just a week), but I am not personally controlling how the resources I need are extracted. Nor am I in any position to develop cleaner alternative resources, even though I engage my responsibility by advocating for such alternatives as best I can.

I have argued that Baichwal extracts the traumatic underside of the labor ongoing at the sites in Mainland China and Bangladesh that Burtynsky has located—an underside that he holds back from showing. If critics debate the degree to which Burtynsky's lush, awesome, beautiful photography lulls viewers into complacency about the corporate practices he shows, by contrast, without explicit feminist consciousness but with a concerned and caring stance, Baichwal and her camera capture the tragedy of young men's dangerous low-paid work on the sites. She also captures the tragedy of women and children of all ages, who scour the piles of recycled computers and technical devices that the West dumps in China. I have tried to show that, without being didactic and largely through the framing and the soundtrack, Baichwal's film constructs a position for the witness to environmental injustice and its slow violence that goes beyond what we normally consider feminist politics. She mourns the ongoing tragedy of scarring nature and creating monumental caverns by extracting minerals from nature, as well as that of the inhumane labor, pollution, and displacement of people that such extraction and such production of goods entail. Human desire and capitalist greed, harnessed on the back of the first industrial revolution, return on a scale that would have been unimaginable in earlier centuries in order to devastate the planet. Unless empowered humans learn to curb the twin drives for consumption and for its imagined pleasures and learn to work together in order to control overconsumption, life on the planet will degrade. While Baichwal could have gone more deeply into the politics of corporate greed (whether in the West or the East) in the way Naomi Klein has done, this point is implicit in her film. She ends up framing Burtynsky's images so as, at once, to retain their otherworldly brilliance and, by moving with her camera literally *into* the photos, to reveal the trauma the photographs imply but cannot actually show. The film implicitly asks us to consider what hope we can have for the future, if we don't remember what is being lost in incursions into nature and if we don't take responsibility at what levels we can.

AFTERWORD

Humans and Eco-
(or Is It Sui-?) Cide

"Anyone who gives way to the temptation to deliver an opinion
on the probable future of our civilization will do well to remind
himself . . . of the uncertainty that attaches quite generally to
any prophecy."

—Sigmund Freud, "The Future of an Illusion"

I have explored how artists and theorists, following Freud, have
been "tempted to deliver an opinion on the probable future of our civilization." But along the way I have inevitably been tempted to offer my own
anxious views—with my own sense of uncertainty, I confess, sometimes at
levels of pretrauma. My discourse has struggled to integrate at least four levels, which include first, the psychic state of deep cultural anxiety about the
future for the planet and for humans; second, politics in terms of both political meanings within the films and the political work that the films perform
in U.S. culture; third, gender and race perspectives; and finally, the place of
memory (both past and future) in the genre, as this pertains to possibilities
for ethical and empathic engagement in a state of social collapse.

As this book goes to press, several important political, literary, and cinematic events have taken place—all germane to topics I have discussed here.
First, the increase in the amount of newspaper and Internet attention to climate change during the course of my writing this book is remarkable. Reports
of extreme weather events are now routine, as are discussions of climate denial

or scientists' reluctance to speak out passionately about their discoveries.[1] In addition to the crucial IPPC 2013–2014 report with which I began this book,[2] and partly as a result of that report, President Obama finally found the courage not only to veto the Keystone Pipeline that was an environmental hazard but also to make a deal with China to cut greenhouse gas pollution.[3] As I write, nations of the world are meeting in Lima, Peru, for the United Nations Climate Change Conference, aiming to revisit the Kyoto Protocol and to address the dangerous rise in fossil fuel emissions said to be nearing the sustainable limit.[4] Meanwhile, the 2015 U.N. climate change conference, COP 21, will be held in Paris, France, from November 30 to December 11. As Michael Greenstone puts it, "Nations comply only with the treaties they deem to be in their interest."[5] On December 15, 2014, a climate change agreement was announced among 196 nations represented in Lima. For the first time in history, this would commit every nation to lower its rate of greenhouse gas emissions. While this still will not solve the problem (a far stronger deal would be needed for that), it is a least a start.[6] A *New York Times* article, published on November 3, 2014, and exemplifying the new public awareness about dangers of climate change, noted that "without immediate action, flooding, food shortages and mass extinctions are likely."[7] Another article published on November 12, 2014, reiterated a similar warning, only now, for the first time baldly stated, the piece claimed that, unless humans take extreme measures, our species may become extinct.[8]

In a similar vein, Naomi Oreskes and Eric M. Conway's new book, *The Collapse of Western Civilization: A View from the Future* (2014) adopts an effective strategy similar to that used by Michael Madsen in *Into Eternity*. They construct the narrative voice of a human who is addressing the reader from four hundred years in the future and reflecting back on the collapse of Western societies. They present the details of each misstep humans have taken as evidence mounted as to the extreme damage that fossil fuel was doing to the planet and human life on it. The future human says, "Historical analysis . . . shows that Western civilization had the technological know-how and capability to effect an orderly transition to renewable energy, yet the available technologies were not implemented in time."[9] Oreskes and Conway's book provides details of developments in science clearly showing the grim dangers and equally details the astounding political denial of climate change that Oreskes and Conway had already written about in *Merchants of Doubt*. The distance from a position in the future allows readers to absorb the mistakes and hopefully take heed now before it is too late.

Christopher Nolan's new film, *Interstellar*, opened in November 2014 and appears to respond to the growing public awareness of climate change in the past five or so years. It's a stunning and ambitious film, evidently drawing on both Alfonso Cuarón's *Gravity* (the term "gravity" is much touted and central to the film's plot) and Kim Stanley Robinson's *Mars Trilogy*. There's also a dash of *Snowpiercer*, Joon-ho Bong's 2013 sci-fi thriller—a film that also shows more awareness of human causation than in films studied here, since a failed climate-change experiment has ironically cooled the world too much. Such bio-engineering is in fact being debated by scientists today, and its dangers (as the film shows) exposed.[10] *Interstellar* combines elements of all these with the dystopian genre I study, adding to it by detailing the gradual decline of life on Earth. The film focuses on a farming family in the Midwest, living on corn (the only sustainable crop at this time), which they grow across vast acres of land. Nolan tracks the slow violence involved in this family's decline, very much in Rob Nixon's sense, as each generation is worse off than the one before. As the dust-bowl effect increases, the small children's lungs are affected, and the corn increasingly fails to grow well. Conditions in the house deteriorate, and tempers fly as a result of all the continuing deprivations.

The film also poses directly a moral question not addressed in other films, which has to do with thinking about the future of humans as a species. Whereas other films track humans trying to survive in dire conditions of infrastructural collapse, *Interstellar* dares to suggest that in order to save humans as a species, those currently living on Earth must be sacrificed. Dr. Brand (played by Michael Caine) is the moral center of the film, and it is he, a brilliant physicist, who engineers a plan to send astronauts on a mission through a wormhole and into another galaxy. There, he calculates, one of three tracked worlds would support human life. The astronauts carry crates of human sperm and eggs to jump-start humanity in the new world, leaving Earth to its own tragic fate.

Third, among the cascade of volumes on the environment in recent years, two related and important books were published in 2014, with themes very much in line with what I discuss. Written by two writer-reporters, Naomi Klein and Elizabeth Kolbert, these books offer contrasting, but I think ultimately complementary, perspectives on the climate catastrophe that faces humans. In line with the documentaries we studied in the last chapter, these works report, now from an environmental humanities position, on the science, economics, and politics of global warming. Naomi Klein's brilliant if belated entry into climate change debates, in her *This Changes Everything: Capitalism vs. the Climate* (debates which, she admits, she long avoided), focuses on those responsible for damage to the planet, namely, international corporations and colluding governmental authorities. In hopeful mode, Klein looks at how climate change could inspire positive change—the kind of changes that leftists over the decades have been arguing for. These include taking back ownership of essential infrastructures, like water and electricity, and "reclaiming our democracy from corrosive corporate influence." Klein summarizes the by-now-well-known science data warning of catastrophe, she documents global corporate crimes against the environment, and analyses how damaging the World Trade Organization has been in regard to accommodating green industrial practices. She has an informative chapter on the "Heartlanders," namely, the climate change deniers, before turning to the enormity of the challenges facing humans and the urgent need for everyone to reduce their carbon footprint. Klein believes that humans can find alternative energy resources if they just put their minds to it.

Meanwhile, Elizabeth Kolbert (a longtime authority and writer on climate change) has a new exhaustive and careful analysis of humanity's fateful impact on the planet in her *The Sixth Extinction*.[11] Drawing on the work of many researchers who have studied ecosystems globally, Kolbert reveals the role of man-made climate change in causing animal and plant losses. She presents us with the convincing evidence she's gathered, often firsthand but, unlike Klein, offers no solutions. In her review of Klein's book, Kolbert initiates a debate about the best way to approach the looming catastrophe. Kolbert appreciates Klein's detailed analysis of the current climate change situation but critiques what she sees as her "fuzzy" optimism. Klein's leftist-style reporting seems to irk Kolbert, whose own approach is very different. While supporting Klein's call for a carbon tax, Kolbert points out that this hardly challenges capitalism, and she is unconvinced by Klein's idea of "managed degrowth." Most of all, she notes, "when you tell people what it would actually take to radically reduce carbon emissions, they turn away."[12]

Klein asks us to see a possible upside to challenges of global warming, that is, the catastrophe might force societies to abandon greed and profit-mongering. Kolbert prefers us to come to terms with the reality that change is impossible. Readers are left to decide between a utopian impulse and realistic aims, whether such an impulse is indeed better than coming to terms with the reality that change is impossible.

The published exchange between these two in the January 8, 2015, issue of the *New York Review of Books* following Kolbert's review simply confirmed that the two writers approach the deep dilemma caused by climate change from different perspectives. And I see both of these as valuable. We need both hope and courage in order to change our ways of being, as we seek solutions and adapt to the new world. But we also need to understand and admit the reality of the dire situation—to take that in fully and try to understand the history of how we got here as we seek to deal with it.

Possibly in line with Kolbert's realism, in her earlier work on feminist dystopias Sally Kitch suggests that the utopian impulse "reflects hard-wired human dissatisfaction with the status quo" (which is useful) but that "the utopian impulse gives humanity an illusion of control over its destiny." This is what we perhaps saw in Klein, and which Kolbert resisted. Kitch has argued in favor of resisting the utopian/dystopian duality endemic to the fantasies I have studied here and of finding a third kind of thought, which she calls "realist."[13] Problematic as this term is, what Kitch means here is that social thought would put "less stock in principles and ideals alone" and would allow for the complexities and vagaries of human action.[14]

In my terms, we need to be able to demonstrate how we will get to any future we think of—from where we are now. Vital to any such movement toward a future will be learning not only to tolerate difference (extremely hard to do) but also, as a second step, being able to collaborate. Global collaboration among all nations, coming as they are from divergent situations along the path to climate catastrophe, is the only way to begin to mitigate what is already in place. This third route—which requires pragmatic thinking and thoughtful leadership about plans for a future based on where we are now—is a hard road to travel. That should not prevent us from trying.

Looked at from the perspectives of psychology, philosophy, and deep personal being that have been offered in some chapters, these films, whether intentionally or not, also implicitly produce a wake-up call to audiences—to attend to what human actions are doing to the species and the Earth. Part of the point in making environments almost recognizable is precisely to help audiences glimpse the decline into a deprived "bare" life that is just a click away. Calling this a "climate pretrauma" suggests the need to pay attention to the psychic issues of living in dangerous times. First, we need to think carefully about what it means to live with radical doubt—uncertainty about the security of the natural as well as political and social worlds.

The antidote to climate trauma is denial. Alan Weisman warns that "we may be undermined by our survival instincts . . . to ignore catastrophic portents lest they paralyze us with fright." He continues, "If those instincts dupe us into waiting until it's too late, that's bad. If they fortify our resistance in the face of mounting omens that's good."[15] Unfortunately, denial usually prevails. I am tempted to read such climate denial as requiring the travel from melancholia to mourning that is so familiar in trauma studies. In Freud's classic work, melancholia signals that the subject is unable to let the lost object go, in a sense denying that the person has died. The subject internalizes the lost object, fuses with it, and the result is a kind of blocked state, which is a severe form of denial; the subject in a sense keeps the object alive through incorporating the absent person into the subject's psychic world. Mourning, however, signals that the subject's loss is being worked through—the lost object is seen as separate and the subject grieves an irreparable loss while moving forward with his or her life.

In their discussion of what they call "the intrapsychic tomb," Nicholas Abraham and Maria Torok take Freud's position further to argue that there are some losses "that one cannot acknowledge as such." In this case, one is not only unable to mourn, but one cannot even admit the inability. Incorporation of the lost object prevents this: "Without the experience of somehow conveying our refusal to mourn, we are reduced to a radical denial of the loss, to pretending that we had absolutely nothing to lose. . . . Everything will be swallowed along with the trauma that led to the loss." Abraham and Torok go on to describe the situation with a powerful metaphor: "Inexpressible mourning erects a secret tomb inside the subject . . . affect, the objective correlative of the loss, is buried alive in the crypt as a full-fledged person, complete with its own topography. The crypt also includes the actual or supposed traumas that made introjection impracticable."[16]

Freud's theories, together with those of Abraham and Torok, may well describe how many viewers watching pretrauma films are situated in regard to climate change and to losses already happening around the world. However, one problem with these theories, as Susannah Radstone pointed out, is the absence of attention to sexual difference. The Freudian theory of mourning and melancholia assumes a male subject and indeed describes a male malady. Radstone's exhaustive analysis deals with a different film genre from mine—the "boyhood film"—but interestingly her argument supports my contention that the pretraumatic climate film mainly addresses a white male audience afraid of what climate catastrophe means for them in terms of loss of control, power, and wealth. Radstone stresses the universality of the postmodern, post-holocaust subject in writers such as Eric Santner who rely on psychoanalysis. "All concerns with sexual difference fall away," she says. Through detailed analysis of the theories of Freud, Winnicott, and Lacan, Radstone concludes that loss is "the foundation of both masculinity and patriarchy." She further claims that, instead of recognizing loss and difference, male communities "project their losses onto the body of woman or . . . onto those relegated to the position of women and who come to stand for castration." Radstone shows how, in the "boyhood film," male protagonists are preoccupied with nostalgia for their own childhoods, revealing what Radstone calls "patriarchal nostalgic melancholia" instead of "postmodern mourning."[17]

This theory may explain why so many climate sci-fi films feature male protagonists and why often symbolic father-son relationships are referenced (they are not always literally male fathers in relation to male sons).[18] Female sci-fi heroines in the pretrauma genre are hard to find—hence the importance of Meirelles's film *Blindness*, which features a female protagonist. We have to turn to female science fiction such as that by Margaret Atwood (here I studied a film adaptation of her *Handmaid's Tale* with its strong female central character), Ursula Le Guin, or Octavia Butler in order to find female protagonists, and ways of dealing with the end of the world other than via prevailing nostalgia and melancholy. Female authors engage readers with utopian fantasies of renewal or the development of new kinds of bodies in other worlds—bodies that replace the Western male/female binary with new kinds of sexualities. It seems that, while male fantasies dwell on nostalgia and melancholy, female authors seek ways to envision moving on.

Nevertheless, it seems to me we need to keep active two different kinds of analysis so that both the micro and the macro levels can be kept in play at the same time. This is something that Dipesh Chakrabarty aims to do as he integrates climate change into postcolonial and leftist analyses of history. Looking on the micro level, the lack of attention to sexual difference in sci-fi films and the dominance of white male protagonists requires understanding and notice. We can learn about how gender relations in our culture are constructed from these narratives. However, on the macro level, humans as a species, together with the planet, are in danger.

It is on this macro level that we might reintroduce the Freudian concept of mourning and melancholia, looking to the cultural context and to the psychological changes that have to take place for moving forward. Here Susann Moser's thoughtful research on climate change might be useful, although this comes from existential psychology rather than psychoanalysis. Arguing that we are living in what she calls "a world in distress," Moser implicitly calls for us to move toward mourning—from what is possibly a dysfunctional state of melancholia, or what she calls "unaffordable denial about climate change."[19] Unlike the humans in many of the films we've seen here, we are still able to imagine a future. So we still have the possibility to move from what Moser implies is a state of melancholia to a much more productive state of mourning, for what we are in the process of losing and for what many have already lost. In her chapter "Getting Real about It: Meeting the Psychological and Social Demands of a World in Distress," Moser notes that "psychologists . . . have begun to research people's emotional distress caused by environmental change and climate disruption." As disasters unfold, she says, there will be "a lot of confusion, a lot of not-knowing, uncertainty, and probably a good deal of hanging onto hope-against-hope and denial." Films in this project offer perhaps an invitation to readers and to viewers to move from a melancholic position on our world-in-distress to the position of mourning—a position Moser advocates as a start toward dealing with the crisis.[20] Futurist dystopian films offer a wealth of provocations to precisely such thought and emotion about images of the future and about the psychoanalytic, political, and cultural meanings involved.

NOTES

PROLOGUE: CLIMATE TRAUMA AND HURRICANE SANDY

1 For incredible images of damage to New York City and surrounding areas, see Alan Taylor, "Hurricane Sandy: The Aftermath," In Focus with Alan Taylor, *The Atlantic*, November 1, 2012, http://www.theatlantic.com/infocus/2012/11/hurricane-sandy-the -aftermath/100397/.

2 See the image of a theatre group in lower Manhattan that also set up a generator where people could charge devices. Ibid.

3 See Emily Fleischaker, "Hungry New York Families Dig Food out of Dumpsters after Sandy," *Buzzfeed*, November 2, 2012, http://www.buzzfeed.com/emofly/hungry-new -york-families-dig-food-out-of-dumpsters/.

4 For pictures of the evacuation, see J. David Goodman and Colin Moynihan, "Patients Evacuated from City Medical Center after Power Failure," *New York Times*, October 30, 2012, http://www.nytimes.com/2012/10/30/nyregion/patients-evacuated-from-nyu -langone-after-power-failure.html. Unfortunately a website that included a video documenting the crisis brought on by the power surge flooding the Langone Medical Center, showing the loss of research data in the labs in the flooded area and the danger to patient records, is no longer available.

5 Viewing these sites to prepare for this prologue, I realized what we had missed in not having access to any media during the entire time of the power outage. News had been going on elsewhere, while we were without.

6 Rubenstein, *Public Works*, 136.

7 Ibid., 134.

8 Ibid., 138. There is an ironic twist in comparing the early situation of electricity coming newly into people's homes in the early twentieth century, and our situation today. While then people were at first terrified of this new unseen power entering their homes, today we are terrified if we lose this unseen power.

9 "Hurricane Sandy," Wikipedia, last modified November 13, 2014, http://en.wikipedia .org/wiki/Hurricane_Sandy/.

10 Malcolm Bowman, "Predicting and Preparing for the Next 100-Year Storm," *Stony Brook Magazine* (Spring 2014): 8–9. See the following websites for Bowman's articles and debates about such storm-surge barricades: "Hurricane Sandy Provides 'Wake-up Call' for Cities at Risk of Flooding," *NBC News*, November 1, 2012, http://rockcenter.nbcnews .com/_news/2012/11/01/14862174-hurricane-sandy-provides-wake-up-call-for-cities -at-risk-of-flooding?lite/; "Storm Center," SoMAS, Stony Brook University, http://somas .stonybrook.edu/storm/sandy/; Jeff Tollefson, "Hurricane Sweeps US into Climate

-Adaptation Debate," *Nature*, November 6, 2012, http://www.nature.com/news/hurricane-sweeps-us-into-climate-adaptation-debate-1.11753/.

11 See Tollefson article and websites in previous note for details of these responses.

12 This information is a summary of the information on the Hurricane Sandy Wikipedia site.

13 Even conservative Republicans are finally beginning to realize that their profits are at stake if we continue to use fossil fuels. See Justin Gillis, "Bipartisan Report Tallies High Toll on Economy from Global Warming," *New York Times*, June 24, 2014, A18.

14 Hoffman's aim is to find, on one hand, traits that point in the direction of species suicide and, on the other, human traits that are prolife. So far, the suicidal traits seem to point to greed, which may paradoxically have self-interest (survival) as its ultimate source.

15 Al Gore, "Without a Trace," review of *The Sixth Extinction: An Unnatural History*, by Elizabeth Kolbert, *New York Times*, February 10, 2014, Sunday Book Review, http://www.nytimes.com/2014/02/16/books/review/the-sixth-extinction-by-elizabeth-kolbert.html.

INTRODUCTION: PRETRAUMA IMAGINARIES

1 Justin Gillis, "U.N. Panel Issues Its Starkest Warning Yet on Global Warming," *New York Times*, November 2, 2014, A8; Paul Crutzen and Eugene F. Stoermer, "The 'Anthropocene,'" in *The Global Warming Reader*, ed. Bill McKibben, 69–74.

2 Kaplan, *Trauma Culture*.

3 The article is only available online for now, but it will appear in print in 2015 in *Clinical Psychological Science*. As of November 26, 2014, it can be found at http://aps.psychologicalscience.org/members/login.cfm?end_location=/members/CPSSsage.cfm?endlocation%3Dhttp%3A%2F%2Fcpx.sagepub.com%2Fcontent%2Fearly%2F2014%2F11%2F22%2F2167702614551766.ful.

4 See Heise, *Sense of Place and Sense of Planet* and her later essays, "Invention of Eco-Futures" and "Globality, Difference and the International Turn in Ecocriticism."

5 Berntsen and Rubin note that "Having pretraumatic stress reactions . . . does not imply that the person has had no prior traumatic events." Rather, they go on to argue that people who have had PTSD are likely to be subject to PreTSS; yet those who have not had PTSD may still be vulnerable to PreTSS.

6 See Elizabeth Kovach's in-progress dissertation research on "Novel Ontologies after 9/11: The Politics of Being in Contemporary Theory and U.S. American Narrative Fiction." Her research is being completed at the International Graduate Center for the Study of Culture, Giessen, Germany.

7 Katherine Sugg, "*The Walking Dead*: Crisis, Late Liberalism, and Masculine Subjection in Apocalypse Fictions," *Journal of American Studies* (forthcoming).

8 Buck-Morss, *Dreamworld and Catastrophe*, ix.

9 Agamben, *State of Exception*.

10 David Harvey's *A Brief History of Neoliberalism* has also influenced my thinking about the new political era, which was initiated in Eurocentric nations but is increasingly adopted globally. As he puts it, "Neoliberalism is . . . a theory of political economic

practices that proposes that human well-being can best be advanced by liberating individual entrepreneurial freedoms and skills within an institutional framework characterized by strong private property rights, free markets, and free trade" (2).

11 Chakrabarty, "Climate of History," 207, 210, 212, 212.

12 Medavoi, "Biopolitical Unconscious," 136–137.

13 Roth, "Trauma as Dystopia," 233.

14 Moser, "Getting Real about It," 437–438.

15 Nicholas Mirzoeff, "Visualizing the Anthropocene," *Public Culture* 26.2 (2014): 213–232.

16 Buck-Morss, *Dreamworld and Catastrophe*, ix.

17 Yusoff, "Excess, Catastrophe, and Climate Change," 1010–1011.

18 Justin Gillis, "Panel's Warning on Climate Risk: Worst Is Yet to Come," *New York Times*, March 31, 2014.

19 Medavoi, "Biopolitical Unconscious," 126.

20 This phrasing comes from a document written by Sarah Buie for a collaborative project. I do not locate my project in the genre of "ecocriticism," even if there are overlaps.

21 Morton, *Hyperobjects*, 103.

22 Cohen, "Introduction: Murmurations," 15–17. I appreciate Cohen's statement that "the impasse between today's spellbound and rapacious present and supposed future generations, the rupture of any imagined moral contract to or recognition of same, has been in circulation for a while" (20).

23 Kristeva, *Black Sun*, 223. Interestingly, *Snowpiercer* nicely combines the two subgenres offered in this book, namely, that of a pretraumatic climate event (humans accidently have frozen Earth in their attempt to mitigate global warming) and that of the dystopian political thriller (in which fascist leaders have taken control of the humans who have survived, subjugating the majority to pitiable and degrading lives).

24 Roth, "Trauma as Dystopia," 235.

25 In fall 2008, for example, the cover of *U.S. News and World Report* read "How Scared Should You Be?" and in 2009, a cover of the *New York Times' Magazine* had a large image of a woman's terrified face with the word *"Anxiety"* writ large. Underneath were the words "Is it the economy, terrorism or where your children are?"

26 Here is a quick example of such circularity: political interventions by the United States in the Middle East created intense anti-Western emotions on the part of the nations invaded; Hollywood fantasized aliens destroying major cities; terrorists (filled with fantasies of heavenly rewards and perhaps inspired by Hollywood) take down the Twin Towers on 9/11; the United States invade Iraq for revenge; the cycle then starts over.

27 Freud, "Future of an Illusion," 46–59.

28 Slavoj Žižek, *Welcome to the Desert of the Real* (London: Verso, 2002), 15–16.

29 Grusin, *Premediation*, 2.

30 Žižek, *Living in the End Times*, 315–352.

31 Wilkinson, "The Cryonic Castle," 44.

32 As Wikepedia puts it: "*Cold Lazarus* is set in the 24th century, in a dystopian Britain where the ruined streets are unsafe, and where society is run by American oligarchs in charge of powerful commercial corporations. Experiences are almost all virtual, and

anything deemed authentic (such as coffee and cigarettes) has either been banned or replaced by synthetic substitutes."

33 See Levy and Sznaider, *Human Rights and Memory.*

34 See Gutman et al., *Memory and the Future.*

35 See also the long entry on *dystopia* in Wikipedia, which includes discussions of etymology, dystopian fiction, and more.

36 For Jameson's use of the terms *utopia* and *anti-Utopia*, see his *Archaeologies of the Future* and "Future City."

37 I found this definition in the Free Online Dictionary, citing the *Collins English Dictionary.*

38 Jameson, *Archaeologies of the Future*, xvi.

39 Atwood, *In Other Worlds*, 85. See Freud's well-known pair of essays from 1915, "Thoughts for the Times on War and Death."

40 In Frank Kermode's critique of the focus on crisis in European modernism, *The Sense of an Ending*, he takes exception to what he calls "apocalyptic utopianism" in fantasies of political revolution (98). Kermode is suspicious of apocalyptic thinking because, as he puts it, "such a myth, uncritically accepted, tends like prophecy to shape a future to confirm it" (94). In this respect, Kermode anticipates Grusin's "premediation" and Žižek's futurist conspiracy theories.

41 Žižek, *Living in the End Times*, 350.

42 The bee problem continues as this book nears completion. In his *New York Times* report of March 29, 2013, Michael Wines informs readers of the drastic expansion of a mysterious malady, started in 2005, that "has been killing bees en masse for several years." While the conclusive cause remains in doubt, beekeepers attribute it to a "powerful new class of pesticides, neonicotinoids, incorporated into the plants themselves." Finally, in 2014, some states are taking action to require that farmers plant the kinds of vegetation that bees can thrive on.

43 Nixon, *Slow Violence*, 3.

44 Jameson, *Archaeologies of the Future*, 199.

45 Zipes, "Introduction," xl.

46 Jacoby, *Picture Imperfect*, xx.

47 Moylan, *Scraps of the Untainted Sky*, 193.

48 Baccolini and Moylan, introduction, *Dark Horizons*, 7.

49 Moylan, *Scraps of the Untainted Sky*, 149, 150.

50 Bill Carter, reporting in the *New York Times* on March 17, 2012, that Fox canceled *Terra Nova* due to high costs, mentions as well that the high-profile creators, including Steven Spielberg, are seeking another venue.

51 See Sugg, "*The Walking Dead.*"

52 David Itskoff, "It's Never Really Dead in Zombieland: After Off-Screen Turmoil, 'The Walking Dead' Returns to Fight for Civilization," *New York Times*, October 6, 2011. This statement requires a longer and more in-depth argument than I can make here but seems to make intuitive sense.

53 Michael Springer, formerly a graduate student at Arizona State University and now at Bryan University, has researched a new series of environmental video games intended

for educational purposes—to help young students understand the need for change in how we relate to the environment.

54 For images and a discussion of the "Apocalist" art show, see Waverly Mandel and Dan Teran, "Spring/Break: End of the World in Art," Show Alert, *The Artsicle Blog*, March 15, 2013, http://www.artsicle.com/blog/spring-break-end-of-the-world-in-art/.

55 The 2012 *Hunger Games* phenomenon is a case in point. The narrative of a frightening future world—in which children, under the authority of sadistic adults, fight each other in order to survive—caters specifically to teenagers. *New York Times* film critic Manohla Dargis, in the *New York Times* (March 22, 2012), argues that Suzanne Collins relies on an old American myth, that of Natty Bumppo (resexed, of course), and the film recalls Michael Mann's *The Last of the Mohicans*. The 2014 film *Divergent* continues the vicious theme.

56 Ridley Pearson, "Dystopia," review of *Legend*, by Marie Lu, Sunday Book Review, *New York Times*, December 4, 2011. See also John Schwartz's review of Ryan Boudinot's *Blueprints of the Afterlife*. Schwartz notes that "in Boudinot's world humanity has all but extinguished itself in a blaze of environmental disaster and a revolt of cyborg slaves." Schwartz adds, "It is an apocalypse of synergistic losses: of species, of environmental balance, then of whole cities, large disasters extrapolating inevitably from smaller ones. . . . It's already started, in other words, and the enemy is us." *New York Times*, January 25, 2012.

57 University curricula continue to include many classes specifically designated as film courses, and texts continue to be needed for such offerings.

58 Chakrabarty, "Climate of History," 207.

59 In *Children of Men*, for example, we find a dichotomy between a suppressed body of people in the workforce and the "thugs" living outside the city in a no-man's land, whose only weapon is rage at the existing order. Meanwhile, leftist terrorists use violence in battles with the authorities, seemingly without a clear theoretical basis, class analysis, or organized revolutionary aims. They simply protest what is; and once the pregnancy is found, they grab the fetus for their ends.

60 Ortiz and Schwab, "Memory Is Key," 68.

61 In fact, this is what happens in Saramago's sequel to *Blindness*, titled *Seeing*. See my brief discussion in Chapter 5.

62 See Guha, *Environmentalism, How Much Should a Person Consume?* and *Unquiet Woods*; Nixon, *Slow Violence*.

63 The report of the UN Intergovernmental Panel on Climate Change (IPCC), entitled *Climate Change 2014: Impacts, Adaptation and Vulnerability*, is unusually confident in its negative predictions and stresses more than prior reports the unequal burden of global warming on those least able to cope with it.

64 Susannah Radstone, "Nostalgia, Masculinity and Mourning," in *Sexual Politics of Time*, by Susannah Radstone, 159–191.

CHAPTER 1   TRAUMA STUDIES MOVING FORWARD

1 Dori Laub, MD is a psychoanalyst and Holocaust survivor whose clinical work led to his theories on trauma and bearing witness to testimony. See his two influential essays, "Bearing Witness, or the Vicissitudes of Listening" and "An Event without a Witness."

2 I do not intend here to pursue arguments I have made elsewhere about differences between a viewer's experiencing vicarious trauma or empty empathy in responding to different media representations of catastrophe. See Kaplan, *Trauma Culture* and "Global Trauma."

3 See Kansteiner, "Genealogy of a Category Mistake"; Alexander, "Toward a Theory."

4 See Massumi, "Future Birth of the Affective Fact," 52–70.

5 Radstone, "Screening Trauma," 89.

6 Alexander, "Toward a Theory," 2.

7 Poole, "Misremembering the Holocaust," 33.

8 Freud, *Group Psychology*, 1.

9 In the context of rising anti-Semitic mass hysteria around Nazism, Freud's concern makes perfect sense. See my discussion of Teresa Brennan's theories, in *The Transmission of Affect*.

10 Roth, *Psychoanalysis as History*, 142–145.

11 Jung, "The Structure of the Psyche," in *Collected Works*, 8 §325.

12 Coman, et al., "Collective Memory from a Psychological Perspective," 100.

13 Brennan, *Transmission of Affect*, 13–14.

14 I have in mind abuses in regard to a local Native American tribe, for example; abuses in an African American community, known locally but not getting national notice; familial sexual abuse, which rarely makes the headlines but around which collectives develop; and so on.

15 For those who concede to a public discourse of forgetting, see Kansteiner's study of the postwar German refusal to confront directly a Nazi past through an analysis of television shows from the 1960s to the 1980s. His 2004 article argues (to quote the abstract) that, "In the 1960s, television recycled the apologetic plot structures of West Germany's postwar historical culture. As a result, the programs all but ignored the Holocaust and provided a very schematic, self-serving image of the past for the benefit of viewers who had themselves experienced the Third Reich. In the 1980s a more complex and self-critical vision of the Nazi past appeared on the screen and was appreciated by a more diverse audience, including a majority of viewers who shared no personal responsibility for the crimes of the regime. But even the improved programming of the 1980s for the most part avoided any direct confrontation with the perpetrators and bystanders of the 'Final Solution.'" Kansteiner, "Genealogy of a Category Mistake," abstract.

16 Poole, "Misremembering the Holocaust," 34.

17 Alexander, "Toward a Theory."

18 See Rothberg, *Multidirectional Memory*.

19 Annie Murphy Paul, "Your Brain on Fiction," *New York Times*, March 18, 2012.

20 Alexander, "Toward a Theory," 17.

21 Gledhill, Introduction, 11. See also her "Rethinking Genre."

22 Gledhill, "Rethinking Genre," 222.

23 Although she is talking about novels rather than film, what Margaret Atwood has to say about this definitional difficulty is pertinent. See Atwood, *In Other Worlds*, 56–64.

24 In later research, I will explore related imaginaries in media other than film. Especially pertinent are select video games (*Half Life 2*, for example), but graphic novels, YouTube videos, and so on also have proliferating futurist fantasies linked to those on film.

25 The only tentatively liberal note in the film is that the persons who save the planet are Jewish and African American. Levinson, a lowly worker in the scientific group monitoring outer space, figures out how the aliens got into the human computers and then how to insert a virus into those same computers using their signals. Meanwhile, Will Smith plays a military officer who is a brilliant pilot. One is used to token African Americans in this genre, less so to token Jews.

26 Eagleton, "Utopia and Its Opposites," 33.

27 Sontag, "Imagination of Disaster," 42, 48.

28 The outburst of post-disaster filmmaking includes Americans living in or visiting Japan, such as *3.11: Surviving Japan*, by Christopher Noland; *Pray for Japan*, by Stuart Levy, and *In the Grey Zone* and *A2-B-C* by Ian Thomas Ash. Given the lack of information coming from authorities, these films, which show victims' suffering and which provide more details of the impact, were deemed necessary. A new Fukushima documentary: *We've been deceived . . . We've been betrayed* (video) was announced by ENENews on February 27, 2013. See an article by Ian Thomas Nash, "Eighteen Months after the Nuclear Meltdown in Fukushima," in ENENnews, February 3, 2013, at http://enenews.com/new-fukushima-documentary-weve-been-deceived-weve-been-betrayed-video. See also *Fukushima: Memories of a Lost Landscape* directed by Yoju Matsubayashi, Tatsuya Mori, Takeharu Watai, and Takuji Yasuoka and *Odayaka na nichijo*, directed by Nobuteru Uchida.

29 See King, *Washed in Blood*.

30 Atwood, *In Other Worlds*, 5.

31 See Sontag, "Imagination of Disaster." Her discussion of science fiction films is still relevant, even though some of her prescient comments do not hold up today given dramatic changes in US culture: in addition, destruction of the environment rather than nuclear disaster is now portrayed as most dangerous. Her summary of the plots of 1950s sci-fi and horror films reveals how dependent today's sci-fi often is on these earlier narrative structures. Today's digital technologies, however, make a difference in experiencing the films, as noted earlier.

32 Bould and Vint, *Concise History of Science Fiction*, 184; Agamben, *What Is an Apparatus?* 22.

33 Uncannily, these films anticipate the world we confront in Laura Poitras's remarkable 2014 film, *Citizen Four*. In this film, Edward Snowden graphically presents us with a world in which people's privacy is daily invaded by technologies capturing every phone call, email message, or website search. "Freedom" no longer means anything since privacy no longer exists. Government officials rationalize this invasion as necessary for the security of the United States.

34 Agamben, *State of Exception*, 2–3.

35 Atwood, *In Other Worlds*, 6

36 Ibid., 86–91.

37 Oates, "Where No One Has Ever Gone," 41.

38 Morton, *Hyperobjects*, chapter 1,"A Quake in Being," 1–24. Indeed, as Margaret Atwood puts it, "I don't write about Planet X, I write about where we are now." She adds that her "speculative fictions [such as *The Year of the Flood*] showcase scenarios that spring from current realities, such as the creep of corporations into many aspects of society, environmental decay, high-tech reproductions, the widening cleavage between the haves and have-nots." Atwood, *In Other Worlds*, 4–5.

39 A very early example of the genre may be found in Richard Fleischer's *Soylent Green*, made in 1973 from a short story by Harry Harrison. While it has a similar dark vision, something about the film's 1970s cinematic style ultimately prevents it from producing quite the same kind of shock effect now as it did in its own time. See Chapter 3 for a discussion of *Soylent Green*.

40 Markus and Nurius, "Possible Selves."

41 Brown et al., "The Impact of Perceived Self-Efficacy."

42 Markus and Nurius, "Possible Selves," 954–955.

CHAPTER 2   PRETRAUMA CLIMATE SCENARIOS

1 Morton misses the point in *Hyperobjects* when he dismisses apocalyptic fantasies such as those I study here. He claims that "all those apocalyptic narratives of doom about 'the end of the world' are . . . part of the problem not the solution." His point is that the narratives "inoculate" us against "the very real object that has intruded into ecological, social and psychic space." My position is that these narratives awaken us to what is—to what, Morton himself agrees, we can't see. These futurist dystopian fantasies make us see. Morton, *Hyperobjects*, 103.

2 For extended discussion of vicarious, or secondary, trauma, see Sakvitne and Pearlman, *Trauma and the Therapist*. See also Hoffman, "Empathy and Vicarious Traumatization in Clinicians"; Kaplan, "Global Trauma."

3 See also Heise, *Sense of Place, and Sense of Planet*.

4 For a preliminary discussion of the shift from the term *world* to *planet*, see Kaplan, "Age Studies and Environmental Humanities." See also Heise, "Invention of Eco-Futures," and Morton's chapter, "End of the World," in *Hyperobjects*. Ken Hiltner's edited volume, *Ecocriticism: The Essential Reader*, has an entire section of first-wave ecocriticism with essays pertinent to historical discussions about concepts of nature in this chapter. Carolyn Merchant's *The Death of Nature: Women, Ecology, and the Scientific Revolution* is an essential pioneering volume pertinent here.

5 Chakrabarty, "Climate of History," 218.

6 For a good summary of this well-traveled history, see Mathieu Roy and Harold Crooks's *Surviving Progress*. The short collage of images that acts as a prologue to *Soylent Green* is also a good way to remember the rapidity of technological change and its related impact on social lives (see Chapter 3). For an international perspective showing links between colonialism and environmental devastation in India, see Guha, *Unquiet Woods* and *How Much Should a Person Consume?* Rob Nixon's *Slow Violence* also deals with links between colonialism and the corporate invasion of developing nations, with particular focus on Africa.

7 Elliott, "Suffering Agency."

8 Guha, *Environmentalism*, 98–124.

9 Lyn White, "The Historical Roots of Our Ecological Crisis." For extensive study of how one Western idea of nature emerged from the Romantic Movement, see Morton, *Ecology without Nature* and *Hyperobjects*. See also Guha's description of Wordsworth's (and more generally English) opposition to industrialism in *Environmentalism*, 10–24; Merchant, *The Death of Nature*.

10 For a useful summary of critical research on Wordsworth's concept of nature's morality, see Joplin, "The Moral Quality of Wordsworth's Nature."

11 Lefebvre, introduction, xv. I take his use of "we" to refer to Western subjectivities.

12 Pratt, *Imperial Eyes*, 200.

13 See Freeman, "Happy Memories under the Mushroom Cloud."

14 See, for example, Ursula Heise, *Sense of Place, and Sense of Planet*.

15 Or we could reverse it and say these things are happening because of the "instructions" humans have given to nature. Either way, and even in Oates's own discourse, the symbiosis between nature and humankind is evident. See Oates, "Against Nature," 621–627.

16 Alan Weisman, *The World without US*, 3, 15.

17 The archive in relation to the development of the environmental humanities is now enormous and cannot be addressed here as such. Ecocriticism has a fairly long history but came into its own with work by Lawrence Buell and Greg Garrard in the mid-1990s. Ecofeminist critics followed, spearheaded in 1980 by Carolyn Merchant's pioneering *The Death of Nature* and including Rachel Stein's memorable edited collection in 2004. In Cultural Studies too since 2010, scholars have seen the need to develop programs dealing with what humanists can contribute to scientific debates about drastic climate change. For leading texts in this field and relevant bibliography, see Guha, *Environmentalism*; Nixon, *Slow Violence*; Heise, *Sense of Place*; Morton, *Ecology without Nature* and *Hyperobjects*; and Moser and Drilling, *Creating a Climate for Change*. The interesting thing is that these two strands of interest in environmentalism didn't relate to one another. Scholars didn't necessarily know the research of the other camp. Only now are the groups finding one another and starting to collaborate. The divide is partly among the disciplines of literary studies, history, and philosophy.

18 In March 2013, as part of the "Figuring Sea Level Rise" project, organizers at UC Santa Barbara's Carsey-Wolf Center held "A Scavenger Hunt to Locate Your Water Relationships on the UCSB Campus." Students were encouraged (perhaps tongue in cheek) to "have a heartfelt desire to understand water and overcome [their] tendencies to ignore it." Students were asked to "say something affectionate and grateful to water as a daily habit." Daleiden and Kelly, *I Heart H2o*.

19 Richard Louv, "The Nature Principle: Reconnecting with Nature in A Virtual Age."

20 Morton, *Hyperobjects*, 105, 103.

21 Ibid., 124.

22 In a fascinating passage, Morton cites the famous moment in *The Prelude* when, as a boy, Wordsworth steals a boat. The looming mountain terrifies him and seems to be punishing him for stealing. But Morton uses this example to discuss the mountain as representing the viscosity of hyperobjects—the way they stick to people. Again, characteristically, Morton examines the experience as a traumatic rupture in Wordsworth's continuity of being. He concludes that "the self, in this respect, is nothing more than the history of such wounds and the secretions we exuded to protect ourselves from them." Psychoanalysis, like deconstruction, informs Morton's arguments throughout the book. Morton, *Hyperobjects*, 51.

23 To make this point (apparently important to Nichols's aims for the film), several sequences deal with the difficulty Samantha experiences in getting Curtis's insurance to pay for cochlear surgery in order to correct Hannah's impaired hearing. We also find Curtis having to pay a $47 co-pay for his sedative later on, and the loan of $6,000 to make the storm shelter serviceable nearly breaks the family bank.

24 There's a telling sequence in which Curtis's building of the dog cage in the yard is intercut with Samantha and Hannah at the local Saturday open market, where Samantha is selling her home-made silk pillows and handkerchiefs for the extra cash the family badly needs for its middle-class desires.

25 Commentary on the DVD for *Take Shelter* details the technical difficulty involved in creating this sequence, especially in regard to allowing viewers to experience the entire living-room furniture suite rise up into the air.

26 Sarah Lauro, "The Eco-Zombie"; see also Graham, "Post-9/11 Anxieties"; Dendle, "Zombie as Barometer."

27 We hear a mournful rock song telling a story of a big storm coming, of the sky going black, of the lovers needing to find somewhere to hide, of their never having seen anything like it before.

28 Lefebvre, "Between Setting and Landscape."

29 Might we see here a subtle reference to Chakrabarty's noting, along with scientists, that as humans destroy the environment, they destroy themselves, taking away aspects of the planet that they rely on to sustain human life? Is Shyamalan's film hinting that humans are a suicidal species?

30 Once again, I am reminded of Morton's research and his concept of humans having long interacted with nonhumans as hyperobjects. Plant life on planet Earth would, I think, qualify as such an object.

31 In the commentary on the DVD, John Hillcoat notes that he didn't want to shoot in a studio but searched for desolate places to film (in the end the film was shot in New Orleans, Pennsylvania, Mount St. Helens, and Oregon). He says that in these places we "see the world we are in becoming that of the film." It's interesting that the principals of the team making the film are Australian and British, from nations far more attentive to global warming than the United States.

32 I juxtapose film and novel not, as in the old days, in order to argue which is better or to evaluate what the film lacks that the novel has. Rather, I use the juxtaposition to stimulate discovery of new meanings in each work, or meanings that I might not have found through analyzing one of the modalities alone.

33 McCarthy, *The Road*, 130.

34 Ibid., 48, 47.

35 Pagels, *Revelations*.

36 Atwood quoted in Oates, "Where No One Has Ever Gone," 40.

37 Carter and McCormack, "Film, Geopolitics," 228.

38 Ibid.

CHAPTER 3 PRETRAUMA POLITICAL THRILLERS

1 See Stefan Klein, *The Secret Pulse of Time: Making Sense of Life's Scarcest Commodity*. Klein deals with the biological underpinnings of concepts of past, present, and future. See also Nicholas Kristof's article "When Our Brains Short-Circuit," *New York Times*, July 1, 2009. Anticipating this book's conclusion, let me note that Kristof suggests we try to compensate for our neurological shortcomings with rational analysis.

2 See Roth, "Trauma as Dystopia," 235. As Roth puts it, "To treat something as historical means at least to connect it via chronology to events before or after."

3 I will address the future for memory in Chapter 4 and will continue to think about memory for the future.

4 Höhler, "Carrying Capacity," 2. She goes on to note that some of these writers "predicted that, with the present rate of population growth, 'in 600 years the entire earth would provide only one square yard of land per person.'"

5 Ibid., 4.

6 See Gresser, "Inventing for Humanity."

7 Indeed, a *New York Times* article published on January 24, 2014, discussed problems caused by climate change at Coca-Cola's outsourced factories in India and Vietnam. The article indicates that it is only when a corporation's bottom line is affected that such a business will take seriously what's happening in the developing nations far more at risk than Western industrialized nations. See also the Risky Business website on "The Economic Risks of Climate Change, Change for Businesses, Change for Corporations." See http://riskybusiness.org/report/overview/executive-summary/ and www.climateprospectus.rhg.org. These websites do not take a position on the causes of climate change but are run by businessmen (such as Michael Bloomberg) for businessmen. If an overriding concern with profit pushes businessmen to change disastrous practices, that's fine with me as a start. But as a *New York Times* article noted in 2015, Republican governors are refusing to implement global warming regulations mandated by President Obama. See Coral Davenport, "McConnell Urges States to Defy U.S. Plan to Cut Greenhouse Gas." March 5, 2015, A12.

8 See Justin Fox, "Head Count," review of *Malthus*, by Robert J. Mayhew, *New York Times*, August 1, 2014, Sunday Book Review. http://www.nytimes.com/2014/08/03/books/review/malthus-by-robert-j-mayhew.html.

9 How far imaginaries of futurist catastrophe in these dystopian films unconsciously take the form of a catastrophe Western cultures have known already—but often repress—is something I will examine in future projects.

10 Cannibalism is a complex issue and needs to be distinguished from zombie monstrosity. In certain dire situations, people have been known to eat dead people. The debate continues about ancient tribal rituals that included eating human flesh. See William Arens, *The Man-Eating Myth: Anthropology and Anthropophagy*.

11 The Malthusian point behind the film (Harrison's story is titled "Make Room! Make Room!") is not repeated in any of the other films I study. But the 2014 Joon-ho Bong film *Snowpiercer* emphasizes the problem of overpopulation. As the fascist leader (played by Ed Harris) puts it, "The population must always be kept in balance." He notes, sardonically, that he realized they had to control the population and could not wait for natural selection; drastic measures were necessary given the limited space available for the last survivors on Earth, circling the frozen globe in their class-divided train.

12 Roger Ebert, "Review of *Soylent Green*." Interestingly, Cuarón's London also looks the same, only more run down—another synergy between the projects.

13 Atwood clearly put a great deal of herself into this character. She is known on the lecture circuit for her humor and playfulness with words as well as for her lively interchanges and trenchant observations.

14 Tsai, "*Traumatic Memory*."

15 It was hard to read this novel without thinking of Charlotte Perkins Gilman's "The Yellow Wallpaper," whose heroine is also basically imprisoned and ordered not to read or write or go out. Perkins's earlier *Herland* imagining a world without men is the novel that *The Handmaid's Tale* is demanding, in a sort of weird time-reversal process.

16 Atwood here uncannily anticipates the arrival of the Tea Party wing of the Republican Party in 2006.

17 Atwood, *The Handmaid's Tale*, 178.

18 Originally an art-house director, Cuarón came to notice with his feature film *Y Tu Mamá También*, shown at the New York Film Festival in 2001. He went on to have an interesting on-again-off-again relationship with Hollywood, acting as a "mercenary" director for mid-size Hollywood productions in the 1990s and continuing with the Harry Potter film *Harry Potter and the Prisoner of Azkaban* (2010).

19 Thanks go to my colleague Adrián Pérez-Melgosa for the insight about Cuarón. Many women in the United States have difficulty conceiving and either have many expensive treatments to give birth or use the surrogate wombs of less privileged women. See DasGupta, "(Re)conceiving the Surrogate."

20 Cuarón has been evasive as to whether he actually read the novel himself (in one interview he allows us to infer he has; in another he states that his co-writer Tim Sexton read the book, not he). However that may be, Cuarón agrees that he was inspired by James's book and that the idea of infertility haunted him. In the end, he claims he wanted it to be only a "metaphor"—something that feminist scholars have objected to. See DasGupta, "(Re)conceiving the Surrogate," and Latimer, "Bio-reproductive Futurism."

21 Cuarón, interview by Kim Voynar, *Moviefone*, December 25, 2006, http://news .moviefone.com/2006/12/25/interview-children-ofmen-director-alfonso-cuaron/; Cuarón, interview by Sheila Roberts, *Movies Online*, December 19, 2006, http://www .moviesonline.ca/movienews_10790.html.

22 Žižek, *Audio Commentary*.

23 See Shaw, *Three Amigos*. In her book, Shaw talks at some length about this film and the limits of Cuarón's politics in *Children of Men*.

24 Once again, Cuarón shares such concerns with Naomi Klein, who in 2011 turned her attention specifically to climate change as she continued to worry about corporate power and the exploitation of people made vulnerable by crisis. In an article, "The Fight against Climate Change Is Down to Us—the 99%," Klein notes, "The point is, today everyone can see that the system is deeply unjust and careening out of control. Unfettered greed has trashed the global economy. And we are trashing the natural world. . . . The new normal is serial disasters: economic and ecological." *Guardian*, October 7, 2011. http://www.theguardian.com/commentisfree/2011/oct/07/fight-climate-change-99. See also Klein, *This Changes Everything*.

25 The future rarely looks good; humans of every generation believe that things are getting worse and yet cannot help hoping that things will improve.

26 See Cuarón, *Audio Commentary*.

27 Udden, "Child of the Long Take." I am unable within the limited parameters of this chapter to discuss Cuarón's amazing cinematography. Cuarón's crew discusses the by now famous long take in the scene where Julian is killed, but (as Udden argues) the film relies on unusually long takes throughout to give its special atmosphere and immediacy.

28 Slavoj Žižek saw this scene as figuring the film's end-of-history ideology, but I suggest that time/history in the film is more complicated.

29 The original Pink Floyd pig was designed by Roger Waters and built in December 1976 by the artist Jeffrey Shaw with help of design team Hipgnosis, in preparation for shooting the cover of the *Animals* album. Plans were made to fly the forty-foot, helium-filled balloon over Battersea Power Station on the first day's photo shoot, with a marksman prepared to shoot the pig down if it broke free. However, the pig was not launched.

30 See Gabbard, *Black Magic*. As Gabbard has pointed out, only too often in dominant narratives the "savior" comes in the form of a "black angel."

31 The couple kiss briefly as they play a sexy Ping-Pong game in the car. Theo also mentions that his ex-wife had promised him "some action," but she dies before anything can happen.

32 I am grateful for discussion with Jackie Stacey and Heather Latimer at the Research Unit at Manchester University (where I delivered a paper on *Children of Men*) for their insights about the absence of sexuality in the film. I take responsibility for how I have framed the issue here.

33 Edelman, *No Future*. Critiques of Edelman's position include Muñoz, *Cruising Utopia*, and Ahmed, *The Promise of Happiness*.

34 See Latimer, "Bio-reproductive Futurism," 56; and DasGupta, "(Re)conceiving the Surrogate," 193.

35 LaCapra, "Trauma, Absence, Loss," 43–85.

36 My UCSB colleague Greg Burris reminded me that in Klein and Cuarón's film, there is not only an analogy between psychiatric experiments in the 1950s and CIA interrogation tactics. The CIA actually financed the psychiatric experiments in the first place.

37 Naomi Klein, *Shock Doctrine*; Naomi Klein, "The Fight against Climate Change Is Down to Us—the 99%," *The Guardian*, October 7, 2011. http://www.theguardian.com/commentisfree/2011/oct/07/fight-climate-change-99.

38 Part of Cuarón's point in making London almost recognizable was precisely to make audiences glimpse the decline into a deprived, "bare" life that is just a click away. For discussion of "bare life," see Agamben, *Homo Sacer.*

39 As this book goes to press, yet one more dystopian film opens, *Interstellar,* this time directed by Christopher Nolan. According to A. O. Scott's pre-release review, "Off to the Stars, with Dread and Regret," the film functions partly as "a plea for forgiveness on behalf of our foolish, dreamy species. We messed everything up, and we feel really bad about it. Can you please give us another chance?" *New York Times,* November 5, 2014, C1. Should we conclude that public consciousness is starting to change, as films now deal more directly with humans being the cause of global warming? Why is there no mention here of capitalist greed as part of the equation—something that Naomi Klein confronts in her book, *This Changes Everything?*

CHAPTER 4 MEMORY AND FUTURE SELVES IN PRETRAUMA FANTASIES

1 Ortiz and Schwab, "Memory Is Key," 69. It is in Ortiz's sections that the phrase "What good is memory for?" is repeated like a refrain in music.

2 Baccolini quoted in Moylan, *Scraps of Untainted Sky,* 149–150. Moylan is quoting Bacconini's essay, "Journeying through the Dystopian Genre," 345.

3 Ortiz and Schwab, "Memory Is Key," 69.

4 Will Smith is another rare example as the protagonist of *I Am Legend* (2007).

5 I'll return to the issues regarding utopian thinking vis-à-vis climate change in the conclusion, when I look at the debates between Elizabeth Kolbert and Naomi Klein in addressing the Anthropocene.

6 Interestingly, the destruction of the world in *The Road* also starts with a flash. Although this genre (I think productively) deliberately avoids any precise causes for the climate catastrophe, horrendous fires seem to be a trope adopted by directors.

7 As in all genres, similar tropes recur across the films. As far back as *Soylent Green,* the precious quality of simple lotion or soap was emphasized (for example, when Thorn first enters the rich man's apartment), and a bit later on, in *The Handmaid's Tale,* Offred too is delighted to get lotion she misses from the Commander. The coast, as escape fantasy, appears often. At the end of *The Book of Eli,* for example, there is a high-angle shot of Eli rowing across the San Francisco Bay to the island where Western culture is being restored, sitting with Solara in the boat. The (also utopian) ending of *Children of Men* shows Theo rowing Kee to the ship *Tomorrow.* In *The Road,* Boy and Man arrive at the coast and steal from an abandoned boat. Common tropes then help define the pretrauma film as a genre.

8 In a deleted scene, there's an image of a *Time* magazine with a picture of an atomic bomb on it, suggesting that at some point in the film's construction the directors wanted to be more specific about the catastrophe. Other deleted scenes suggest the bomb resulted from a war in the Middle East.

9 Joe Penhall, "Last Man Standing: What Cormac McCarthy Made of My Adaptation of *The Road*," *The Guardian*, January 4, 2010, http://www.theguardian.com/film/2010/jan/04/the-road-cormac-mccarthy-viggo-mortensen/.

10 Google Images offers many opportunities to see photos of wastelands *avant la lettre*, before the whole world becomes a wasteland. See for example the website: spongebobandfriends.wikia.com/wiki/Dark_Wastelands.

11 See Skutnabb-Kangas, *Linguistic Genocide in Education*, and Skutnabb-Kangas and Heugh, *Multilingual Education and Sustainable Diversity Work*, for their work on the links between biodiversity and linguistic diversity. This is the crux of a long argument they make for these links. It's provocative and contested research, but many adhere to there being such connection in practice— if hard to theorize.

12 Zombies have moved to the center of popular discourse in the millennium as never before, partly because of the increasing number of zombie movies but because of a new fascination with creatures who are neither fully human nor nonhuman. Their in-between status captures the imagination. The figures in *The Road* are closer to humans than those in Curtis's hallucinations in *Take Shelter*. But many of the futurist dystopias include zombie images that seem to go back to the Charlton Heston trilogy starting with *The Omega Man* (1971). *I Am Legend* perhaps started the trend of zombie renewal.

13 McCarthy, *The Road*, 18.

14 Ibid.

15 Ibid., 131.

16 Ibid., 26. While this is one of the scenes that is shown in the film, there is no way that the image of Man and Boy in the house can communicate what's going on in Boy's mind as he watches his father remembering his long lost past and struggles to grasp what it means for his father.

17 Ibid., 54, 43.

18 Ibid., 12–13.

19 Ibid. 19. Doesn't this sound like an homage to Gerard Manley Hopkins and his poem "The Windhover"?

> I caught this morning morning's minion, king-
>> dom of daylight's dauphin, dapple-dawn-drawn Falcon, in his riding
>> Of the rolling level underneath him steady air, and striding
> High there, how he rung upon the rein of a wimpling wing
> In his ecstasy! then off, off forth on swing,
>> As a skate's heel sweeps smooth on a bow-bend: the hurl and gliding
>> Rebuffed the big wind. My heart in hiding
> Stirred for a bird,—the achieve of, the mastery of the thing!

20 Ibid., 77.

21 Ibid., 51, 54. I'll return to this scene when discussing memory in the film. Hillcoat chose in the film adaptation to make quite clear the novel's implicit meaning regarding no future for memory.

22 Ibid., 18.

23 Ortiz and Schwab, "Memory Is Key," 79. I find the synergy between my reading of McCarthy's novel and Ortiz's profound 2008 essay fascinating. His piece clarified what I have been trying to say about the future for memory and its impact on future selves. A colleague responding to my talk on this chapter remarked that some of Hillcoat's scenes looked like what one could find out West around Native American reservations as per the landscape in Ortiz's essay.

24 More than *Take Shelter*, *The Road* recalls the zombie film of all time, *Night of the Living Dead*, in which infected humans are driven to eat the flesh of surviving people.

25 It was this relationship together with a veneer of Christianity that drew Oprah Winfrey to the novel, which was selected as one of the books featured on her show. She even managed to get McCarthy to do an interview about the novel.

26 Maureen Turim, *Flashbacks in Film: Memory and History*, 110.

27 Ibid. The flashbacks in *The Road* combine two categories of the cinematic device studied with such depth and historical overview by Margaret Turim. The biographical flashback became a staple of Hollywood narrative technique, but Turim, before the concept of PTSD entered into film scholars' discourse, discussed "Holocaust flashbacks," looking at trauma and repression in flashbacks in films about World War II. See her chapter "Disjunction in the Modernist Flashback," in *Flashbacks in Film*.

28 Penhall, "Last Man Standing." As Penhall notes, neither Hillcoat nor Viggo Mortensen liked the voice-over Penhall had created. But when McCarthy was shown an early print, he praised the voice-over, and so it remained.

29 There are just a few flashbacks in the film after the bridge sequence. One happens when the two finally hit gold with the deep bomb shelter filled with unbelievable amounts of food. Searching through Boy's bag, Man finds a hair comb that belonged to his wife. As he smells it, we get a flashback of them happily watching a concert and making secret sexual contact. At the end of the film, as Man is dying, there's a final flashback to tenderness between him and his wife. These scenes do not occur in the novel. Penhall, since he is making a commercial film, here departs somewhat from the idea of memory presented by McCarthy because of the need to tug at viewers' heartstrings.

30 A colleague suggested that perhaps Man's behavior is not so much a matter of being freed from the social contract as such, although this is part of what's going on with survivors on the rampage for food and resources. In Man's case there is guilt in freeing himself from his wife's memory, and my colleague has suggested that this left scars that emerge in Man's cruel behavior. The fact that Hillcoat chose to have an African American actor play the thief, with the resulting humiliation, is troubling. Or does Hillcoat intend to make a deliberate comment about slavery?

31 McCarthy, *The Road*, 41.

32 Ortiz and Schwab, "Memory Is Key," 68.

CHAPTER 5 MICROCOSM

1 Saramago, *Blindness*, 1.

2 The narrator continues to describe the car that has suddenly stopped in the middle of the road but then adds more detail than necessary for the fact of the car stopping,

suggesting a variety of possible reasons before continuing. Soon the Japanese Man speaks, "I am blind, I am blind." As people gather around, more comments are injected into the narrative, and people make suggestions for what could be the cause, the comments running one after another without a break.

3 Saramago, *Blindness*, 243.

4 Chang, review of *Blindness*.

5 Ebert, review of *Blindness*.

6 Nixon, *Slow Violence*, 2.

7 Derrida, *Memoirs of the Blind*. Derrida's haunting text traces some of this history as he reflects on diverse portraits of largely blind men in Western art. One could find numerous parallels in other arts—drama, performance, sculpture, and more—and blindness as punishment for immoral acts is at the root of Western culture, from Sophocles to Shakespeare and beyond, as I will suggest below.

8 Žižek, *Living in the End Times*.

9 I say "fittingly" because Saramago belongs to the generation of brilliant French Marxist—and then structuralist—scholars who reworked Marx for their time. His brand of communism would have been shared by others in Europe.

10 The world of the film also memorializes worlds that have been (concentration camps) and are now (refugee camps). The big difference in *Blindness* is that these worlds now become all that there is, instead of being limited to specific communities.

11 Saramago only belatedly received the recognition he deserved as an original writer, because of his criticism of Portugal's dictatorship over the years and his ties to communism. Starting out as somewhat of an idealist, he was never an ideologue or a supporter of Stalin. Yet his view of the world got darker as he grew older, and his despair about modern life sometimes seems uncannily similar to that of Freud in his *Civilization and Its Discontents*.

12 Quoted in Vieira, *Seeing Politics Otherwise*, 167n13.

13 Resistance to this lesson can be seen in response to a *New York Times* article published on March 9, 2013, by Graham Hill about a wealthy man who decided to give up his big house, his cars, books, and much more to live simply. Responses ranged from admiration to disbelief and (correctly) to critique of his idealizing deprivation when many homeless people live miserably with "less stuff."

14 There is an interesting parallel to *The Road*, where, as we saw, characters only have generic, not specific, names, and for similar reasons.

15 I say "paradoxically," but perhaps Saramago is making a comment that empathy in fact protects people because of their lack of narcissism.

16 See Fernand Braudel, *Civilization and Capitalism*, trans. Siân Reynold, 3 vols. (Oakland, CA: University of California Press, 1992). This exhaustive study details how the history of capitalism goes back much further than previous scholars believed. It seems that, like the inevitable sequence of past, present, and future that humans rely on, capitalism is also structured into human behavior. The fictions I study support such a view.

17 Saramago, *Blindness*, 131–132.

18 Lee Ben Clarke, *Worst Cases: Terror and Catastrophe in the Popular Imagination*; Karen Cerulo, *Never Saw It Coming: Cultural Challenges to Imagining the Worst*.

19 For Ebert, see http://www.rogerebert.com/reviews/blindness-2008/.

20 Foucault, *Discipline and Punish*. As is well-known, Foucault took the concept of the panopticon from Jeremy Bentham, who had designed structures for prisons and other incarcerating institutions that most economically enabled guards to oversee those incarcerated without the inmates knowing when and if they were being watched. For Foucault, Bentham's panopticon is a symbol for the modern disciplinary society.

21 I'll return later to debates about the film's dehumanization of people and paradoxical humanization of the dogs who appear once the blind are freed. But the issue of the authorities' seeing the people as animals, as lesser beings than themselves, is different from arguing that the novelist or film director presents people as degenerating into animals. The now growing field of animal studies would question closely such a nineteenth-century way of looking at a hierarchy of humans versus animals. This is of course far too big a topic for me to get into here.

22 Canavan, "Hope, but Not for Us," 152.

23 Guha, *How Much Should a Person Consume?*, 221–250.

24 Hayles, "Autonomous Algorithms and Flash Crashes." In this keynote address, Hayles recommends that humanists also learn about and attend to the dangers inherent in this new capitalist model of finance. A financial catastrophe is almost bound to happen, much as a climate-change disaster cannot be avoided.

25 Klein, *This Changes Everything*, 40.

26 Derrida, *Memoirs of the Blind*.

27 As we saw, there is a diversity of relationships—including that of blind people with one another, blind people with sighted people, and people born blind relating to the suddenly blinded.

28 Saramago, *Blindness*, 324.

29 Kolbert, "Can Climate Change Cure Capitalism?"

30 When questioned by Solara at a later point in the film, Eli talks about being called by a voice after he came out of hiding from the flash. The voice led him to the Book hidden in rubble and told him he would be protected from attacks—this in part explains his ability to escape from the shantytown despite a hail of bullets.

31 One of the brothers introduces the story on the DVD by noting their interest in graphic fiction. The drawings are well done, in soft reds and browns. One almost wishes the entire film had been made this way.

CHAPTER 6 GETTING REAL

1 I say "on a scale that has not yet taken place," but such catastrophes are already happening, if on a smaller scale than in the fictions. For example, as this book goes to press, several African nations are struggling with an epidemic of the Ebola virus that authorities seem unable to control. Such an epidemic was already imagined in Wolfgang Petersen's 1995 film, *Outbreak*. The film uncannily contains elements regarding the start of the epidemic in rural Africa, its being carried to the United States via a passenger on a plane, and its rapid spread among people he contacted.

2 See Kaplan, *Trauma Culture*; Jane Elliott and Gillian Harkins, "Introduction: Genres of Neoliberalism"; Christine Gledhill, "Introduction," in *Gender Meets Genre in Postwar Cinemas*; and Jacques Derrida, "The Law of Genre."

3 Kaplan, *Trauma Culture*, 125–135.

4 See http://en.wikipedia.org/wiki/Onkalo_spent_nuclear_fuel_repository/ for details about the repository, the companies involved, and some issues with the design.

5 I refer here to Louis Althusser's concept of "interpellation" as described in "Ideology and Ideological State Apparatuses." Here Althusser shows how each subject is, as it were, "called into being" by the structures of state institutions that "hail" us and in so doing produce us as subjects. The viewer in this film is similarly called into being—but for productive purposes, not to be subjected to the state apparatus. Interestingly, Naomi Oreskes and Eric Conway similarly adopt the position of a future human (this time four hundred years in the future), looking back and analyzing the tragic refusal to pay heed to climate dangers staring humanity in the face. See Oreskes and Conway, *The Collapse of Western Civilization*.

6 As Madsen puts it in a conversation with G. Allen Johnson, "I told the crew from the beginning. We have to think of this as a science fiction film that's shot today. I want the audience to experience a kind of afterworld." I am reminded of Ursula K. Heise's observation (also online) in her essay, "Comparative Literature and the Environmental Humanities," that sociological texts such as Alan Weisman's *The World without Us* or Bill McKibben's *Eaarth* also edge up to science fiction.

7 See Madsen, Interview with Helen Caldicott. When Madsen is asked about what drew him to make the film, he explains that "essentially it was the hundred thousand year aspect, that somebody in Finland is building a facility that has to last in a foolproof manner for a hundred thousand years. That was what caught my attention. . . . And secondly, they will have to have a facility, some kind of scenarios for the future, some ideas about how the future will look like in this time span. That is what got me really, really interested. Then I thought that this has to be the first time in the history of mankind that we are building something like this. And also something which is not in any kind of religious context, as would be the case with the cathedrals of the Middle Ages or the Pyramids."

8 Issues discussed include the "Interim Storage" of waste, a "Permanent Solution" for it, dangers of "Human Intrusion" into Onkalo and what to do about it, "Human Law" related to nuclear waste, and issues about future use in our time of nuclear energy.

9 Madsen here draws upon a 1991 Department of Energy project that involved bringing linguists, scientists, and anthropologists together to devise a conceptual marker system for dangerous waste. See Juliet Lapidos, "Atomic Priesthoods, Thorn Landscapes, and Munchian Pictograms," and ROMAN, "Episode 114: Ten Thousand Years." Roman Mars is one of the founders of Radiotopia, and his article describes the Department of Energy's detailed discussion of how to create markers for far in the future in order to prevent future humans from entering the zone.

10 Madsen, Interview with Helen Caldicott. Madsen notes that experts evidently don't agree on how long the waste is actually dangerous. Madsen also notes that no one knows what reactions will go on inside the waste as it stays underground.

11 Jim Ridley, "More Inconvenient Truths: China's Industrial Footprint, Writ Large," *Village Voice*, June 12, 2007, http://www.villagevoice.com/2007-06-12/film/more -inconvenient-truths/full/.

12 I want to thank my colleague Adrián Pérèz Melgosa for helping me to better articulate what I was trying to say here from the perspective of the relatively new globalized era that is rapidly changing old national hierarchies and relationships.

13 See Clinton, "Zombies as Racialized Pollution."

14 See the DVD's special features for a video of Burtynsky talking about and presenting his huge photos in a Canadian gallery. Burtynsky traces the history of his interest in industrial incursion into the landscape, and he comments on how his ideas progressed as he continued to work. It is the last phase of his interest in large sites that provides the basis for Baichwal's film.

15 Burtynsky and Baichwal, Interview with Michael Guillén. As Guillén puts it, addressing Baichwal, "You didn't make a film *about* Edward Burtynsky, you ceded authorship to him, which as Ed's website puts it, 'extends the narrative stream' of his photographs. *Variety*'s Peter Debruge has written that you have 'deftly use[d] the moving image to reinforce the spirit of Burtynsky's still pictures, expanding the discourse by providing valuable context.' You let Edward's photographs speak for themselves."

16 See Baker, "Form versus Portent," 40–45.

17 There is one remarkable exception (noted below) when Burtynsky catches in close-up an old woman sitting outside her small house next to a huge pile of toxic waste she hopes to profit from. Her face bears witness to her pain.

18 The discipline in the factory is palpable and the atmosphere far different from the often noisy American work site. While perhaps workers knew they were being filmed, nevertheless I am sure their pay depended on how many objects they assembled, hence their studied focus. Certainly, we experience a cultural difference in factory-floor attitude, so to speak, which correlates with the criticism/self-criticism sessions noted earlier.

19 It is possible that, as they worked together, they approached one another's positions to create a middle ground regarding framing and its politics. The many interviews they gave following the release of the film may also, interestingly, have brought their positions closer together. See Burtynsky, Interview with Michael Torosian, and Burtynsky and Baichwal, Interview with Michael Guillén.

20 Ridley, "More Inconvenient Truths."

21 This issue has been discussed by many over the centuries, but perhaps the most recent bibliography stems from Susan Sontag's thoughtful interventions in *On Photography* and again in *Regarding the Pain of Others*. See also Kaplan, "Empathy and Trauma Culture."

22 This argument about whether or not the Holocaust is representable has been taken up time and again by Holocaust scholars. See in particular Brett Ashley Kaplan, *Unwanted Beauty: Aesthetic Pleasure and the Holocaust* (Champaign-Urbana: University of Illinois Press, 2007).

23 LaCapra, "Trauma, Absence, Loss," 47; Hoffman, *Empathy and Moral Development*, 134–135.

24 The full quotation includes the following: "And it's the hubris of humanity that we yearn for that scale. It's almost as if we're trying to make ourselves bigger and bigger and

bigger. Something like the Three Gorges Dam is so massive. It's such a monumentally arrogant act to divert nature on such an enormous scale and yet it's the perfect expression of some—what is it?—is it the yearning of humans to be like gods? Is that what it is?" Burtynsky and Baichwal, Interview with Michael Guillén.

AFTERWORD: HUMANS AND ECO- (OR IS IT SUI-?) CIDE

1 See Naomi Oreskes, "Playing Dumb on Climate Change," *New York Times*, January 4, 2015, 2.

2 See http://www.ipcc.ch/ for both the 2013 Physical Science Basis for the report and the Climate Change Synthesis Report.

3 See Coral Davenport, "In Climate Deal, Obama May Set a Theme for 2016," *New York Times*, November 13, 2014, A1; Michael Shear and Coral Davenport, "Obama Vetoes Bill Pushing Pipeline Approval," *New York Times*, February 24, 2015.

4 See information about the conference at http://unfccc.int/meetings/lima_dec _2014/meeting/8141.php/.

5 Michael Greenstone, "A Voluntary, and Effective, Climate Treaty." *New York Times*, February 15, 2015.

6 See Coral Davenport, "A Climate Accord Based on Global Peer Pressure." *New York Times*, December 14, 2014, A3.

7 Justin Gillis, "U.N. Panel Issues Its Starkest Warning Yet on Global Warming," *New York Times*, November 3, 2014, A8.

8 Coral Davenport, "In Climate Deal, Obama May Set a Theme for 2016," *New York Times*, November 12, 2014, A1.

9 Naomi Oreskes and Eric M. Conway, *The Collapse of Western Civilization: A View from the Future*, 34.

10 See Clive Hamilton, "Risks Of Climate Engineering," *New York Times,* Op-Ed, February 12, 2015. See also "Fighting Back against Climate Change," Letters to the Editor, February 24, 2015.

11 See also Elizabeth Kolbert, *Fieldnotes from a Catastrophe*. This text was well received and widely reviewed when it came out.

12 Kolbert, "Can Climate Change Cure Capitalism?," 16.

13 Kitch, *Higher Ground*, 40.

14 Ibid., 9.

15 Weisman, *The World without Us*, 3.

16 Abraham and Torok, *The Shell and the Kernel*, 130.

17 Susannah Radstone, *The Sexual Politics of Time*, 167, 172, 173. Richard Linklater's *Boyhood* (2014) came later than Radstone's book, but much of what she theorizes would fit this film as well.

18 For example, in *Children of Men*, Cuarón changes a symbolic father-son relationship in P. D. Jame's novel into a father-daughter one, but the child is named after the hero's dead son. And in *Soylent Green,* this relationship is between an older man and a younger one. But the structure of feeling is the same nostalgic one that Radstone theorizes.

19 Moser and Drilling, *Creating a Climate for Change*.

20 Moser's article "Getting Real about It" is available on line at http://www
.climateaccess.org/sites/default/files/Moser_Getting%20Real%20About%20It
.pdf. Internationally, humanities institutes like the one I have directed for twenty-seven
years are currently developing projects specifically to address the kinds of issues that
Moser raises. Following the lead of Clark University, the Humanities Institute at Stony
Brook is planning to establish local councils of interdisciplinary scholars and activists
to address what it means to live in uncertain times. As Sarah Buie puts it, in her summary of the Higgins School of Humanities Climate Change project at Clark University,
"while our knowledge of the scientific consensus on climate and its wider contexts has
grown substantially, as a society we are largely reluctant or unable to address the implications of what we face." She continues, "a conversation that would begin to address our
circumstances must both integrate and transcend the specific environmental, moral,
political, and intellectual dilemmas posed by them. It will engage issues of perception,
uncertainty, speculation, fear, values, and agency. Such a conversation may take partici-
pants into fearsome aspects of imagination and psyche, through questions requiring
both intellectual and spiritual courage."

BIBLIOGRAPHY

Abraham, Nicholas, and Maria Torok. *The Shell and the Kernel: Renewals of Psychoanalysis.* Translated by Nicholas T. Rand. Chicago: University of Chicago Press, 1994.

Agamben, Giorgio. *Homo Sacer: Sovereign Power and Bare Life.* Translated by Daniel Heller-Roazen. Stanford: Stanford University Press, 1998.

———. *The State of Exception.* Translated by Kevin Attell. Chicago: University of Chicago Press, 2005.

———. *What Is an Apparatus?* Translated by David Kishik and Stefan Pedatella. Stanford: Stanford University Press, 2006.

Ahmed, Sara. *The Promise of Happiness.* Durham and London: Duke University Press, 2010.

Alexander, Jeffrey. "Toward a Theory of Cultural Trauma." In *Cultural Trauma and Collective Identity*, edited by Jeffrey Alexander et al., 1–30. Berkeley and London: University of California Press, 2004.

Althusser, Louis. *For Marx.* London: Verso, 1990.

Arens, William. *The Man-Eating Myth: Anthropology and Anthropophagy.* London and New York: Oxford University Press, 1980.

Atwood, Margaret. *The Handmaid's Tale.* Toronto: McClelland and Stewart, 1985.

———. *In Other Worlds: SF and the Human Imagination.* London and New York: Doubleday, 2011.

———. *The Year of the Flood.* New York: Doubleday, 2009.

Baccolini, Raffaella. "Journeying through the Dystopian Genre." In *Viaggi in Utopia*, edited by Rafaella Baccolini, Vita Fortunati, and Nadia Minerva, 343–357. Ravenna: Longo, 1996.

Baccolini, Rafaella, and Tom Moylan. Introduction. In *Dark Horizons: Science Fiction and the Dystopian Imagination*, edited by Rafaella Baccolini and Tom Moylan, 1–12. London and New York: Routledge, 2003.

Baker, Kenneth. "Form versus Portent: Edward Burtynsky's Endangered Landscapes." In Pauli, Burtynsky, Haworth-Booth, Baker, and Torosian, *Manufactured Landscapes*, 40–45.

Barnes, Brooks. "Carpetbagger: Quirk Meets Bleak at Sundance." *New York Times,* December 12, 2012, C1, C8.

Barry, Ellen, and Andrew E. Kramer. "Meteor Explodes, Injuring over One Thousand in Siberia." *New York Times,* February 16, 2013, A1.

Bermingham, Ann. *Landscape and Ideology: The English Rustic Tradition, 1740–1860.* Berkeley and London: University of California Press, 1986.

Berntsen, Dorthe, and David C. Rubin. "Pretraumatic Stress Reactions in Soldiers Deployed to Afghanistan." In *Clinical Psychology Science.* Published online before print, November 26, 2014.

Bloch, Ernst. *The Principle of Hope.* Translated by Neville Plaice, Stephen Plaice, and Paul Knight. 3 vols. Boston: MIT Press, 1995.

———. *The Spirit of Utopia*. Translated by Anthony A. Nassar. London and Palo Alto: Stanford University Press, 2000.

———. *The Utopian Function of Art and Literature: Selected Essays*. Translated by Jack Zipes and Frank Mecklenburg. Cambridge, MA, and London: MIT Press, 1988.

Bloom, Harold. Introduction. In *José Saramago*, edited by Harold Bloom, ix–xviii. Philadelphia: Chelsea House, 2005.

Bolt, David. "Saramago's *Blindness*: Humans or Animals?" *The Explicator* 66.1 (Fall 2007): 44–47.

Bould, Mark, and Sherryl Vint. *Routledge Concise History of Science Fiction*. London and New York: Routledge, 2011.

Brennan, Teresa. *The Transmission of Affect*. Ithaca and London: Cornell University Press, 2004.

Brown, Adam D., Michelle L. Dorman, Charles R. Marmar, and Richard A. Bryant. "The Impact of Perceived Self-Efficacy on Mental Time Travel and Social Problem Solving." *Consciousness and Cognition* 21.1 (2011): 299–306.

Brown, Adam D., J. C. Root, T. A. Romano, L. J. Chang, R. A. Bryant, W. Hirst. "Overgeneralized Autobiographical Memory and Future Thinking in Combat Veterans with Posttraumatic Stress Disorder." *Journal of Behavior Therapy and Experimental Psychiatry* 44.1 (March 2013): 129–134.

Buck-Morss, Susan. *Dreamworld and Catastrophe: The Passing of Mass Utopia in East and West*. Cambridge, MA, and London: MIT Press, 2002.

Buell, Lawrence. *Writing for an Endangered World: Literature, Culture, and Environment in the U.S. and Beyond*. Cambridge, MA: Belknap Press, 2001.

Burtynsky, Edward. Interview with Michael Torosian. "The Essential Element." In Pauli, Burtynsky, Haworth-Booth, Baker, and Torosian, *Manufactured Landscapes*, 46–55.

Burtynsky, Edward, and Jennifer Baichwal. Interview with Michael Guillén. *The Evening Class*, June 4, 2007. Webcast. http://theeveningclass.blogspot.com/search?q=burtynsky/.

Butler, Octavia. *Xenogenesis*. New York: Guild America, 1989.

Canavan, Gerry. "Hope, but Not for Us: Ecological Science Fiction and the End of the World in Margaret Atwood's *Oryx and Crake* and *The Year of the Flood*." *Literature Interpretation Theory* 23.2 (Summer 2012): 138–159.

Carter, Sean, and Derek P. McCormack. "Film, Geopolitics, and the Affective Logics of Intervention." *Political Geography* 25 (2006): 228–245.

Cerulo, Karen. *Never Saw It Coming: Cultural Challenges to Imagining the Worst*. Chicago: University of Chicago Press, 2006.

Chakrabarty, Dipesh. "The Climate of History: Four Theses." *Critical Inquiry* 35.2 (Winter 2009): 197–222.

Chang, Justin. Review of *Blindness*, directed by Fernando Meirelles. Variety.com. May 14, 2008. Web. http://variety.com/2008/film/reviews/blindness-2-1200522472/.

Clarke, Lee Ben. *Worst Cases: Terror and Catastrophe in the Popular Imagination*. Chicago: University of Chicago Press, 2006.

Clinton, Greg. "Zombies as Racialized Pollution: *World War Z*, *Wretched of the Earth*, and Chinese Carbon Dioxide." Cultural Studies Association Annual Conference. University of Utah, Salt Lake City, May 29, 2014. Conference presentation.

Cohen, Tom. "Introduction: Murmurations—'Climate Change' and the Defacement of Theory." In *Telemorphosis: Theory in the Era of Climate Change*, edited by Tom Cohen, 1:13–42. Ann Arbor, MI: Open Humanities Press, 2012.

Cole, Kevin L. "Saramago's *Blindness*." *The Explicator* 64.1 (2006): 109–113.

Coman, Alin, Adam Brown, Jonathan Koppel, and William Hirst. "Collective Memory from a Psychological Perspective." *International Journal of Politics, Culture and Society* 22 (2009): 125–141.

Crutzen, Paul, and Eugene F. Stoermer. "The 'Anthropocene.'" In McKibben, *Global Warming Reader*, 69–74.

Cuarón, Alfonso. Audio Commentary. *Children of Men*. Directed by Cuarón, with performers Michael Caine, Julianne Moore, Clive Owen, and Juan Gabriel Yacuzzi. 2006. Universal, 2006. DVD.

———. Interview by Sheila Roberts. In Sheila Roberts, *Movies Online*, December 19, 2006. Web. http://www.moviesonline.ca/movienews_10790.html.

———. Interview by Kim Voynar. *Moviefone*. AOL Inc. December 25, 2006. Web. http://news.moviefone.com/2006/12/25/interview-children-of-men-director-alfonso-cuaron/.

Curren, Lindsay. "Nukes Are Forever." Review of *Into Eternity*, directed by Michael Madsen. *Transition Voice*, June 8, 2011. Webcast. transitionvoice.com/2011/06/nukes-are-forever/.

Daleiden, Sarah, and Therese Kelly. *I Heart H20: A Scavenger Hunt to Locate Your Water Relationships on the UCSB Campus*. 2013. PDF file.

DasGupta, Sayantani. "(Re)conceiving the Surrogate: Maternity, Race, and Reproductive Technologies in Alfonso Cuarón's *Children of Men*." In *Gender Scripts in Medicine and Narrative*, edited by Marcelline Block and Angela Laflen, 178–213. Newcastle upon Tyne: Cambridge Scholars, 2010.

Davenport, Coral. "A Climate Accord Based on Global Peer Pressure." *New York Times*, December 14, 2014, A3.

———. "In Climate Deal, Obama May Set a Theme for 2016." *New York Times*, November 12, 2014, A1.

———. "McConnell Urges States to Defy U.S. Plan to Cut Greenhouse Gas." *New York Times*, March 5, 2015, A12.

———. "Optimism Faces Grave Realities at Climate Talks." *New York Times*, December 1, 2014, A1.

Davis, Mike. "Welcome to the Next Epoch." TomDispatch.com/, June 26, 2008. Web. http://www.tomdispatch.com/blog/174949/tomgram%3A_mike_davis%2C_welcome_to_the_next_epoch/.

———. "Who Will Build the Ark?" *New Left Review* 61 (January–February 2010): 29–46.

Dendle, Peter. "The Zombie as Barometer of Cultural Anxiety." In *Monsters and the Monstrous: Myths and Metaphors of Enduring Evil*, edited by Niall Scott, 45-60. Kenilworth, NJ: Rodopi, 2007.

Derrida, Jacques. "The Law of Genre." Translated by Avital Ronell. *Critical Inquiry* 7.1 (Autumn 1980): 55–81.

———. *Memoirs of the Blind: The Self-Portrait and Other Ruins.* Translated by Pascale-Anne Brault and Michael Nass. Chicago and London: University of Chicago Press, 1993.

Eagleton, Terry. "Utopia and Its Opposites." *Socialist Register* 36 (2000): 31–40.

Ebert, Roger. Review of *Blindness*, directed by Fernando Meirelles. RogerEbert.com/, October 2, 2008. Web. http://www.rogerebert.com/reviews/blindness-2008/.

———. Review of *Soylent Green*, directed by Richard Fleischer. RogerEbert.com/. April 27, 1973. Web. October 8, 2013. http://www.rogerebert.com/reviews/soylent-green-1973/.

Edelman, Lee. *No Future: Queer Theory and the Death Drive.* Durham and London: Duke University Press, 2004.

Elliott, Jane. *Popular Feminist Fiction as American Allegory: Representing National Time.* New York: Palgrave Macmillan, 2008.

———. "Suffering Agency: Imagining Neoliberal Personhood in North America and Britain." *Social Text* 31.2 115 (2013): 83–101.

Elliott, Jane, and Gillian Harkins. "Introduction: Genres of Neoliberalism." *Social Text* 31.2 115 (2013): 1–17.

Feuer, Alan. "The Capitalism of Catastrophe: At Survivalists Expo, Items for Everything Short of the Zombie Apocalypse." *New York Times*, April 7, 2014, A11, A13.

Fitting, Peter, ed. *Subterranean Worlds: A Critical Anthology.* New York: Wesleyan Press, 2004.

Foucault, Michel. *Discipline and Punish: The Birth of the Prison.* Translated by Alan Sheridan. New York: Vintage, 1995.

Fox, Justin. "Head Count." Review of *Malthus*, by Robert J. Mayhew. *New York Times*, August 1, 2014, Sunday Book Review.

Freeman, Lindsey A. "Happy Memories under the Mushroom Cloud: Utopia and Memory in Oak Ridge, Tennessee." Gutman et al., *Memory and the Future*, 158–178.

Freud, Sigmund. *Beyond the Pleasure Principle.* 1920. Translated and edited by James Strachey. London and New York: W. W. Norton, 1961.

———. *Civilization and Its Discontents.* 1929. Translated and edited by James Strachey. London and New York: W. W. Norton, 1961.

———. *Collected Papers.* Edited by James Strachey, translated by Joan Riviere. London: Hogarth Press, 1948–1950.

———. "The Future of an Illusion." 1927. In Strachey, *Standard Edition*, 21:5–59.

———. *Group Psychology and the Analysis of the Ego.* 1922. In Strachey, *Standard Edition*, 18:67–134.

———. *Inhibitions, Symptoms, Anxiety.* 1926. Edited by James Strachey, translated by Alix Strachey. London and New York: W. W. Norton, 1989.

———. *Moses and Monotheism.* 1939. Translated and edited by James Strachey. New York: Vintage, 1955.

———. "Mourning and Melancholia." 1917. In Strachey, *Standard Edition*, 14:243–258.

———. "Psycho-analysis and the War Neuroses." 1919. In Freud, *Collected Papers*, edited by James Strachey, 5:92–97.

———. "Thoughts for the Times on War and Death." In *Collected Papers*, edited by Ernest Jones, translated by Joan Riviere, 4:288–317. New York: Basic Books, 1959.

————. "Thoughts on War and Death." 1915. In Freud, *Collected Papers*, 4:307.

Frier, David G. *The Novels of José Saramago: Echoes from the Past, Pathways into the Future.* Cardiff: University of Wales Press, 2007.

Gaard, Greta. *The Nature of Home: Taking Root in a Place.* Tucson: University of Arizona Press, 2007.

Gaard, Greta, Simon C. Estock, and Serpil Oppermann., eds. *International Perspectives in Feminist Ecocriticism.* London and New York: Routledge, 2013.

Gabbard, Krin. *Black Magic: White Hollywood and African American Culture.* New Brunswick, NJ: Rutgers University Press, 2004.

Gillis, Justin. "Panel's Warning on Climate Risk: Worst Is Yet to Come." *New York Times,* March 31, 2014.

————. "U.N. Panel Issues Its Starkest Warning Yet on Global Warming." *New York Times,* November 2, 2014, A8.

Gilman, Charlotte Perkins. *The Yellow Wallpaper and Other Stories.* (Includes *Herland*). New York: Dover Publications, 1997.

————. *Herland.* In *The Yellow Wallpaper and Other Stories*, by Charlotte Perkins Gilman. New York: Dover Publications, 1997.

Glassner, Barry. *The Culture of Fear.* 1991. New York: Basic Books, 2010.

Gledhill, Christine. Introduction. In *Gender Meets Genre in Postwar Cinemas*, edited by Christine Gledhill, 1–11. Urbana, Chicago, and Springfield: University of Illinois Press, 2012.

————. "Rethinking Genre." In *Reinventing Film Studies*, edited by Christine Gledhill and Linda Williams, 221–243. New York and London: Sage, 1997.

Graham, Becki A. "Post-9/11 Anxieties: Unpredictability and Complacency in the Age of New Terrorism in *Dawn of the Dead* (2004)." *Race, Oppression, and the Zombie: Essays on Cross-Cultural Appropriations of the Caribbean Tradition,* edited by Christopher M. Moreman and Cory James Rushton, 124–138. Jefferson, NC: McFarland, 2011.

Greenstone, Michael. "A Voluntary, and Effective, Climate Treaty." *New York Times,* February 15, 2015.

Gresser, Julian. "Inventing for Humanity—A Collaborative Strategy for Global Survival." March 13, 2012. PDF file.

Griffin, Susan. *Woman and Nature: The Roaring inside Her.* New York: Harper and Row, 1978.

Grusin, Richard. *Premediation: Affect and Mediality after 9/11.* London and New York: Palgrave MacMillan, 2010.

Guha, Ramachandra. *Environmentalism: A Global History.* London: Pearson, 2000.

————. *How Much Should a Person Consume? Environmentalism in India and the United States.* Berkeley and London: University of California Press, 2006.

————. *The Unquiet Woods. Ecological Change and Peasant Resistance in the Himalaya.* Berkeley and London: University of California Press, 1989.

Gutman, Yifat, Adam D. Brown, and Amy Sodaro, eds. *Memory and the Future: Transnational Politics, Ethics and Society.* London and New York: Palgrave MacMillan, 2010.

Hamblin, Jacob Darwin. "Ecology Lessons from the Cold War." *New York Times,* May 30, 2013, A23.

Hamilton, Clive. "The Risks of Climate Engineering." *New York Times*, February 12, 2015.

Harrison, Harry. "Make Room! Make Room!" In *50 in 50: A Collection of Short Stories One for Each of Fifty Years*, by Harry Harrison. New York: Tom Doherty Associates, 1966.

Harrison, Robert Pogue. "The Book from Which Our Literature Springs." *New York Review of Books*, February 9, 2012, 40–45.

Harvey, David. *A Brief History of Neoliberalism*. New York: Oxford University Press, 2007.

Hayles, N. Katherine. "Autonomous Algorithms and Flash Crashes: The Role of the Nonhuman in Finance Capital." Conference on *Mediating the Nonhuman and the Sixth Annual Digital Humanities Research Slam*, University of California–Santa Barbara, Interdisciplinary Humanities Center, Santa Barbara, March 15, 2013. Keynote address.

Heighton, Steven. "Crimes without Punishment." Review of *Raised from the Ground*, by José Saramago. *New York Times*, December 30, 2012, BR14.

Heise, Ursula K. "Comparative Literature and the Environmental Humanities." *State of the Discipline Report*. American Comparative Literature Association, 2014. Web. April 10, 2014. http://stateofthediscipline.acla.org/entry/comparative-literature -and-environmental-humanities/.

———. "Globality, Difference, and the International Turn in Ecocriticism." *PMLA* 128.3 (May 2013): 636–642.

———. "The Invention of Eco-Futures." *Ecozon@: European Journal of Literature, Culture and Environment* 3.2 (Autumn 2012): 1–10.

———. *Sense of Place and Sense of Planet: The Environmental Imagination of the Global*. New York and Oxford: Oxford University Press, 2008.

Hendershot, Cindy. *Paranoia, the Bomb, and 1950s Science Fiction Films*. Bowling Green, OH: Popular Press, 1999.

Hillcoat, John. Audio Commentary. *The Road*. Directed by John Hillcoat, with performers Viggo Mortenson, Charize Theron, and Kodi Smit-McPhee. 2008. Dimension, 2009. DVD.

———. Interview with Peter Keough. "Outside the Frame." *Boston Phoenix Blogs*, November 29, 2009. Web. http://blog.thephoenix.com/blogs/outsidetheframe/ archive/2009/11.aspx.

Hodgkin, Katharine, and Susannah Radstone, eds. *Memory, History, Nation: Contested Pasts*. London and New Brunswick: Transaction Publishers, 2006.

Hoffman, Martin L. *Empathy and Moral Development: Implications for Caring and Justice*. Cambridge: Cambridge University Press, 2000.

———. "Empathy and Vicarious Traumatization in Clinicians." Lecture presented at Psychology Department, Simon Fraser University, British Columbia, Canada. 2002.

Höhler, Sabine. "Carrying Capacity: The Moral Economy of the 'Coming Spaceship Earth.'" 4S & EASST Conference, Paris, France, August 25–28, 2004. Conference presentation.

Holden, Stephen. "Dear Humans: The Planet Needs Your Help." Review of *Force of Nature: The David Suzuki Movie*, directed by Sturla Gunnarsson. *New York Times*, December 2, 2011, C10.

Jacoby, Russell. *Picture Imperfect: Utopian Thought for an Anti-utopian Age*. New York: Columbia University Press, 2005.

James, P. D. *The Children of Men*. New York: Warner Books, 1992.

Jameson, Fredric. *Archaeologies of the Future: The Desire Called Utopia and Other Science Fictions*. New York: Verso, 2007.

———. "Future City." *New Left Review* 21 (May–June 2003): 65–79.

Johnson, G. Allen. "Into Eternity: Effort to Store Nuclear Waste." *San Francisco Chronicle*, May 25, 2011. Web. April 10, 2014. http://www.sfgate.com/thingstodo/article/Into-Eternity-Effort-to-store-nuclear-waste-2370462.php.

Joplin, David D. "The Moral Quality of Wordsworth's Nature." 2007. Web. PDF file. March 3, 2013. http://barfieldsociety.org/Wordsworth-Moral%20Nature_Conference.pdf.

Jung, Carl. *Collected Works*. Translated by Gerhard Adler and R.F.C. Hull. Princeton, NJ: Princeton University Press, 1969.

Kansteiner, Wulf. "Genealogy of a Category Mistake: A Critical Intellectual History of the Cultural Trauma Metaphor." *Rethinking History* 8.2 (June 2004): 193–221.

———. *In Pursuit of German Memory: History, Television, and Politics after Auschwitz*. Athens: Ohio University Press, 2006.

Kansteiner, Wulf, and Harald Weinlböck. "Against the Concept of Cultural Trauma." In *A Companion to Cultural Memory Studies*, edited by Astrid Erll and Ansgar Nünning, 229–240. Berlin and New York: Walter de Gruyter, 2008.

Kaplan, E. Ann. "Age Studies and Environmental Humanities." Modern Language Association Annual Conference, Sheraton Hotel, Chicago, IL, January 7, 2014. Conference presentation.

———. "Empathy and Trauma Culture: Imaging Catastrophe." In *Empathy: Philosophical and Psychological Perspectives*, edited by Amy Coplan and Peter Goldie, 255–276. New York and Oxford: Oxford University Press, 2011.

———. "Global Trauma: Viewing Images of Catastrophe." *Consumption Markets & Culture* 11.1 (March 2008): 3–24.

———. *Trauma Culture: The Politics of Terror and Loss in Media and Literature*. New Brunswick, NJ: Rutgers University Press, 2005.

Kaplan, E. Ann, and Ban Wang. *Trauma and Cinema: Cross-cultural Explorations*. Hong Kong: Hong Kong University Press, 2004.

Kermode, Frank. *The Sense of an Ending: Studies in the Theory of Fiction*. New York: Oxford University Press, 1967.

King, Claire Sisco. *Washed in Blood: Male Sacrifice, Trauma, and the Cinema*. New Brunswick, NJ: Rutgers University Press, 2012.

Kitch, Sally. *Higher Ground: From Utopianism to Realism in American Feminist Thought*. Chicago and London: University of Chicago Press, 2000.

Klaic, Dragan. *The Plot of the Future: Utopia and Dystopia in Modern Drama*. Ann Arbor: University of Michigan Press, 1991.

Klein, Naomi. *The Shock Doctrine: The Rise of Disaster Capitalism.* New York: Metropolitan Books, 2008.

———. *This Changes Everything: Capitalism vs. the Climate.* New York: Allen Lane, 2014.

Klein, Naomi, and Elizabeth Kolbert. "'Can Climate Change Cure Capitalism?': An Exchange." *New York Review of Books,* January 8, 2015.

Klein, Stefan. *The Secret Pulse of Time: Making Sense of Life's Scarcest Commodity.* Boston, M.A.: Da Capo Lifelong Books, 2009.

Kolbert, Elizabeth. "Can Climate Change Cure Capitalism?" Review of *This Changes Everything: Capitalism vs. the Climate,* by Naomi Klein. *New York Review of Books,* December 4, 2014. Web. http://www.nybooks.com/articles/archives/2014/dec/04/can-climate-change-cure-capitalism/.

———. *Fieldnotes from a Catastrophe.* New York: Bloomsbury, 2006.

———. *The Sixth Extinction: An Unnatural History.* New York: Henry Holt, 2014.

Kovach, Elizabeth. "Novel Ontologies after 9/11: The Politics of Being in Contemporary Theory and U.S. American Narrative Fiction." Dissertation, International Graduate Center for the Study of Culture, Giessen, Germany. Forthcoming.

Kristeva, Julia. *Black Sun: Depression and Melancholia.* Translated by Leon S. Roudiez. New York: Columbia University Press, 1989.

Kristof, Nicholas D. "A Poverty Solution that Starts with a Hug." *New York Times,* January 8, 2012, SR11.

———. "When Our Brains Short-Circuit." *New York Times,* July 1, 2009.

LaCapra, Dominick. "Trauma, Absence, Loss." In *Writing History, Writing Trauma,* by Dominick Capra, 43–85. Baltimore: Johns Hopkins University Press, 2000.

Lapidos, Juliet. "Atomic Priesthoods, Thorn Landscapes, and Munchian Pictograms: How to Communicate the Dangers of Nuclear Waste to Future Civilizations." http://www.slate.com/articles/health_and_science/green_room/2009/11/atomic_priesthoods_thorn_landscapes_and_munchian_pictograms.html/.

Larsen, Lars Bang. "Zombies of Immaterial Labor: The Modern Monster and the Death of Death." *e-flux* 15 (04/2010). Web. October 11, 2012. http://www.eflux.com/journal/zombies-of-immaterial/.

Latimer, Heather. "Bio-reproductive Futurism: Bare Life and the Pregnant Refugee in Alfonso Cuarón's *Children of Men.*" *Social Text* 29.3 108 (2011): 51–72.

Laub, Dori. "Bearing Witness, or the Vicissitudes of Listening." In *Testimony: Crises of Witnessing in Literature, Psychoanalysis, and History,* by Shoshana Felman and Dori Laub, 57–74. New York and London: Routledge, 1992.

———. "An Event without a Witness: Truth, Testimony and Survival." In *Testimony: Crises of Witnessing in Literature, Psychoanalysis, and History,* by Shoshana Felman and Dori Laub, 75–92. New York and London: Routledge, 1992.

Lauro, Sarah Juliet. "The Eco-Zombie: Environmental Critique in Zombie Fiction." In *Generation Zombie: Essays on the Living Dead in Modern Culture,* edited by Stephanie Boluk and Wylie Lenz, 54–67. Jefferson, NC: McFarland, 2011.

Lee, Dan P. "After the Rapture." *New York Magazine,* October 24, 2011, 28–30.

Lee, Felicia B. "Back to the Scary Future and the Best-Seller List." *New York Times,* September 22, 2009, C1, C6.

Lefebvre, Martin. "Between Setting and Landscape in the Cinema." In Lefebvre, *Landscape and Film*, 19–60.

———. Introduction. In Lefebvre, *Landscape and Film*, xi–xxi.

———, ed. *Landscape and Film*. London and New York: Routledge, 2006.

Le Guin, Ursula K. *The Word for World Is Forest*. New York and London: Macmillan, 2010.

Levitas, Ruth. *The Concept of Utopia*. Syracuse, NY: Syracuse University Press, 1990.

Levy, Daniel. "Changing Temporalities and the Internationalization of Memory Cultures." In Gutman et al., *Memory and the Future*, 15–30.

Levy, Daniel, and Natan Sznaider. *The Holocaust and Memory in the Global Age*. Translated by Assenka Oksiloff. Philadelphia, PA: Temple University Press, 2006.

———. *Human Rights and Memory*. University Park: Pennsylvania State University Press, 2010.

Louv, Richard. "The Nature Principle: Reconnecting with Life in a Virtual Age." *Noeti* 23 (June 2012). Web. http://www.noetic.org/noetic/issue-twenty-three-june/the-nature-principle/. Now printed as a book with the same title. Chapel Hill: Alonquin Books, 2012.

———. "Nature's Neurons: Do Early Experiences in the Natural World Help Shape Children's Brain Architecture?" *The New Nature Movement*. Children & Nature Network, July 26, 2012. Web. http://blog.childrenandnature.org/2012/07/26/natures-neurons-do-early-experiences-in-the-natural-world-shape-childrens-brain-architecture/.

Lyman, Stanford M. *Roads to Dystopia: Sociological Essays on the Postmodern Condition*. Fayetteville: University of Arkansas Press, 2001.

Madsen, Michael. Interview with Helen Caldicott. "The Journey Our Nuclear Waste Must Take: Into Eternity." *If You Love This Planet*, July 15, 2011. Webcast. http://ifyoulovethisplanet.org/?p=4732/.

Markus, Hazel, and Paula Nurius. "Possible Selves." *American Psychologist* 41.9 (September 1986): 954–969.

Martinez, Alanna. "Spring/Break Art Show's School House Experience Makes a Splash Downtown." *New York Times*, March 17, 2012: C3.

Massumi, Brian. "The Future Birth of the Affective Fact: The Political Ontology of Threat." In *The Affect Theory Reader*, edited by Melissa Greg and Gregory J. Seigworth, 52–70. Durham and London: Duke University Press, 2010.

McCarthy, Cormac. *The Road*. New York and London: Vintage International, 2006.

McKibben, Bill. *Eaarth: Making a Life on a Tough New Planet*. New York: St. Martin's Griffin, 2011.

———, ed. *The Global Warming Reader*. London: Penguin Books, 2012.

McNeil, Donald, Jr., and Denise Grady. "How Hard Would It Be for Avian Flu to Spread?" *New York Times*, January 3, 2012, D1, D6.

Medavoi, Leerom. "The Biopolitical Unconscious: Toward an Eco-Marxist Literary Theory." *Mediations: Journal of the Marxist Literary Group* 24.2 (Spring 2010): 122–139.

———. "A Contribution to the Critique of Political Ecology: Sustainability as Disavowal." *New Formations* 69.7 (2010): 129–143.

Merchant, Carolyn. *The Death of Nature: Women, Ecology, and the Scientific Revolution.* New York: HarperCollins, 1980.

Mirzoeff. Nicholas. "Visualizing the Anthropocene." *Public Culture,* 26.2 (2014): 213–232.

More, Sir Thomas. *Utopia.* Translated from the Latin by Paul Turner. London and New York: Penguin, 1965.

Morton, Timothy. *Ecology without Nature: Rethinking Environmental Aesthetics.* Cambridge, MA: Harvard University Press, 2007.

———. *Hyperobjects: Philosophy and Ecology after the End of the World.* London and Minneapolis: University of Minnesota Press, 2013.

Moser, Susanne C. "Getting Real about It: Meeting the Psychological and Social Demands of a World in Distress." In *Environmental Leadership: A Reference Handbook,* edited by Deborah Rigling Gallagher, 432–440. London and New York: Sage, 2012.

Moser, Susanne C., and Lisa Drilling, eds. *Creating a Climate for Change: Communicating Climate Change and Facilitating Social Change.* Cambridge: Cambridge University Press, 2010.

Moylan, Thomas. *Scraps of the Untainted Sky: Science Fiction, Utopia, Dystopia.* Boulder, CO: Westview Press, 2000.

Muñoz, José Esteban. *Cruising Utopia: The Then and There of Queer Futurity.* London and New York: New York University Press, 2009.

Nagourney, Adam. "For Californians, Two Earthquakes Have Put Preparedness Back on the Map." *New York Times,* March 31, 2014, A11.

Nietzsche, Friedrich Wilhelm. *The Birth of Tragedy.* Translated with notes and introduction by Douglas Smith. New York: Oxford University Press, 2000.

Nixon, Robert. *Slow Violence and the Environmentalism of the Poor.* Cambridge, MA: Harvard University Press, 2010.

Oates, Joyce Carol. "Against Nature." In *The Norton Reader: An Anthology of Nonfiction,* edited by Linda H. Peterson and John C. Brereton, 621–627. 11th ed. New York: W. W. Norton, 2004.

———. "Where No One Has Ever Gone." Review of *In Other Worlds: SF and the Human Imagination,* by Margaret Atwood. *New York Review of Books,* March 12, 2012, 39–40.

Oreskes, Naomi. "Playing Dumb on Climate Change." *New York Times,* January 4, 2015, Sunday Review, 2.

Oreskes, Naomi, and Erik M. Conway. *The Collapse of Western Civilization: A View from the Future.* New York: Columbia University Press, 2014.

———. *Merchants of Doubt.* New York: Bloomsbury, 2010.

Ortiz, Simon J., and Gabriele Schwab. "Memory Is Key." *Kenyon Review* 30.4 (Fall 2008): 68–81.

Oz, Mehmet. "When Panic Goes Viral." *Time,* November 7, 2011, 40.

Pagels, Elaine. *Revelations: Visions, Prophecies, and Politics in the Book of Revelations.* New York: Viking, 2012.

Passerini, Luisa. Introduction. In *Memory and Totalitarianism: International Yearbook of Oral History and Life Stories,* edited by Luisa Passerini, 1–20. New York and Oxford: Oxford University Press, 1992.

Pauli, Lori, Edward Burtynsky, Mark Haworth-Booth, Kenneth Baker, and Michael Torosian. *Manufactured Landscapes: The Photographs of Edward Burtynsky*. New Haven, CT: Yale University Press, 2003.

Pearson, Patricia. "Things to Fear and Loathe." *New York Times*, March 4, 2012, SR1, SR7.

Penhall, Joe. "Last Man Standing: What Cormac McCarthy Made of My Adaptation of *The Road*," *The Guardian*, January 4, 2010. http://www.theguardian.com/film/2010/jan/04/the-road-cormac-mccarthy-viggo-mortensen/.

Penley, Constance. *The Future of an Illusion: Film, Feminism, and Psychoanalysis*. Minneapolis: University of Minnesota Press, 1989.

Pollack, Andrew. "A Genetic Entrepreneur Sets His Sights on Aging and Death." *New York Times*, March 5, 2014, B1, B4.

Poole, Ross. "Misremembering the Holocaust: Universal Symbol, Nationalist Icon, or Moral Kitsch?" In Gutman et al., *Memory and the Future*, 31–49.

Porter, Eduardo. "Old Forecast of Famine May Yet Come True." *New York Times*, April 2, 2014, B1, B3.

Pratt, Mary Louise. *Imperial Eyes: Travel Writing and Transculturation*. 2nd ed. London and New York: Routledge, 2007.

Radstone, Susannah. "Screening Trauma: *Forrest Gump*, Film, and Memory." In *Memory and Methodology*, by Susannah Radstone, 79–110. Oxford: Berg, 2000.

———. *The Sexual Politics of Time: Confession, Nostalgia, Memory*. London and New York: Routledge, 2007.

Rascaroli, Laura. "Time Travel and Film Spectatorship in *12 Monkeys* and *Strange Days*." In *The Science Fiction Film Reader*, edited by Gregg Rickman, 355–368. New York: Limelight Editions, 2004.

Rickety, Carrie. "Female Directors Gain Ground, Slowly." *New York Times*, January 13, 2013, AR17.

Ridley, Jim. "More Inconvenient Truths: China's Industrial Footprint, Writ Large." *Village Voice*, June 12, 2007. http://www.villagevoice.com/2007-06-12/film/more-inconvenient-truths/full/.

Roberts, Adam. *The History of Science Fiction*. Basingstoke and New York: Palgrave, 2006.

Roberts, Sam. "U.N. Says 7 Billion Now Share the World." *New York Times*, November 1, 2011, A4.

Robinson, Kim Stanley. *Mars Trilogy*. New York: Random House, 1993.

Roman [Roman Mars]. "Episode 114: Ten Thousand Years." In SLATE, May 12, 2014. http://99percentinvisible.org/episode/ten-thousand-years/

Rose, Mark. *Alien Encounters: Anatomy of Science Fiction*. Cambridge, MA: Harvard University Press, 1981.

Roth, Michael, S. *Psychoanalysis as History: Negation and Freedom in Freud*. 1987. Ithaca: Cornell University Press, 1995.

———. "Trauma: A Dystopia of the Spirit." In *Thinking Utopia: Steps into Other Worlds*, edited by J. Rüsen, J. and M. Fehr, 230–245. London: Berghan Books, 2005.

Rothberg, Michael. *Multidirectional Memory: Remembering the Holocaust in the Age of Decolonization*. Stanford: Stanford University Press, 2009.

Rubenstein, Michael. *Public Works: Infrastructure, Irish Modernism, and the Postcolonial.* Notre Dame, Ind.: University of Notre Dame Press, 2010.

Sakvitne, Karen W., and Laurie Pearlman. *Trauma and the Therapist: Countertransference and Vicarious Traumatization.* New York: W. W. Norton. 1995.

Santner, Eric. *Stranded Objects: Mourning, Memory, and the Film in Postwar Germany.* Ithaca, NY: Cornell University Press, 1990.

Saramago, José. *Blindness.* Translated by Giovanni Pontiero. London and New York: Harcourt, 1997.

Scott, A. O. "Father and Son Bond in Gloomy Aftermath of Disaster." *New York Times,* November 25, 2009, C1.

———. "Number Crunching at the Apocalypse." *New York Times,* October 21, 2011, C1.

———. "Off to the Stars, with Dread and Regret." *New York Times,* November 5, 2014, C1.

Shaw, Deborah. *Three Amigos: The Transnational Filmmaking of Guillermo del Toro, Alejandro González Iñárritu, and Alfonso Cuarón.* Manchester: Manchester University Press, 2013.

Shear, Michael, and Coral Davenport. "Obama Vetoes Bill Pushing Pipeline Approval." *New York Times,* February 24, 2015.

Shiva, Vandana. "Diversity and Democracy: Resisting the Global Economy." *Global Dialogue* 1.1 (Summer 1999): 19–20.

Skutnabb-Kangas, Tove. *Linguistic Genocide in Education or Worldwide Diversity and Human Rights.* Mahwah, NJ: L. Erlbaum Associates, 2000.

Skutnabb-Kangas, Tove, and Kathleen Heugh. *Multilingual Education and Sustainable Diversity Work: From the Periphery to Center.* New York: Routledge, 2012.

Smith, Damon. "Made in China: Jennifer Baichwal and Edward Burtynsky on Their Travels across *Manufactured Landscapes.*" *Bright Lights Film Journal* 58 (November 2007). Web. http://brightlightsfilm.com/58/58landscapesiv.php#.VCTrLVeTFSE/.

Smith, Daniel. "Anxiety: It's Still the 'Age of Anxiety.' Or Is It?" *New York Times,* January 15, 2012. Web. http://query.nytimes.com/gst/fullpage.html?res=9C06E2D91E31F936A25752C0A9649D8B63/.

Snyder, Gary. "The Place, the Region, and the Commons." In *The Practice of the Wild,* by Gary Snyder, 25–48. San Francisco: North Point Press, 1990.

Sontag, Susan. "The Imagination of Disaster." *Commentary* 40.4 (Fall 1965): 42–48.

———. *On Photography.* New York: Farrar, Straus and Giroux, 1979.

———. *Regarding the Pain of Others.* New York: Farrar, Straus and Giroux, 2013.

Soper, Kate. *What Is Nature? Culture, Politics and the Non-Human.* London and New York: Wiley-Blackwell, 1995.

Staels, Hilde. "Margaret Atwood's *The Handmaid's Tale*: Resistance through Narrating." *Margaret Atwood's* The Handmaid's Tale. Edited by Harold Bloom. Philadelphia: Chelsea House Publishers, 2001: 113–126.

Stein, Rachel, ed. *New Perspectives on Environmental Justice: Gender, Sexuality, and Activism.* New Brunswick, NJ: Rutgers University Press, 2004.

Strachey, James, ed. *Standard Edition of the Complete Psychological Works of Sigmund Freud.* Translated by James Strachey. 24 vols. London: Hogarth Press, 1959.

Sugg, Katherine. "*The Walking Dead*: Crisis, Late Liberalism, and Masculine Subjection in Apocalypse Fictions." *Journal of American Studies*. Forthcoming.

Suvin, Darko. *Positions and Presuppositions in Science Fiction*. Basingstoke and London: Macmillan, 1988.

Tsai, Yun-Chun. "Traumatic Memory, Gender Melancholia, and Prospective Multiplicity: Negotiating with the Dead in Margaret Atwood's *The Handmaid's Tale*." 2009. Master's thesis. Stony Brook University, Stony Brook, NY.

Turim, Maureen. *Flashbacks in Film: Memory and History*. London: Routledge, 1989.

Udden, James. "Child of the Long Take: Alfonso Cuarón's Film Aesthetics in the Shadow of Globalization." *Style* 43.1 (Spring 2009): 26.

United Nations. Intergovernmental Panel on Climate Change. *Climate Change 2014: Impacts, Adaptation, and Vulnerability*. n.d. Web. October 15, 2014. http://www.ipcc.ch/report/ar5/wg2/.

Valentine, Stephen. *Timeship: The Architecture of Immortality*. Victoria, Australia: Images Publishing Group, 2012.

Vieira, Patrícia, *Seeing Politics Otherwise: Vision in Latin American and Iberian Fiction*. Buffalo, London, and Toronto: University of Toronto Press, 2011.

Wagner, Cynthia. "Theatrical Visions: Playwrights and the Future." Review of *The Plot of the Future: Utopia and Dystopia in Modern Drama*, by Dragan Klaic. *Futurist* (July–August 1992): 45.

Weisman, Alan. *The World without Us*. New York: St. Martin's Press, 2007.

White, Lyn Jr. "The Historical Roots of Our Ecological Crisis." *Science* 155, no. 3767 (1967):1203–1207.

Wilkinson, Alec. "The Cryonic Castle: Can an Architect Design a Building for a Man Who Wants to Live Forever?" *New Yorker*, January 19, 2004, 44.

Yusoff, Kathryn. "Excess, Catastrophe, and Climate Change." *Environment and Planning D: Society and Space* 27 (2009): 1010–1029.

Zipes, Jack. "Introduction: Toward a Realization of Anticipatory Illumination." In Ernst Bloch, *Utopian Function of Art and Literature: Selected Essays*, xi–xliii. Cambridge, MA, and London: MIT Press, 1988.

Žižek, Slavoj. Audio Commentary. *Children of Men*. Directed by Alfonso Cuarón, with performers Michael Caine, Julianne Moore, Clive Owen, and Juan Gabriel Yacuzzi. 2006. Universal, 2006. DVD.

———. "The Clash of Civilizations at the End of History." *Scribd*, n.d. Web. March 10, 2013. http://www.scribd.com/doc/19133296/Zizek-The-Clash-of-Civilizations-at-the-End-of-History/.

———. *Living in the End Times*. London and New York: Verso, 2011.

———. *Violence: Six Sideways Reflections*. New York: Picador, 2008.

———. *Welcome to the Desert of the Real*. London: Verso, 2002.

FILMOGRAPHY

Blindness. Dir. Fernando Meirelles. Perf. Danny Glover, Don McKellar, Julianne Moore, and Mark Ruffalo. Canada: Rhombus Media, 2008.

The Book of Eli. Dir. Albert Hughes and Allen Hughes. Perf. Denzel Washington, Mila Kunis, and Ray Stevenson. United States: Alcon Entertainment, 2010.

Children of Men. Dir. Alfonso Cuarón. Perf. Michael Caine, Julianne Moore, Clive Owen, and Juan Gabriel Yacuzzi. Canada: Universal, 2006.

Contagion. Dir. Steven Soderbergh. Perf. Matt Demon, Kate Winslet, Jude Law, Gwyneth Paltrow. United States: Warner Bros., 2011.

Force of Nature: The David Suzuki Movie. Dir. Sturla Gunnarsson. Canada: Legacy Lecture Productions, 2010.

4:44 Last Day on Earth. Dir. Abel Ferrara. Perf. Willem Dafoe, Shanyn Leigh, Natasha Lyonne. United States, Switzerland, France: Fabula, Wild Bunch, 2011.

Fukushima: Memories of a Lost Landscape or *311*. Dir. Yoju Matsubayashi, Tatsuya Mori, Takeharu Watai, Takuji Yasuoka. Japan: Yasuoka Film, 2011.

Gravity. Dir. Alfonso Cuarón. Perf. Sandra Bullock, George Clooney, Ed Harria. United States, United Kingdom: Warner Bros. 2013.

The Handmaid's Tale. Dir. Volker Schlöndorff. Perf. Natasha Richardson, Faye Dunaway, Aidan Quinn, and Robert Duvall. United States: Bioskop Film, 1990.

The Happening. Dir. M. Night Shyamalan. Perf. Mark Wahlberg, Zooey Deschanel, and John Leguizamo. United States: Twentieth Century Fox, 2008.

I Am Legend. Dir. Francis Lawrence. Perf. Will Smith, Alice Braga, Charlie Tahan. United States: Warner Bros., 2007.

Interstellar. Dir. Christopher Nolan. Perf. Matthew McConaughey, Anne Hathaway, Jessica Chastain. United States: Paramount Pictures, 2014.

Into Eternity: A Film for the Future. Dir. Michael Madsen. Finland: Magic Hour Films, 2010.

Manufactured Landscapes. Dir. Jennifer Baichwal. Canada: Foundry Films, 2006.

Melancholia. Dir. Lars Von Trier. Perf. Kirsten Dunst, Charlotte Gainsbourg, Kiefer Sutherland. Denmark: Zentropa Entertainment, 2011.

Night of the Living Dead. Dir. George A. Romero. Perf. Duane Jones, Judith O'Dea, Karl Hardman. United States: Image Ten, 1968.

Odayaka na nihijo. Dir. Nobuteru Uchida. Perf. Kiki Sugino, Yuki Shinohara, Takeshi Yammamoto. Japan: Wa Entertainment, 2012.

The Omega Man. Dir. Boris Segal. Perf. Charlton Heston, Anthony Zerbe, Rosalind Cash. United States: Warner Bros., 1971.

Outbreak. Dir. Wolfgang Petersen. Perf. Dustin Hoffman, Rene Russo, Morgan Freeman. United States: Warner Bros., 1995.

The Road. Dir. John Hillcoat. Perf. Viggo Mortensen, Charlize Theron, and Kodi Smit-McPhee. United States: Dimension Films, 2009.

Snowpiercer. Dir. Joon-ho Bong. Perf. Chris Evans, Jamie Bell, and Tilda Swinton. South Korea: Moho Film, 2014.

Soylent Green. Dir. Richard Fleischer. Perf. Charlton Heston, Edward G. Robinson, and Leigh Taylor-Young. United States: Metro-Goldwyn-Mayer, 1973.

Surviving Progress. Dir. Mathieu Roy and Harold Crooks. Canada: Big Picture Media Corporation, 2011.

Take Shelter. Dir. Jeff Nichols. Perf. Michael Shannon, Jessica Chastain, and Shea Whigham. United States: Hydraulx Entertainment, 2011.

INDEX

ABOUT THE AUTHOR

E. ANN KAPLAN is distinguished professor of English and comparative literary and cultural studies at Stony Brook University, where she also founded and directed The Humanities Institute. Kaplan has written many books and articles on topics in cultural studies, media, and women's studies, from diverse theoretical perspectives including psychoanalysis, feminism, postmodernism, reproductive politics, and post-colonialism. Kaplan's many books include *Women and Film: Both Sides of the Camera; Motherhood and Representation: The Mother in Popular Culture and Melodrama;* and *Looking for the Other: Feminism, Film and the Imperial Gaze.* Her many edited and co-edited books include *Women in Film Noir; Playing Dolly: Technocultural Fantasies of Assisted Reproduction* (co-edited with Susan Squier); and *Feminism and Film* (2000). Kaplan's more recent research focuses on trauma, as evident in her books *Trauma and Cinema: Cross-Cultural Explorations* (co-edited with Ban Wang in 2004), and her 2005 monograph, *Trauma Culture: The Politics of Terror and Loss in Media and Literature* (2005). Her new monograph, *Climate Trauma: Foreseeing the Future in Film and Fiction,* continues her trauma research. Completing her "trauma trilogy," Kaplan's new book project will focus on an "aging as trauma" trope in Western media and literature.